Religion: a Humanist Interpretation

Religion: a Humanist Interpretation represents a lifetime's work on the anthropology of religion from a rather unusual viewpoint. Raymond Firth treats religion as a human art, capable of great intellectual and artistic achievements, but also of complex manipulation to serve human interests of those who believe in it and operate it. Religion may also be used as a symbol or cloak for violence, with political or economic aims. The study is comparative, drawing material from a range of well-known and lesser-known religions around the world, and giving the results of much anthropological research. Its findings are a challenge to established beliefs.

The book explores notions of the divine, both as a single person and in a multiplicity of gods. It considers ideas and practices of communication with the supernatural, as in spirit possession, the roles of religious leaders and the function of prayer, offering and sacrifice. Thoughts on the relation between religion and politics include a critique of Karl Marx's idea of religion as 'spiritual aroma'. Examples are given of the subtleties of theological controversy and of the difficulties faced by religious organizations in coming to terms with modern economic and political developments.

Professor Sir Raymond Firth was a pupil and colleague of Malinowski at the London School of Economics and is internationally regarded as one of this century's great anthropologists. His books include *Human Types* (1938), *Malay Fishermen* (1946), *Symbols Public and Private* (1973) and range from *We, the Tikopia* (1936) to *Tikopia Songs* (1991).

Religion: a Humanist Interpretation

Raymond Firth

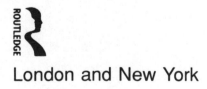

London and New York

First published 1996
by Routledge
11 New Fetter Lane, London EC4P 4EE

Simultaneously published in the USA and Canada
by Routledge
29 West 35th Street, New York, NY 10001

Phototypeset in Times by Intype, London

Printed and bound in Great Britain by
TJ Press (Padstow) Ltd, Padstow, Cornwall

British Library Cataloguing in Publication Data
A catalogue record for this book is available from the British Library

Library of Congress Cataloguing in Publication Data
A catalogue record for this book has been requested

ISBN 0–415–12896–x (hbk)
ISBN 0–415–12897–8 (pbk)

For
Hugh and Melinda,
Nicholas and Emma

Contents

Preface

This book gives some of the results of my thinking about religion over many years. In particular, its gives my own personal view on the nature and origin of religion more openly than I have tended to do previously, to a degree unusual among anthropologists who have written on the subject.

Six of the nine chapters in the book reproduce with slight modifications articles which I have published in a variety of more specialized books and journals. They have been descriptive and analytical, and they have been meant to depict aspects of religion as studied from an anthropological comparative base. By contrast, the first and last two chapters, more general in form, have been freshly written, and discuss the problems of religion from my own personal humanist point of view. They are somewhat of a challenge to the religious establishment. The results may be provocative to some of my anthropological colleagues, and even more so to some other readers for whom religion still represents supreme, absolute sacred values.

Acknowledgements

I am indebted to the following sources for re-publication:
Chapter 2: *Journal of the Royal Anthropological Institute* **78** (1948), Henry Myers Lecture.
Chapter 3: *American Anthropologist* **83** (1981), Distinguished Lecture to American Anthropological Association for 1980.
Chapter 4: *The Humanist Outlook* (1968); *R.A.I. News* **14** (1977); *The Times Literary Supplement*, 23 May 1986.
Chapter 5: *Journal of the Royal Anthropological Institute* **93** (1963).
Chapter 6: *Comparative Studies in Society and History* **9** (1967), Jane Harrison Lecture.
Chapter 7: Roff, William R. (ed.) (1974) *Kelantan: Religion, Society and Politics in a Malay State*, Kuala Lumpur: Oxford University Press.

The list of references at the end of the book shows the range of sources consulted. For the last chapters in particular, apart from authors cited in the References I am indebted for general enlightenment to *A New Dictionary of Christian Theology* edited by Alan Richardson and John Bowden, London, SCM Press, 1983.

For discussion of the general form of this book I am indebted to my colleague Peter Loizos, of the London School of Economics and Political Science.

To accord with modern literal-minded literary fashion I have used he/she to indicate inclusiveness when no particular gender is intended. But in some early chapters 'he', 'his', 'him' should be understood figuratively to include both male and female.

Chapter 1

An anthropological approach to the study of religion

A major problem in modern thought is the existence and survival of religion. In a world of rapidly developing technology and radically changing social and political institutions, is religion in peril? Opinions on this vary greatly. Some people hold that secularism and rationalism are sweeping irresistably across the world of belief. In many Western countries they see organized church congregations greatly shrunk, and the forces of modernism and the international market threatening to reduce religious institutions to a negligible dimension. Events in communist countries seemed for a time to bear out this view also. But an opinion which now seems better founded is that organized religion can be eliminated only in special cases, and diffuse religious belief may continue in the absence of overt ritual practice. Belief and ritual relating to the transcendent, it is thought therefore, will not only survive in the face of adversity and indifference, but may even develop in protest against the materialistic thrust of secular values.

Yet bitter controversy has arisen regarding the relation of religion to the secular world, even among religious people themselves. Animosity has also been manifest between followers of different religions, and even of members of sects, denominations, churches within any particular religion. Sometimes these come to expression in continued acts of violence, as between Catholics and Protestants in Northern Ireland. Sometimes they are evident in struggles for adherents, as in the wasteful duplication of missionary efforts of Christianity and Islam in Africa. Often argument about ideas has been deeply divisive within religious bodies, as entrenched positions on say the teaching of religion in school;

the ordination of women to priesthood; the dominance of religious or secular law in a nation-state.

Many theories about the nature and origin of religion try to account for the persistence of faith and ritual. They also explore reasons for the changes that religions have undergone in the course of their history. Two contrasted positions are common. Believers argue that their religion is simply accounted for by the existence of God or whatever spiritual entities they worship. Sceptics hold that religion is just a human illusion. But clearly the matter is more complex. Religion cannot be understood simply as a response of men to divine revelation, or alternatively as a case of mistaken perception. For religions show enormous variety, in types of belief, degrees of belief, kinds of ritual procedures, spiritual concepts and symbolic imagery. Religions also vary greatly in the kind of relationship they bear to the social, economic and political structures of the communities in which they are practised. Any 'theory' then has to be many-armed, multi-factorial, to take account of this range of variation. Ideally, the theory should be explanatory, showing why the given forms and processes originated. But the ultimate 'Why?' of any religion may be thought to be too elusive. Any simple affirmation of divine presence and revelation will not do; assertion has to stand the test of evidence. Metaphysical problems enter here at every turn. All that may be possible in a theory of religion may be interpretation, a demonstration of the nature and meaning of rites and beliefs for those people who hold and practise them, of their value for the people in the context of their lives. As part of the interpretation, the theory must deal with nonrational as well as rational elements in belief patterns and practice.

Anthropologists have contributed in a unique way to theories of the operations and meaning of religions, over a wide comparative range. In earlier times the work of Edward Burnett Tylor, Robertson Smith, James Frazer, R. R. Marett, Jane Harrison and E. O. James was of pioneering character. More recently Edward Evans-Pritchard, Godfrey Lienhardt, S. F. Nadel, John Middleton, Victor Turner, Monica Wilson – to mention only a few Africanists – have provided detailed analytical studies of particular religious systems. They and many other anthropologists in other regions have examined notions of God; concepts of the soul, ghosts, ancestral and other spirits; cults of the dead; the operations of priests and prophets; shrines, offerings, sacrifices; purification and pollution; ideas of sin and salvation. My own studies in the religious field have included a demonstration of the close fit between economic and religious operations in the traditional seasonal ritual cycles of a western Polynesian community (Firth 1967) and a more general examination of the relation between the political structure and the religion of these people (Firth 1970).

Though anthropologists have focused largely on the comparative study of the small-scale so-called 'primitive' religions of the technically less developed peoples, many of us have also examined aspects of the major universalistic religions. Following a lead of E. O. James in his historical study of Christian myth and ritual (1933a), Victor Turner has written of Christianity, S. J. Tambiah of Buddhism, Dale F. Eickelman, Clifford Geertz and Ernest Gellner of Islam. Nearly all the dozen anthropological contributions to a book on religious organization and religious experience edited by John Davis (1982) dealt with aspects of the great religions. My own studies of religious symbolism (1973) have included comment upon the ethnicity of Jesus, the concept of the Sacred Heart of Jesus, and the Eucharist.

The value of any theory of religion depends not only on the logical development of the argument, but also upon the validity of the evidence produced in support. The approach of social anthropologists to the study of religion, unlike that of historian, theologian, psychologist or even sociologist, has been based largely upon unique experience, that of field enquiry. This has consisted in personal observation, often involving actually taking part in the religious practices of the people being studied, and systematic discussion of their religious beliefs with them. This has also involved studying the religion in its social setting and noting the economic and political parameters to religious ideas and operations. Combined with a training in the comparative scholarship of religious belief and institutions, this has given social anthropologists a special perspective and a powerful body of evidence for examining religion.

Since the study is so unfamiliar to many people, in the next part of this chapter I give an outline of a social anthropological approach, its aims, its difficulties and the kind of results it hopes to get. But social anthropologists have approached the subject of religion and formulated their theories about it with many different interests and diverse assumptions about the reality of the phenomena studied. Hence in the latter part of this chapter I describe my own personal position, as a preface to the general theoretical statements of the book as a whole.

GENERAL CHARACTER OF SOCIAL ANTHROPOLOGY

Anthropology, from the Greek, means the study of man. Social anthropology, my own specialism, was the latest main branch of the subject to develop explicitly, about seventy years ago. It is concerned with men's and women's relationships to one another in society, with the behaviour patterns, institutions and beliefs which characterize people in different types of society. Social anthropology has two important features which distinguish it from other fields of social study. It is essentially comparative, studying human behaviour in all forms of society in any part of the world, its variations and the meaning of such variants. In such comparisons social anthropology tends to take a wider range than sociology, with which it has shared a considerable theoretical history. Social anthropology is also distinguished by the directness and intensity of the relationship of its fieldworkers to the people among whom they work. Often described as 'participant observation', the situation of the fieldworker is apt to be unique, living in a hunter's camp, village or urban ward among the people, sharing food with them, attending their marriage ceremonies, initiation rites and funerals, speaking their vernacular tongue. The anthropologist is in communication with them throughout the day – and often well into the night – listening to their gossip and tales of joy or woe, getting to understand their loves, their jealousies and rivalries, their expectations and their fears, their religious beliefs and forms of symbolic behaviour. Such experiences, even if lasting for only a year or so, but sometimes repeated periodically, can be very significant for the anthropologist, with aesthetic and emotional as well as intellectual values. Vividly meaningful, the record of these experiences forms the basis for much analytical anthropological study.

There is another feature of peculiar importance in an anthropological study of religion. Unlike many of those, such as missionaries or government officials, who have been in contact with members of an alien society, anthropologists have been trained not to attach a moral evaluation to their record of what they see and hear. Personally, an anthropologist may feel approval or revulsion at some religious practice or belief, but his/her job is to describe it and reveal its meaning, not to class it on some moral scale. One may expect from an anthropologist then a more dispassionate, more neutral, perhaps more sympathetic and more understanding account of a religious system than that provided by another outside observer.

Considering the unique character of the anthropological experience in studying religion, some questions may arise about the methods used and the validity of the findings.

A general question in all fieldwork, not particularly in a study of religion, is how far an anthropologist can really have access to the ways of thinking and feeling of the alien, often 'exotic' people studied? Complete access is impossible. One can observe, even share another person's overt behaviour. One cannot observe, let alone directly experience another person's thoughts and emotions; one can only infer them. An anthropologist may watch a Polynesian religious ritual of offering a libation of *kava* (an infusion of pepper root) liquid, where the officiating chief-priest raises the coconut shell cup to his brow before pouring out the liquid upon the ground before him. The anthropologist infers that the act is an offering to invisible spirits of gods and ancestors, and this is confirmed by statements of priest and other elders, and by the behaviour of respect shown to symbols of the spirits. The lifting of the cup to the brow is then clearly an act of obeisance, of acknowledgement of dependence upon the spirits, and such an interpretation fits into the whole passage of the ritual. But it is impossible for the anthropologist to know *exactly* what is passing through the mind of the priest as he lifts the cup to his brow. There are various possibilities known to the anthropologist – the chief is thinking with respect to the spirits, he is anxious about food supplies for the rite, he is worried about the health of his family which depends upon the goodwill of the spirits, or he is concerned with some more mundane problem such as to whom will be distributed the food brought as offering, once the rite is over. Later discussion with the priest may let the anthropologist check as to whether such thoughts may have been in the priest's mind. This means that anthropological inferences about religious belief, as distinct from accounts of religious behaviour, must always be approximate. But this is not a situation confined to anthropology; it is so with all forms of human encounter and communication. In every phase of everyday life we have to make an effort at interpreting what is being thought by others, or felt, with varying degrees of success. Claims of writers and speakers of all kinds, from poets to preachers, to 'understand' what other people think and feel, or what they mean by what they do, rest upon such broad interpretation.

The question of how far an anthropologist's findings are governed by his or her personality, temperament and experience is important for any study of religion. There has been much professional emphasis in recent years upon the 'reflexive' or 'autobiographical' components of an anthropological interpretation. The idea of objectivity has been scorned. It has been held that all anthropological accounts are subjective, reflections of the self of the investigator, as imaginative constructs.

But recognition of such personal elements in anthropological findings is not new. Some thirty years ago I myself wrote that the observer's experience is always viewed through his personal lens; that if one wished to use Cassirer's terms there is no content which is not construed according to some form which is supplied by the human understanding at the start of apprehension. The primary experience is itself form-selected. A scientist cannot immediately grasp or communicate reality; he can only mediate it. In knowledge, truth itself must be in accord with the form of understanding. But while we may grant that the form-giving and symbolizing activities of consciousness mean that we can never reproduce the 'crude facts' of Malay or Tikopia social life, this does not justify intellectual retreat (Firth 1964: 41). We can continually learn from experience, and the field experience of the anthropologist is continually being built into his/her framework of ideas. So these ideas are continually being modified, not simply emerging as a kind of pre-formed straitjacket upon the construction and interpretation of what is observed, thought and felt in the field. Too much preoccupation with the anthropologist's own role and state of mind can blur the clarity of observation and record.

There is undoubtedly some relation, however faint, between the temperament and personality of an anthropologist and his/her interpretation of the data gathered. But it may be hard to identify this relation adequately; even in a study of religion I think I can identify some aspects of my own early religious and moral upbringing in my writings about religion (see chapter 3).

But what about aesthetic make-up? In the attraction which Romanesque painting and sculpture have for me, with their grotesque, hieratic and symbolic forms, I can perceive a kind of general link with some of the more idiosyncratic, bizarre religious practices of people studied by anthropologists. But not so in my preference for Western 'early music'. It has a curious appeal for me, from Machaut's first setting of the Mass through Dufay's lament for the fall of Constantinople and the work of Josquin des Prés, Ockhegem, Dunstable, Tallis, Byrd, Schütz, Monteverdi to the supreme beauty of J. S. Bach. This musical commitment clearly fits into a historical interest in Christian religion. But I cannot trace its effect in any of my interpretation of the religious sayings and doings of the Tikopia or of the Kelantan Malays. What I am arguing is that the elements of temperament and experience of any anthropologist are so complex, so subtly composed and intertwined that only at a most superficial level can any identification of them be usually seen in his or her professional work. In judging such work the primary criteria are those of internal validity – amount and quality of evidence, degree of checking manifest, systematic approach in putting counter-questions to see if the propositions formulated can be falsified, consistence of inference from the record.

What I am defending is the claim of social anthropology to present an acceptable ethnography of religion, not a fictionalized, fantasized account of what has been studied. But, as will be seen later, when it comes to more general interpretation of religious matters, the personal assumptions of the anthropologist may be highly significant.

An important set of problems in any anthropological study of religion involves language. The treachery of language as a mode of reference is well-known. To express thought in language often creates great difficulties. A Slav poet, Fyodor Tyutchev, has said 'A thought when uttered is a lie', in despair at the inadequacies of language to convey the intricacies of mental process. For an anthropologist there is the problem of rendering in verbal form, in words, images many of which have been presented to the fieldworker in non-verbal, visual or aural terms. There is also the special problem of glossing in one language utterances which have originally been made in another language. Anthropologists are now generally expected to 'speak the vernacular'. But there are many stages or levels of being able to handle an alien vernacu-

lar tongue. During my time in Malaya I became fairly competent
in speaking and understanding the Kelantan dialect of Malay,
carrying on extensive conversations with fishermen and rice
farmers, and local magicians, on a variety of topics from net-
making and catching fish to shadow-play drama and beliefs about
the bounty of Allah (see chapter 7). But I was not equipped to
deal easily either with the linguisitic niceties of court etiquette
or the more abstract theological and philosophical discussions
with the more learned men of the neighbourhood. Over the
years, I have become highly competent in the Tikopia language.
Uncommonly for an anthropologist, I have published a dictionary
(Tikopia–English), in which I have been able to gloss Tikopia
words very extensively in terms of their social context of use. Yet
I would never claim that I have had the complete fluency of a
native Tikopia speaker. Deep questions, including those relating
to unstated philosopical and religious assumptions, lie behind the
anthropologist's choice of glosses in his/her translations of many
esoteric vernacular terms. From the linguistic angle, then, I insist
on the approximate, illustrative nature of any ethnographic
account of a religious system.

Granted these qualifications, I would still contend that an
anthropologist is probably better equipped than most observers
to give an account of an alien religious system, and to offer an
original, comparative theoretical view of religion in general.

PERSONAL STANDPOINT

I now turn to my own more personal standpoint in anthropological analysis, with particular reference to the ideas and practices
of religion. In my collection and interpretation of anthropological
data I have been guided by a basic curiosity about the nature of
the human condition, with all its complexities of individual belief
and action as affected by a network of social relationships,
norms and obligations. In shaping my enquiries I have been led
by two themes which to a degree have marked my work off
from that of some of my colleagues. These are empiricism and
humanism.

It has been a fashion in much modern or 'post-modern' social
anthropology to decry what has been termed a positivist, empiricist approach. By contrast, I call myself an empiricist, accepting
in general the validity of sensory experience as a guide to knowl-

edge. I reject claims to knowledge by revelation. But I am a modified empiricist, a neo-empiricist. I accept the possibility that ultimately the results of sensory experience may be illusory, that their unreality is a logical alternative. As J. N. Findlay and others have pointed out, there is always a possibility of error in any material-object statements, including those about the nature of material existence itself (Findlay 1963: 36). I also accept as significant in thought what may be called 'intuition', a cohering activity of the mind not apparently due to any action of the senses. (But what is called 'intuition' in my view is often only an unconscious inference from subliminal observation, often relying on previous experience, or an analogy in experience.) My empiricist position has been closely bound to my conviction of the importance of evidence in anthropological propositions. I am sceptical of assertions of knowledge not backed up by empirical evidence; in religious matters they are often no more than assertions of privilege or claims to power. That the evidence must be open to critical scrutiny applies to any study of religion as to that of any other social phenomenon.

My approach to religion has been distinguished from that of some of my colleagues by my humanism. There are alternative approaches to the recognition of reality. Some Western anthropologists have clearly professed a Christian faith, while others elsewhere have adhered to Hinduism, Buddhism, Judaism or Islam. The term 'humanism' is rather suspect in Western intellectual circles, since it suggests an old-fashioned rationalism. But some other social anthropologists such as Ernest Gellner and the late Edmund Leach, as I myself, have been honorary associates of the Rationalist Press Association, the major humanist association in Britain, as well as other distinguished thinkers such as Karl Popper and Joseph Needham. In social anthropology other colleagues are probably of much the same temper, though preferring not to bear the humanist label. (Philosophers who share the same general trend of thought may call themselves 'realists', such as 'internal realists' or 'scientific realists'.)

Any social anthropologist studying religion must have some basic assumptions about the nature of the phenomena. My own assumptions are humanistic, based on the view that a central part of reality for people everywhere lies in the existence of human individuals in their social matrix, and that it is comprehensible only by human cognition and expressible only in human language.

The universe holds many mysteries, from the behaviour of quasars in space, to the sexual attraction between two persons. Many human problems are obscure, and the fate of individuals unpredictable. But I assume that whatever be the nature of the external world, there is no reality of another order beyond that world, no revelation of divine plan or divine values, no creative supersensible transcendent mind that can give meaning and sense to human experience and human endeavours.

To an anthropologist such as myself, therefore, religion, including ideas of God, is clearly a human construct. It grows and is maintained by the wish to have answers to fundamental human problems. Religion supplies reasons for the forms of nature, for human existence. It faces questions of pain and suffering and the ultimate fate of the human personality. According to its particular tenets, it encourages love, charity and respect for others. It can also provide a great pillar of strength, both by the alleged certainty of the propositions it proclaims, and by a body of faithful who support one another. But religion is a human art. It has produced, like other arts, some of the greatest literary and intellectual constructs, analyses of thought and emotion, and stirring aesthetic experiences of a creative order in painting, poetry and music. But it has also been treated as a ladder to personal and group advancement, as an instrument of manipulation in ideas and behaviour, the purveyor of ready-made solutions to traumatic issues of human conduct. In its corporate aspect, a church, it can be a sociological force of great impact. It can be of positive value in helping to maintain moral standards. But it can also offer a field for controversy about doctrine and ritual, for divisive sectarian activity and opposition. It can even act as a force of destruction, as violent collisions of religious wars have demonstrated in many faiths.

A humanist approach to religion, within an anthropological framework of enquiry, means that rational study can go much further than religious people are often prepared to allow. 'Science' may be able to give no final answers to such problems as the origin of the universe, the nature and fate of a soul, the occurrence of miracles. The answers of religion are assertions, no more capable of proof. But if the answers given by either science or religion are untestable, one can speak in terms of probabilities. On this basis, the asserted existence of an invisible, transcendent, omniscient, omnipotent being known as God is highly improbable. It is much more probable that such an assertion fits the highly complex world of human imagining, and serves an array of human purposes not always consciously realized by people themselves. It corresponds in figurative and symbolic language to an attempt to meet basic human problems involved in mental and physical anxiety and pain, the certainty of death, the uncertainties of life in the complicated relations with other human beings. The propositions of religion, despite claims to any divine origin, are all formulated by human beings. Its asserted transcendental origins do not mean that these propositions are *true* in any external, objective sense. One does not speak of a musical composition as true (unless in a highly technical sense) but as beautiful, powerful, aesthetically and emotionally satisfying. And so it should be with the imaginative creations of religion.

Such a humanist viewpoint is unpalatable to many religious people. Most theologians object to what they have termed such a reductionist, projectionist approach to religion. A professor of theology, John Kent, has singled out Emile Durkheim, author of a book on what he called the elementary forms of religious life, and an early proponent of a humanist view of religion, for critical treatment (in Richardson and Bowden 1983, 'Reductionism'). 'When Durkheim, the French sociologist, attempted to "reduce" the idea of God to society's sense of its own oneness, he did so, the historian may say, because he was a frightened moralist anxious to detect social forces which might be relied upon to unite what he saw as a disintegrating French society in the early twentieth century.' But to anyone familiar with Durkheim's work this interpretation seems an odd paraphrase of his own statement of his objective: 'to lead to an understanding of the religious nature of man, that is to say, to show us an essential and permanent aspect of humanity'. Durkheim's proposition that God is society divinized can be criticized on various grounds, as over-simplified. But striking examples of how it may apply in some conditions do occur. In some aspects of Israeli fundamentalism, the modern concept of Eretz Israel – 'a land promised to the Jews by Abraham' – claims that God Himself is the author of the sanction for settlement in Palestinian lands. Such an interpretation by the extreme nationalist group Gush Emunim clearly identifies God as the justificatory sanctified projection of their own sense of pressing community territorial needs. The crude community drive is given spiritual cloak.

The following chapters deal with selected aspects of religion, from a broad comparative point of view. They combine the results of deep analysis by anthropologists, including myself, with the critical use of documentary sources. They include examination of individual and corporate religious beliefs and ritual forms. They range in evidence from relatively simply organized 'primitive' religious systems to the highly sophisticated complex 'universalistic' religious systems. And above all, they demonstrate how 'pure' religion hardly exists; how closely religion is bound to a social, economic and political framework in an essentially human construction.

My treatment in this book moves primarily from studies of belief to those of ritual and daily practice. After my introductory discussion of scope and method, chapter 2 deals with a basic problem: how far can religious belief fit an individual's personal constitution and circumstances? What part do nonrational ideas play in the coherence of a person's life? But an individual is not alone in his religion. In chapter 3 the title 'Spiritual Aroma' is taken from an essay on Karl Marx's view of religion. I have not accepted Marx's opinion that religion has been a shield for a capitalist society and class exploitation. But while Marx's theories are now highly unpopular (especially among those who have not read his work) one of his basic approaches is still sound – that man is a social being, and religion is a social product.

Chapter 4 deals with a (some would say *the*) basic religious concept – the idea of God. But it also takes into account an anthropological perspective – that many religious systems are polytheistic, and some can not be credited with a concept of God but operate with a set of much vaguer Forces or Powers. Implications from this are explored. The burden of this chapter is then that the god-concept is variable and humanly constructed according to context.

Chapter 5 turns from belief to ritual. It takes for analysis the key rites of offering and sacrifice, which are at the base of much religious practice. Contrary to much anthropological treatment, of an ideological character, I stress here the basic economic parameters of such rituals.

Chapters 6 and 7 are illustrative of complexities in religious ritual and practice. They stem directly from my own field experience and that of my wife Rosemary Firth, in the Malay state of Kelantan, both before and after the Second World War. The chapters deal specifically with variations in religious behaviour of Malay peasants. Good Muslims, these Malays still retained elements of traditional, possibly pre-Islamic thinking and behaviour in their rituals of agriculture, fishing and personal healing, which tended to mark them out from more sophisticated co-religionists of Islam. Such admixture of traditional folk beliefs and rituals from outside the main doctrinal field of the faithful has been characteristic of many rural Muslim, Christian and Buddhist congregations in the Orient, Europe and elsewhere in the world.

The penultimate chapter, recently written, is a synoptic analysis. It examines generally the diversity of religious systems, and the kinds of paradox that arise within them, showing the richness and complexity of thought and behaviour in the religious field as products of human intelligence, emotion, imagination and fantasy. The last chapter is a re-affirmation of my general humanist position.

Chapter 2

Religious belief and personal adjustment

An anthropologist addressing an audience on the subject of religion realizes that he is probably facing great divergences of view. While some may regard all religious professions as illusory, others, like More's Utopians, may hold that it falls below the dignity of human nature to believe that the soul perishes with the body or that the world is governed by chance and not by divine providence. The anthropologist trusts that his scientific inquiry will reveal something of the nature of religious phenomena, but he knows that he does not stand as the sole interpreter. Apart from the theologian who claims a proprietary right, historian and sociologist, philosopher and psychologist, and even an occasional natural scientist, all proffer their interpretations of what William James summarized as the feelings, acts and experiences of people apprehending themselves to stand in solemn relation to what they consider to be the divine. Through the scope of his comparative method the anthropologist has contributed a universalism which the study lacked before. His primary observation of 'primitive' cults has added much to its depth. Yet where so much is clouded over by emotion and feeling in the study of those heights of the human spirit which we call religious, the anthropologist's first justification is his sincerity in his attempt to gain as clear an intellectual comprehension of it as possible. His approach has been for the most part humanistic, seeking to understand on the plane of peoples' activities. It has also been socially positivist, in attributing to religious phenomena important social functions irrespective of the nature of their reality.

My subject is religious belief. My basic hypothesis is that religious beliefs are related, in content, form and expression, to the attempts of individuals to secure coherence in their universe

of relations, both physical and social. Many anthropological studies of religion have concentrated more on the analysis of ritual
than on that of belief. Religious beliefs appear less stable than
ritual, more open to personal variation and modification. Their
vagueness and lack of definition are seen in two respects. Different individuals in the same religious communion vary in their
beliefs on a given topic, which makes it difficult to assign to any
synoptic expression a truly representative value. Again, a single
individual is often unable to formulate clearly his belief on even
such fundamental concepts as God, Heaven or the soul. Variation
in ritual is significant in the interpretation of the role which ritual
has in the life of different individuals. Variation and lack of
precision in belief, too, have analogous significance. Though they
may complicate the analyses of the sociologist, they are not fortuitous; they are characteristic and indeed essential to the functions
which religious belief fulfils.

Consider first the notion of belief itself. It has been called the
subjective side of judgement. It is a set of ideas more or less
integrated by reason but held with a conviction that they are
true, that they are meaningful in relation to reality. Elements of
knowledge, of emotion or feeling tone, and of volitional activity
can be distinguished therein, each capable of being present to
varying degrees. But however adequate it may be to isolate belief
as a psychological concept for examination, for sociological analysis it is necessary to consider it in terms of classes. For our
immediate purposes any exact classification is not important. A
convenient grouping comprises: empirical, mathematical, philosophical, aesthetical, ethical and religious. What is noteworthy is
how religious belief differs from the others essentially in its content of the supernatural and in its quality of the sacred. In
religious belief above all, the element of emotion in whatever be
the kind of experience that gives the basis to the belief provides
it with a strong flavour of reality. At one level, the nature of this
experience is a specific question for psychology – as William
James, Leuba and many others have amply shown. At another
level, as a general question for philosophy, it has occupied the
minds of men for over two thousand years. No one wishes deliber-
ately to pass off metaphysics as science. But it has always seemed
to me rather naïve to imagine that a personal metaphysical
position can be entirely irrelevant to the analysis of religious

phenomena. So a little later I shall say something about what I think is the object of religious belief.

For my present analysis it is primarily the content of belief as expressed in verbal behaviour with which I am concerned. One can study belief in its non-verbal expression as well. But one interest of the word, either spoken or written, as an index of belief, is that it can be studied at different levels – overt, or indicative of much that the author does not suspect is revealed. What I want to emphasize here is that religious beliefs, in their immediate expression, are a mode of action. They are not merely passive fixed items of mental furniture; their emotional component alone would suggest this cannot be so. They are active weapons in the process of adjustment by the person who holds them. What I mean by personal adjustment is the continual process of striving for order by the individual in his relations on the one hand with his physical and social universe, and on the other with his own logical system of categories of thought and his own set of impulses, desires and emotions. I think it will be admitted that there is a continual and real need for such adjustment or adaptation on the part of every individual. In this respect the vagueness and lack of precise definition of religious belief is, up to a point, an asset. It allows of a plastic treatment. Modification takes place in detail, often almost imperceptibly to the external observer, and it may be unconsciously by the individual himself.

If this be agreed, then certain implications can be considered. As greater precision in the definition of belief occurs, the greater is the necessity to cope with the change in external circumstances by reinforcing the belief. We shall be concerned with some examination of the processes of reinforcing or buttressing religious belief later. An alternative process is to make a radical alteration in belief by what is known as conversion. In any process of adjustment the content of belief, which varies according to the cultural situation, may be of considerable importance. For example, a belief in an ancestor cult is not of such a type as to allow easily the affiliation of other persons from a different society, who can have the original ancestors ascribed to them only by a series of elaborate fictions. Moreover, the range of religious belief can be expected to vary according to the range of possible social situations. In a simple society the personal adjustments which an individual may have to make are as great in magnitude as in a highly differentiated society such as our own, but are less in diversity.

Each individual has a configuration of religious beliefs corresponding to or representing a configuration of his personal adjustments. These adjustments can have degrees of completeness or adequacy according as the situation to which adjustment is required is more or less adequately conceived. To the degree that there is ignorance or error so there is imperfect adjustment, either recognized or not recognized as such. This conception of the individual's relation to the situations he has to meet is very different from that of a system of equilibrium. It is possible, in fact probable, that each individual has a configuration of more or less imperfect adjustments to reality – always lagging behind or varying from the current situation that he has to face. To conclude this series of propositions for the moment it is through the continuous operation of personal adjustment in terms of belief that change in religious forms becomes possible.

The attempt to secure personal adjustment rests upon a perception that some degree of adaptation between self and environment is necessary to effective action in view of the ends the individual is pursuing. It rests also upon the emotional drive for sympathy and inter-communion. In the process of adjustment various motivations are at work. These include the search for order, for certitude, for self-expression and for feeling for others, for the exercise of intellectual curiosity. It is conceivable that individuals in any society might be content to place reliance on themselves or on their fellows alone for these elements of adjustment; some do so, especially in the more highly differentiated social systems. A young child presumably relies on its parents for these matters. But the obvious human insufficiency to cover all the range of circumstances is only too plain. Peoples' limitations, their fallibility, their exercise of their own individualistic impulses, are soon discerned, even where sentiment of a strong kind may lead to trust. The requirements demanded are secured in the highest degree by the postulates of religious belief.

Such belief is always culturally defined, whether explicitly recognized as such or not. It has a nucleus or core, which is firmly held and in essentials usually simple to state; a set of ancillaries or personal variations of a fluctuating kind; and a periphery which is vague, involving either difficulties of formulation or lack of certainty or conviction. The nucleus of the belief may be comprised in part by the dogma of the religion concerned, that is, by the set of doctrines regarded as proper to be believed in by all who profess that religion. It may be assisted in utterance by creeds, expressions of the essential dogma in formal terms. But this is not inevitably the case. Most 'primitive' religions have no creeds, and their dogmas are to be inferred from activity rather than from any specific formulation.

For evidence of this let me briefly refer to material from my own studies. In Tikopia there is a nuclear belief held, as far as could be verified, by all persons, in what may be termed a separable soul-essence of man. Different people have varying ancillaries attributing or denying soul-essence to birds and animals, to stones and trees, and to material goods. There are varying ancillaries also relating to the fate of souls after death. One man, a chief, linked their fate with their interest in life in the basic religious rite, the *kava*. Those who ignored the *kava* in life were themselves ignored after death; their souls, he maintained, were not borne to the spirit world, but left to stand in the path and annoy people. Another man, also a chief and with a similar interest in maintaining the prestige of the *kava*, believed that the souls of the dead came in due course to a stone crossing a void barring the way to the future world. If the soul was that of a man who had sought the *kava*, all was well; the stone stayed firm and the soul crossed it to its future abode. If the man had spurned the *kava*, the stone began to rock and finally precipitated the soul down into the gulf, to be lost. A question as to where the soul goes then showed belief on the periphery – on one occasion the chief said he didn't know, the soul simply vanished; on another occasion he said the soul wandered blindly about. A third man, son of a chief, was not so concerned to interpret the stone in terms of moral or ritual duties. He regarded it as a matter of paying dues, as to a Cerberus. The soul arrives with bark-cloth, areca-nut, oil and valuables. If he wishes to pass, he offers them to the female demon dwelling in the stone. Should he not do this, and try to cross, she makes the stone slippery, the soul loses its footing and tumbles down below. As a further ancillary belief, a description was given of certain flying souls. They have 'speed', that is, power, and evade toll by taking wing, rising up above and darting onwards through the air like fish in the sea. The personal interests of the chiefs are clear in these beliefs. They compensate for inability to punish ritual laggards directly, by adjustment of belief to imagine them suffering future punishment. To the extent that such views get popular credence, the ritual obligations are reinforced.

Similar differences of belief occur in regard to those souls that arrive in the afterworld. The general scheme is that of a number of different heavens, stratified. Each set of strata is associated with a major social group and is situated at a different point of the compass. This is nuclear belief. But there are many individual ancillaries, as regards the names and number of the heavens, and the behaviour of the spirits of the dead there. In particular, this type of belief serves in citation of names in tales and songs, thus acting as material of revelation for spirit mediums. A new name is an effort of the creative imagination, which appeals to other people as a piece of new knowledge, in effect, property. Hence there is a tendency for spirit mediums in their recitals to elaborate the furniture of the other world, in nomenclature and activities; in so doing they help to bolster up their own authenticity by the production of such novel information, in which they appear to believe firmly.

Examination of Malay religious beliefs in a fishing community gave analogous data. Every person held nuclear beliefs in spirits, the ubiquitous *hantu*, and in the powers of selected human individuals to control them. But very different beliefs were held about the powers of a specific *hantu*, or specific human controls. Two dramatic events brought this out to me – the advent of a conjurer claiming to produce sugar, biscuits, and even live birds by materialization; and the practices of a religious man who without experience of the sea and its lore, claimed modestly to be able to increase the catch of fish by well-timed rites with a candle and an egg. The resulting controversies illustrated a variety of ancillary beliefs and their dependence on problems of personal adjustment (see chapter 7).

In examining belief in the simpler religious systems, the anthropologist relates the concepts under scrutiny to human needs, desires and emotions. He sees how the various kinds of spirit powers believed in, for example, can be interpreted as essentially socialized projections of the believer's own psychological requirements and faculties. Applied on a comparative basis, such findings may lead him to stress the subjective character of all religious experience and belief. His hypothesis may be that even those concepts which are normally regarded as basic in a religious system are not independent of the individual human believer, but are part of his total adjustment, in common with that of his fellows, to their general field of problems.

Let us pursue this theme in terms of the way in which certain basic beliefs have been formulated. Anthropologists ordinarily study particular religions, that is, those in which the system of beliefs and practices is regarded by the adherents as applying to their particular society alone, and not by implication to mankind as a whole. I propose to draw examples also from the universalist religions, to broaden my generalizations. In this part of the analysis I shall examine some of the beliefs concerning the Deity, as being of crucial interest. (See also Chapter 4.)

It is a commonplace that even in the universalist religions belief in God is often conceived in terms which in providing a definite sanction for behaviour, are appropriate to the particular type of society in which the belief finds expression. For instance, in the Koran, the Faithful are enjoined to fight on God's path. Believers who sit at home free from trouble shall not be treated alike with those who do valiantly in the cause of God with their substance and their persons. God has assigned to the latter a rank and a rich recompense above those who sit at home. If a believer kills a believer by mischance, he is bound to atone by blood-money, setting free a slave who is a believer, or both; or by fasting two months if he has no means otherwise. This is the penance enjoined by God, the Knowing, the Wise. But who shall kill a believer of set purpose shall abide in hell for ever; God shall be wrathful with him, and curse him and prepare for him a great torment.[1] Here the attitudes attributed to God can be regarded as a projection of the Prophet's desires to safeguard the faith of his creation. The religious sanction is invoked to promote unity and amity among the Faithful and compose differences. The Divine sanction was invoked with a more personal flavour to explain the special dispensation by which the Prophet allowed himself to have as many as nine wives, whereas the maximum number allowed to the Faithful was only four. The Prophet by the Koran was allowed not only the wives whom he had dowered and the daughters of his uncle and of his aunts, but also any believing woman who had given herself up to him, if he desired to wed her – 'a Privilege for thee above the rest of the Faithful' as the Prophet's own revelation announced it to him.[2]

Fundamental in the nature of much religious belief is that

characteristic which may be called the process of theo-symbolism. The aims of man and the principles which he seeks or thinks he finds in the universe are given shape in the idea of the Deity, who is made their symbolic expression. Social relations or interests empirically observable are explicitly formulated as inherent or transcendental principles. They are represented as arising not from the nature of social action but from the nature of God. To acquire knowledge is to many people a human good and certainly engages a great deal of their energies. Consequently it is held that it must be God's will that men should use to the full what gifts of intellectual curiosity with which He has endowed them. Guidance is required in one's contacts with one's fellows. Consequently, it is held that God has a will for the world, and that this will, which is perfect and good, sets a pattern for the life of every man.[3]

This theo-symbolism may also assume an inverted form. Some trust and confidence in one's fellow beings is a prerequisite to effective cooperation and sharing of the products of social endeavour. Hence the concept of faith may be expressed as a two-way process. Not only must man have faith in God; he must also believe that God has faith in him. 'God puts His trust in man; He depends upon him; He commits to him the responsibility for carrying out His purposes for the world. . . . God trusts the individual with the raw materials for the formation of character.' God's trust is often abused, by human faithlessness, stupidity and indolence. But God continues to trust; God's trust implies His patience.[4] Here then is an interesting mechanism whereby a man first projects his desire for confidence into divine shape, and then injects this image in turn with a further charge of the desired element. Human frailty can then be interpreted not merely as failure to take advantage of facilities offered, but as betrayal of facilities handed over. The sanction for human action is thus doubled, and guilt is added to laxity. But there is room for selective adjustment. Assurance is given to the shrinking spirit. Where one cannot trust one's fellows, where the course of events belies their fair promise, one can fix one's trust on God, and find that reciprocity which is so craved by feeling that Divinity returns the confidence. Again to him who wishes to feel that he is entrusted with a task, to feel that in a situation of dependence he is the one who is relied upon for action, a belief that God has committed a responsibility to him – even if it be the onerous one of formation of his own character – can be a stimulating and heartening thing. However mean a creature he may be in his own eyes and those of his fellows, he is one on whom God depends. If he has faith, he can set back his shoulders and go forward on his daily business, feeling that every step he takes in the social world is in discharge of a personal duty to the Most High.

The same process of attribution helps to provide man with that sense of order which he desires to see in the flux of events, that he may guide his future actions and have some certainty in what often seems a sorry tangle. One kind of belief which allows this and strengthens the doubter is that which assigns the origin of the world to a Creator who continues to take a controlling interest in his work. Most religious systems, primitive as well as more developed, have concepts of this type. But once the principle of order has been admitted, there is also need for the explanation of contradiction. It is only by the eye of faith that a perfect plan can be discerned. There are several ways in which this can be achieved. One, probably the simplest, is to stress human incapacity to understand. To give a sample citation, 'The divine plan in its totality is utterly beyond human comprehension, though it must include the possibility of moral and physical evil, and contain within it elements of contingency which are inseparable from human freedom.'[5] Another way is to distinguish between the plan or will of God and the imperfection of the human creature as hampering its execution. It is argued that God's will, which stands sure and unshakable through all the ebb and flow of human history, cannot be finally thwarted. But its fulfilment may be hindered and the progress of His kingdom slowed down by human indifference and perversity, and by man's refusal to cooperate with Him.[6] By this interpretation it would seem that the Deity is content to abide by the implications of the freedom which He Himself has vouchasafed to man. He accepts therefore the limitations of His own plan. But contradiction or inconsistency may be faced another way. Those who hold fast to the belief that there is only one proper vehicle for the propagation of the divine message of Christianity are distressed by the way in which the historic Church has been divided by the secession of numerous reforming dissident bodies. The spectacle of a divided Christendom, it is argued, is intolerable to anyone who realizes what God's will is in regard to His Church. Nevertheless the spectacle of good men and of good works proceeding from nests of false doctrine can hardly be denied. An analogous issue which attained wider currency and even some poignancy arose in the First World War when it was discovered that many of the young soldiers who excelled not only in bravery but also in self-sacrifice and in acts of devotion to their fellows did not profess the Christian faith. To such problems many answers have been given. But among them is the view that God is not bound by His own ordinances.[7] Having laid down what shall be the proper procedure in the implementation of the Divine plan for salvation, He is nevertheless prepared to receive all that serves His purposes, whether it is prepared to come under the formal jurisdiction or not. This view can be of course a most flexible instrument since it can be used to justify almost any act of expediency. But its interest to us in this connexion is the way in which it can serve as a means of adjustment for those who believe in the unique value of one religious faith and have to account for virtue in the adherents of others.

One of the most interesting issues in this general theme is that technically known as theodicy, the problem of the vindication of Divine Providence in view of the existence of pain and evil. This offers an intellectual as well as an emotional challenge to the believer in the conception of the Deity as powerful, wise, good, and concerned with the administration of the universe. For the deeply religious person evil is a problem to be overcome when it manifests itself in concrete behaviour. But it is also a phenomenon demanding some kind of explanation in terms of the consistency of the divine supervision of the affairs of men.

In the religions of the simpler societies behaviour, thought and emotion which are injurious or intended as injurious to man are not usually conceptualized as a single abstraction. Conceptualization takes the form rather of separate type events or institutions, such as death or witchcraft or war. Aetiological myths provide their rationale or a defence against them. As Malinowski has pointed out, such myths often treat cosmic events as the product of the simplest human or even animal lapse or omission. Take the myth of death, which is normally regarded as the supreme evil. The ancient Maori people believed that death came from the Goddess Hine-nui-te-po, the Great Lady of Darkness. The culture-hero Maui thought that he could win life for man if he penetrated the body of the Goddess and touched her heart. In due course he made his attempt, entering her while she lay sleeping by the way from which all men are born. But accident intervened. A little bird, the fantail, seeing Maui's legs kicking in the air as he began the perilous passage, was overcome with laughter at the ridiculous sight and the sound of his mirth woke the sleeping Goddess. She closed her body upon Maui and killed him; so death continued its hold over man. One Tikopia myth of death also places man's fate in animal hands. A rat and a crab disputed as to what should happen to man when he grew old. Said the crab, 'Let him cast his skin as I do, emerge freshly and continue to live on'. The rat objected to this, saying, 'No, let him die and be buried in the ground, that his body may rot away'. Here the myths supply explanation and allocate responsibility on a scale and in a way which allows simple comprehension of the great inescapable yet mysterious element in human destiny.

Most 'primitive' societies, in conformity with their lack of effective international relations and emphasis on small group organization, have not proceeded to ideas of a unitary god and a unitary principle of evil. Some of the more advanced religions subsume the phenomena of the universe under integrative principles but do not view these as having any personified character. For the Chinese Confucianist philosopher Hsün Ch'ing, for instance, Heaven, roughly equivalent to Nature, was the unchanging process of action responsible for the final accomplishment of events. 'The true sage does not try to know Heaven' though he sees the results. Man's body and spirit are the work of Heaven. Concerning the fundamental nature of man he and other philosophers were often in disagreement. Mencius maintained the innate goodness of man's nature, with evil as due to bad upbringing. Hsün Ch'ing maintained its basic evil to be corrected by the character acquired through the purposive thinking and practice of the sages and expressed in ritual and rightness.[8] Buddhism proclaims the unitary principle of the universe, but will hardly call it God even as a symbolic expression. The problem of theodicy hardly arises directly then. The issue is handled by admitting the validity of evil as a real phenomenon, but stressing that it is all part of human involvement in desire.[9] The Taoist view, as expressed in the opening of the *Tractate on Actions* (Kan Ying P'ien), is that 'Woe and weal have no gates, men call them on themselves', that is, they are not predestined, but the result of the heart rising to goodness or rising to evil.[10]

In the monotheistic religions various other solutions to the

problem, each allowing a considerable degree of personal interpretation, allocate responsibility differently. The Zoroastrian sees
the problem in terms of two active conflicting principles, Good
and Evil, each of equal validity. They struggle for mastery in a
contest almost indefinitely to be prolonged, though it is hoped
that Good will prevail in the end. The Muslim, following the
Koran, has a fairly clear-cut set of propositions on which to rely,
and which place responsibility for the ills of the world on man's
own shoulders. God has breathed into the soul its wickedness
and its piety, but these are only potentials. Man himself creates
his own ills. The believer is told, 'Whatever good betideth thee
is from God and whatever betideth thee of evil is from thyself.'[11]
In Christianity the existence of evil rests presumably on the
ultimate acquiescence of God. But in terms of human affairs its
application is understood by reference to the doctrine of the
Fall on the one hand, and the principle of human freedom and
responsibility on the other. The myth of the original sin of our
first parents being due to a simple act of yielding to curiosity is
reminiscent of the myths of the more primitive religions. To make
death and the source of all our woe really spring from one single
yielding to caprice by an unsophisticated woman almost at the
beginning of the world is poising this scheme of things on a very
slender foundation. Evil and the fruits of evil must therefore have
entered into the Great Design before the Creation; the Fall was
the symbol, not the source.

Theological argument about the problem of evil has brought
various explanations, including doctrines of self-limitation on the
part of God. It is difficult to keep this separate from the idea
that He is a finite being and therefore not omnipotent. But it
does help to alleviate the burden of the mystery of evil. Another
explanation relies largely on the recognition of the instrumental
worth of evil – the value of physical pain and suffering in mould-
ing character, and that of moral evil as part of the general
discipline of education in combating it. Moral evil has been
described as the 'discord without which there would be no har-
mony, shade without which there would be no light'.[12] Such an
essentially monistic view of the problem preserves the omnipotence of God at the cost of the absoluteness of evil. It is
reminiscent of the Hindu view that good and evil alike are
phenomenal expressions of the one divine substance or energy;
as they operate, often in cyclical opposition, in the world, they

are but manifestations of Māyā, the mirage-like illusory character of all existence.[13]

Here then we have a set of beliefs regarding the nature of evil and its place in the scheme of human life, with several emphases. One is an empiricist attitude, accepting the existence of evil as a given element in the nature of things, whether present as an active principle in the world, or as innate in man's constitution, or the product of his desires. Another associates evil more directly with the permissive control of a Deity, as part of his cosmic plan, either as embedded in the great design or called into operation by some fatal action of man. The more enlarged the conception of the Deity, the more difficult becomes the problem of justification of the Divine providence. In all cases an element of human activity is involved, both in setting the processes of evil in motion and in putting an end to them and their consequences. Freedom from evil and its results can be attained according to some religious beliefs by the acts of self-restraint of a more or less positive kind, forming a virtuous life. According to other beliefs, it is reached by the acts of faith, accompanied by some degree of regret or repentance for what has been done, and leading of themselves to salvation. Emotionally the acts of faith are more attractive and easier as a solution than the acts of self-discipline without reference to Divine grace. Intellectually, it may be more difficult to say honestly 'I believe . . .' than to see the reasonableness of altering one's way of life. With every profession of faith is mingled a modicum of reason. For the man who endeavours to guide himself by thought and not simply by emotion, the sedative of faith is not enough; it must be balanced by the stimulant of argument. For belief to be effective as an instrument of personal adjustment, therefore, one expects to find elaborate intellectual analysis mingled with the statement of what are conceived as the results of experience.

So far we have been examining what may be called public expressions of belief; now let us consider some more individual formulations. These are to be found in particular as far as Christianity goes in the sphere of speculative theism – in arguments for the existence of God, and about the attributes of God. I would emphasize that I am concerned not with the logical validity of the arguments, but with their form and content as sociological expressions, reflecting interests and providing means of action. The ontological argument of Anselm, and its reformulation by

Descartes, the aetiological and other arguments of Leibnitz, the Thomist arguments from motion and so on, are all attempts to buttress by the power of logic those convictions which rest on the basis of faith. The reasoned sequences of propositions regarding the dependence of conception upon existence; the necessity of an Existent which is not contingent but carries within it its own cause or reason; the relation of order and intelligibility in the world to an intelligent, planning Creator are religious as well as metaphysical exercises. The urgency of the argument that in each case the inference *must* be so reveals how the imperative that drives the disputant emerges from his own need for intellectual reassurance, rather than from the rigour of the implications of the premisses.[14] Nowadays, all this brave show brings only feeble applause.

It is true that years ago one daring spirit reformulated the ontological argument, with certain additions relating to emotional content, to give the concept of a personal God what he termed value as well as logical validity. But he surpassed himself by proving by the same line of reasoning that if God marks the upper limit of our conceptions there must be a corresponding lower limit. Rather disconcerted, he concludes that this can only be the Devil. With some relief he affirms that this Devil is not personal, though the impersonal devil, or evil, must be reckoned as eternal. At this point his courage cracks a little and he almost begs to be proved wrong. 'I confess', he says, 'to being uncomfortable over my deduction from Anselm's argument, but perhaps my critics will show that the reality of the devil is after all only a pseudo-reality – a regulative notion, in distinction from the reality of God.'[15]

But ever since Kant's powerful attack, the case for thinking that God's existence can be inevitably demonstrated by reasoning from basic propositions about mind or matter has been greatly weakened. C. C. J. Webb has pointed out that 'the proofs of the existence of God which were so important a factor in the eighteenth century defence of religion are now very largely discredited'. In carefully weighed terms he continues, 'it is vain to suppose that, apart from some specifically religious experience in our hearer we can, so to say, force religion upon a reluctant mind by means of such reasonings.'[16] And J. L. Stocks indicates the singular character of the assertion of the existence of God on *a priori* grounds. 'The proofs themselves rest on the uniqueness of their problem.'[17]

The logical arguments put forward for the existence of God have always in religious history been supported also by the appeal to empirical experience. Events in the external world have been regarded as countersigning, so to speak, the evidence provided on other grounds. Such events are of two types – normal and miraculous. In all religions which base part of their claim to recognition upon the purity of their ethical principles, witness to their truth is sought in the conduct of those who follow their doctrines. Each of the major religions has its saints, whose lives have been marked by an extreme of piety, self abnegation, and moral refinement. But each has been able to count also multitudes of ordinary adherents who have shown such control of themselves and such care for their fellow beings that is concluded they could only be animated by belief of a true kind. One of the arguments put forward not merely for the superiority but also for the correctness of Christian belief, for instance, is the general character of the achievements of Western civilization in liberating people from physical and mental bonds. However, it is difficult for even those who maintain such views to regard them as conclusive or final evidences for the truth of the religion concerned. The achievements of Christian like those of other religious organizations have often been base as well as noble. And people of pure life with ethical systems of a lofty selfless kind are not the prerogative of any one religious faith. In fact many modern theologians are coming to acknowledge that the social influence of Christianity is not the prime argument for its validity, that it is only a by-product. Its aim of promoting social justice on this view, if not illusory, is certainly secondary. The world is impermanent; it is the future, the eternal, that should be sought, by the road to salvation through faith and grace.

The argument of evidence from miracle seems to be at present in a transitional state – at least as far as Christian circles go. Whereas a century ago sceptics were few, there are probably now large numbers of professing Christians who believe that most if not all of the miracles described in the Scriptures are at best allegorical. Miracle, by definition, is an event which stands outside the ordinary processes of nature, is remarkable for its discontinuity, and is not explainable by physical principles. As has often been pointed out, if we could explain it, it would not be a miracle.

Nevertheless there is an attempt to reconcile modern scientific views with Scriptural account as far as possible. This takes three forms. The first is to waive any idea of physical anomalies or variations from natural laws and to treat a miracle as a symbol – an account in terms of physical behaviour of what was in fact mental behaviour. On this view the miracle of feeding the hungry multitude from a small quantity of loaves and fishes is a beautiful story illustrating the importance of compassion, the virtues of sharing, and the way in which the effects of a gift are multiplied manifold. Another view is that the Scriptural account describes an actual event, but in terms somewhat different from what in fact must have happened. Ritchie's explanation, for example, is that the crowd had come to hear the Master already furnished with provender concealed about their garments. But in the character of suspicious Oriental peasantry they were unwilling to take out what they had and share with their neighbours. The Master, knowing this, called up to him a small boy; then, breaking up and dividing the food, by his personal magnetic example He induced the crowd to follow suit. The miracle lay not in multipli-cation of the food itself, but in dissipating suspicion and securing cooperation from the hard-bitten, slow-moving peasant assembly.[18] Still another view is that which tries to save the miracle by an appeal to modern science. The miracles of healing are thus interpreted as an early use of psychotherapy. The miracle of the feeding of the five thousand is explained by concepts analogous to those of atomic fission, of which the Master is believed to have had the secret. The following is one view: 'That Our Lord in creating the solid matter of which the food was formed had at His intuitive disposal and control the vast energy which we now know to have been necessary, gives to the Christian believer a new realisation of His power, and to the unbeliever a further difficulty.'[19] Within the whole range of miracles there are, however, grades in what is treated as matter for belief. Many who give credence to Biblical miracles deny this to the miracles recorded since Apostolic times, regarding them as not supported by evidence of the same weight. The newer the miracle, the less it is believed. Even within the New Testament range a distinction is drawn between such ancillary events as the feeding of the multitude and the cardinal events of the Virgin Birth and the Res-urrection. That which is central to the whole religious system cannot be so easily abandoned, however incredible it may seem.

The surest course to adopt is that which has been hallowed by long usage – to believe even though it is incredible. 'Strange to all our experience and inscrutable to all our science', as one writer has put it, such stupendous miracles are part of the attraction of faith. Belief in them is part of the test of faith istelf. *Credo quia incredibile* becomes a matter of pride (cf. chapter 8, pp. 206–9).

In the last resort, it is not intellectual or moral proofs for belief in the existence of God, or in other religious concepts that have prime validity; it is the emotional proofs. This was demonstrated more than a century ago by the German theologian Schleiermacher. Seeing the inadequacy of basing evidences for the truth of Christianity upon human reason alone, he developed the theme of the importance of man's feeling of dependence on God. This to him was the true basis of dogma. An essentially similar view was put forward as the basis of religion on scientific grounds by Radcliffe-Brown.[20]

But basing belief on emotion, on non-rational attachment of the will, does not mean suspension or abnegation of all reasoning processes. This can be so even in the acceptance of miracles. The view that the events described as miracles actually happened because the Gospel record is based on eyewitness or near eyewitness accounts is interesting. Every anthropologist is familiar with the miracles of magic, faith-healing, spirit-mediumship, and ancestral intervention – apparently much better authenticated from contemporary sources. What impresses is not the value of the evidence adduced. But the mental attitude on the part of the believer indicates the strength of the need that is felt for support to what is believed. It is felt that there should be some demonstration of relation between antecedent and consequent. In the case of the Resurrection, verification is at times held to lie in experiences of the disciples, transmitted to other followers who wrote their words down. The believer in the miracle thus transfers his reasoning – he abandons any attempt to place the event in a physical order, since it is characterized by discontinuity in natural process. But he sets it in the framework of a rational human order by relying on a case for the credibility of witness and faithfulness of the written record. Suggestion has even been made that the evidence would bear scrutiny comparable with that given in a modern court of law.

My point here is that belief is emotionally based but intellectually supported. Its use as part of the processes of personal

adjustment requires that the emotion be organized in an intellectual or para-intellectual system.

The furthest removes from this are the emotional extremes
of frenzy (such as that following on, say, bereavement) or of
transcendental mysticism. It is symptomatic of the general attitudes of believers that though the same propositions of belief
may be shared, there is often an attempt to restrain the exhibition
of transports of emotion by others. And among writers on religion
who are primarily concerned with intellectual analysis, there is a
tendency to deprecate any ranking of transcendental mysticism
too high on the scale of religious experience.[21] On the other hand
there is the simple attitude of the intuitional claim – 'I believe
because I know'. In this, as for example in the identification of
the object of knowing with a transcendent Being, there is a refusal
to carry the intellectual analysis beyond an affirmation.

But let us continue with the arguments which buttress faith.

In line with modern ideas of development is the view that God
is being made known to man more exactly and completely by
progressive relation. Few Christians will go so far, perhaps, as to
admit that the nature of God himself may have changed from
that of a jealous tribal god to one of love for all humanity, even
though it is one implication from the Biblical record.[22] But only
the most ardent fundamentalist nowadays will maintain that the
days of the Creation were spaces of twelve hours or so between
dawn and dusk, that man was formed of the dust of the ground,
and woman from one of the ribs of man, and that the Lord God
walked in the cool of one evening in a garden, eastward in Eden,
which had a tree giving the fruits of the knowledge of good and
evil.[23] The argument for progressive revelation is used in two
ways. One way is in buttressing the general validity of religion,
while meeting the difficulty of the existence of a diversity of
faiths or creeds, each claiming to have the sole key to the truth.
If all are wrong but the one championed by the particular
believer, then intellectually doubt may creep in as to the possibility of error in that one. But if all are admitted to have in some
measure a partial revelation of the Divine, then, to some types
of mind at least, it becomes easier to think that one's own faith
must be right, and being so is the closest to the truth. The
argument can be applied even to the religious conceptions of the
people of the simpler societies, often formerly dismissed as absurd
by Christian missionaries. Thus a few years ago the Moderator

of the Presbyterian Assembly in New Zealand, in opening the annual conference spoke of the ancient Maori conception of Io – represented by European scholars as the supreme god – as remarkable. In his view it 'could only be accounted for by the statement that, while they felt after Him in the darkness, God's spirit revealed to them as much of the Divine nature as could be conveyed to men in their stage of development'.[24] Such an opinion reflects the speaker's conviction of his church's own attainment. But the reverse attitude can also be emphasized.

The second way of using the argument for progressive revelation is in emphasizing the relativity of our own present knowledge, and so warding off criticism. This may be of two kinds. Internal criticism alleges that a change or development in interpretation of doctrine is not an improvement but a perversion, a heresy. External criticism alleges that changes in doctrine are still further evidence that the religion as a whole is a human fabrication – that what are claimed as refinements in understanding the spiritual world are nothing but inevitable adjustments to the flux of events in the material world. The notion of progressive revelation meets both these attacks.

One of the most brilliant achievements in the use of this concept to face internal criticism is given by the Lotus Sutra, the Mahayana Buddhist text. It would appear that this work had in its inception no direct connexion with the Buddha. Though it purports to present the words of the eternal Saviour, his last testament before his departure, it was composed long, perhaps centuries, after his death. Its essential teaching, salvation by faith, is in flat opposition to the ideas of attainment of Nirvana by self-discipline and good works, which are the essence of the older orthodox 'Hinayana' (Theravada) teaching. The Lotus Sutra, in a series of mystical revelations, disclosed through the mouth of the Buddha himself how he had hitherto used the narrow way of doctrine of salvation by works as a preparatory piece of enlightenment, reserving the broad way of salvation by faith for the ultimate gift of knowledge. When asked why he should have first taught and then repudiated the Theravada doctrines, the Buddha answers that he has had to preach the Law as might be expedient. Sinful ignorant men would not have been able to understand the full and wonderful truth at once and therefore he had to use appropriate tactful methods. The Buddha reinforces his argument by the parable of the Burning House. A father sees his children playing about inside, heedless of his warnings, and in danger of burning to death. He lures them outside by promises of rich toys which for the moment he does not have. Overjoyed, they all run outside. Then, when they are in safety, he takes his time and prepares for them the gifts he described. In the Sutra, all his hearers assent that the Buddha's intention and his gift of redemption remove from him all taint of falsehood – that his explanation justifies his message.[25]

The history of the great religions is full of such arguments of progressive revelation. Christianity uses them to justify itself against Judaism; Islam uses them against Judaism and Christianity both. In the early nineteenth century they were used against Islam in Persia by the reformer Saiyid 'Ali Muhammed of Shiraz. As El Bâb, The Door, he put forward what was in effect a new set of religious doctrines about the unity and attributes of God. To the Comte de Gobineau, now rather under a cloud because of his ill-judged essay on the inequality of the races of man, but a sociological observer of acute penetration nevertheless, we owe a valuable record and analysis of the new faith, and its relation to the old. According to Gobineau, El Bâb purported to give not a new conception of the Deity, but only a further development of the knowledge of the Divine nature. All the prophets successively, he argued, had stated more on this subject than their predecessors were commissioned to do. It was only in accordance with this regular progress that El Bâb had had entrusted to him a task more complete than that of Mohammed, which was more complete than that of Jesus, who in turn had known more than his precursors.[26] 'Ali Muhammed, the Door or Mirror of God, met a fate not unlike that of an earlier prophet who had claimed a new revelation; he was put to death by the authorities as an outrage to the orthodox faith and a threat to civil order.

The idea that the revelation of fundamental truths is progressive is a valuable defence against external challenge. It can always be held that what is being attacked is in fact not the real or complete explanation, but only a partial, perhaps even distorted version. The critic thus spends himself fighting a phantom adversary while the real protagonist, the truth in its blinding entirety, will reveal herself, if ever, only at a later time.[27] When the idea of progressive revelation is linked with that of ultimate incomprehensibility in this life of the final religious truths, then the argument of belief takes on one of its strongest forms.

Negatively, it is an aid to rejection of the charge that anthropo-morphic concepts of the Divine are an indication that God is man-made. If the ultimate reality transcends man's capacity for understanding, then how otherwise can he express his attitudes than by using the terminology and concepts of his own experi-ence? Positively, it strengthens the call for faith. If in this world our knowledge is incomplete and our understanding is difficult, the greater is the importance of a faith which holds before us the complete realization of the mystery in the life to come, be it Nirvana, or union with the Divine.[28]

This brings us to the threshold of the perennial dispute as to the relations between religion and science. We are not concerned here to evaluate carefully the respective views, but primarily to indicate their sociological relevance to an understanding of religious belief. The basic religious attitude is to protect its sphere of faith and ritual from what is regarded as unjustified encroach-ment by the principles of reason, particularly reason in what is expressed as the materialistic doctrines exemplified by science. The term science ordinarily refers both to a body of knowledge and to a set of methods of investigation. By religion the body of knowledge is nowadays usually accepted, while the competence of the set of methods to pursue knowledge into the religious sphere is denied. But methods of inquiry must start from assump-tions about the nature of reality, and here is the fundamental divergence. Three main standpoints may be mentioned – that matter is the ultimate reality; that mind is the ultimate reality; that mind, as ultimate reality, has qualities of an extra-human or supra-human order, such as omniscience, omnipotence or power of incarnation. Different scientists adopt different standpoints on this. Some for example do hold that there is a non-empirical reality or sphere of thought, with which a logical-empirical analy-sis cannot cope.[29] But recognition of this need not imply the recognition of that supra-human mind or power, which for religion is the essential assumption. And what some scientists take as assumptions, together with a real or imagined body of knowledge, and set of methods, is in popular usage lumped together and given a quasi-personal, almost magical value. Science in this sense is the voice of authority or that of the false prophets, according to the point of view.

The arguments of religious belief in respect of science take a variety of forms. One is to stress the essential relativity of scientific discovery and principles. This is in order to show that the findings of science, apparently incontrovertible, will in the end be superseded, and in particular the firm grasp of science on matters fringing the religious sphere will slip away. The essence of this approach is given by a recent Muslim economist. 'My belief', he says, 'is that when Quranic theories come into conflict with the modern scientific theories, I find no reason to trouble my conscience. I firmly believe that the science of today may be the mythology of tomorrow, and that what the Quran has said we may not understand today, but it is likely to become quite clear to us tomorrow.'[30]

Another instance of the way in which stress on the relativity of scientific knowledge is used as a buttress to religious faith is the cordial reception given to Heisenberg's enunciation of the uncertainty principle.[31] This and other discoveries in modern physics which have promoted revision of the classical notions of causal laws and determinism of a mechanistic kind are thought to prove the case for the inadequacy of science to grasp fundamental reality. The universe is thought to be indeterminate, mysterious, something more than matter.[32] But as Susan Stebbing has shown, with humour and skill, the physicists' discoveries warrant no such conclusions. Neither idealism nor materialism can benefit.[33] Nor would it seem to follow that the less we know about the seen world the more therefore we know about the unseen world.

Another form of the argument is a denial of the competence of science to pronounce on matters which are regarded as falling within the province of religion. This view is met not only among the professed exponents of religious doctrines, but also among philosophers and among scientists themselves. The real world, it is held, is beyond the shadow-show of space and time. The physical is a manifestation of something other than itself. Religious experience is truly objective, not merely subjective. Contemporary science, including sociology and anthropology, is incapable of passing judgement on any theory concerning the super-sensory or transcendental world, with which religious and philosophical thought deals.[34] A further buttress to religious belief is to claim the reverse – that religion is only another form of science. Made in the most blatant form it is that a religious system is founded on scientific principles primarily because it purports to argue in terms of cause and effect. One such system is Christian Science, alleging that illness, pain and sin can be made to disappear by using the laws of mind properly. Another, an intellectual variety of Saivaism, claims the law of universal causation as its basic postulate. Since this is regarded as being the very foundation of Western science, Saivaism is hailed as embodying the counterpart of the most modern scientific theories of the West. Another view represents science as essentially a part of religion because both are a quest for knowledge and truth in a disinterested way.[35]

An interesting example of the way in which a scientist has worked out his personal adjustment in religious terms comes from an eminent professor of electrical engineering. For him, God is a finite Being, conforming to the laws of mechanics. He has the ether as His abode, and as part of His nature. The visible material uiverse is God's kenosis, the shedding of part of Himself, part of His output of energy. From these views, rather unorthodox, certain corollaries emerge. If God has surrendered part of Himself in creating matter, is it perhaps true that there is some slight justification for the perception of an inner spirit in wood and stone? If the wisdom and foreknowledge of God apply to the laws by which action takes place, and not to the predestination of every fact or event, then must even God try out the laws which He has framed? Can He perhaps not foresee or intend to foresee their consequences in every variant? 'Is He in truth as Creator the Supreme Researcher?' it is argued. 'Is the chemist who makes the compound hitherto unknown or a biologist who succeeds in making new variations of a species, carrying on the work of God as He would have it done?'[36]

Another variant on the same theme is to represent science as only of limited adequacy in its ordinary form and as needing enlargement to take in factors which religion wishes to include in the world view. It is argued, for instance, that a 'bastard' science leaves out all except material factors. 'True' science takes into account the eternal verities, such as character and conscience, religious instinct, parental, conjugal or patriotic love. These cannot be weighed, analysed, dissected, but cannot be excluded from 'true' science.[37]

All these points of view indicate different modes of adjustment whereby, sometimes in most elaborate imaginative constructions, attempts are made to place the facts of emotion within an intellectual system. But whether religion is made to oppose science or to absorb science, the issue needs clarification. Science has as its hallmarks the formulation of hypotheses, testing of them by

observation and experiment, and careful relation of conclusions
to empirical data. In its use of analytical thought, it must always
work with given premises. It is unable to pronounce with certainty on the nature of ultimate reality. From its methods, it is
debarred from mere assertion, unsupported by that degree of
probability which is ordinarily held to constitute proof. But
religion feels no necessity for such limitation. In its certitude lies
its strength. It constantly makes assertions about the nature of
reality. The proofs produced rest either on argument of which
the logic is highly debatable or on further assertion about the
intuitive nature of the revelation or other experiences of a special
order adduced as evidence. Even where the data are regarded as
capable of empirical examination by an external observer, the
initial premises supplied in the interpretation are usually in
excess of those which are the necessary minimum. No social
science may be able to prove or disprove the reality of such
religious categories as God, devil, heaven or angels, apart from
their existence as human concepts. But it can certainly show the
way in which such concepts can be seen to be consistent with
much in human wants and behaviour alone. Revelation and mystical experience, for instance, whether regarded as proceeding from
an external supra-human source or not, are fundamentally human
states. As such they can be analysed and interpreted with significance from the scientific point of view. The anthropologist, like
any other scientist, has to base his work upon some assumptions
of a metaphysical order. Whatever metaphysical position he
adopts it must be such as to allow him the greatest freedom of
exploration of the whole range of phenomena of man's behaviour.

Freedom is a word which every system nowadays, however
authoritarian, likes to inscribe on its banners. And there are
other old labels too, which are borne on unaccustomed packages.
Freedom is held out as a promise by what has been called the
new humanism. It is exemplified in the work of Jacques Maritain,
in whom the neo-Thomists have a philosophical publicist of great
eloquence. The classical humanism, he argues, had an anthropo-
centric idea of man and culture − the idea of human nature as
self-enclosed or self-sufficient. This it put forward instead of what
Maritain would term an open nature and an open reason − which
are man's real nature and his real reason. The classical attitude
towards human existence has been that of the isolation of reason
from all that is supra-rational and irrational in man. Its reaction

inevitably has been the counter-humanism of Kierkegaard and Karl Barth with its emphasis on personal anguish.[38]

The new humanism as conceived by Maritain is of a Christian order; he has termed it 'the humanism of the Incarnation', integral and progressive. It is claimed as springing from the concrete logic of the events of history. It involves the conception of the wholeness of man in his natural and supernatural being and of the descent of the divine into man. Faith supplies the key to fundamental questions of being; the supra-rational is regarded as equally essential as the rational in the interpretation and government of human affairs. This new humanism, it is argued, has its implications not merely for the religious life of the believer. It is conceived as an attitude and doctrine of far-reaching importance – even as affecting our own anthropological science. 'The new humanism', he says, 'must reassume in a purified climate all the work of the classical period; it must re-make anthropology, find the rehabilitation and the "dignification" of the creature not in isolation, not in the creature shut in with itself, but in its openness to the world of the divine and supra-rational.'[39]

This is only one of a group of tendencies which seek to demonstrate the inadequacy of reason not merely for an approach to human contacts and relations with the external world as part of man's everyday behaviour, but also as a mode of analysis of phenomena. One expects to find a championing of the irrational in the sphere of art, where the emphasis upon feeling as a guide and stimulus to aesthetic activity has always been paramount. The abandonment of the medieval artist's subjective attitude to his material in favour of a naturalism derived from the remnants of classical antiquity led inevitably, it is held, to a degeneration of art. By taking nature first as an inspiration for creative form and then as a model the artist was led to become a copyist. As the Church progressively lost her spiritual initiative in Europe the artist progressively became freer from mysticism and religious iconography. In the Renaissance political system this did lead to some of the finest products of art. But the inevitable outcome of this classicism was the translation of the artist into the artisan.[40] But the historian also can exemplify the same attitude. Arnold Toynbee in his monumental study of culture argues that criteria of the growth of civilization are not to be found in increasing command over the human or the physical environment. This, the evidence suggests, is a concomitant of disintegration rather than of growth because of a decline in the spiritual forces which make for purpose and unity. The proper saviour from a disintegrated society is not to be found in the philosophy of detachment like that of Buddhist or Stoic. It is the 'mystery of transfiguration' which alone can work as the effective agent – the God incarnate in a man. This, he argues, represents a truth which we can verify empirically but which is also known to us intuitively.[41] One suspects also that recent work by the psychologists on precognition and extra-sensory perception attracts attention for its religious bearing rather than for its scientific interest. This derives ultimately from the hope that negatively these conclusions will place limitations on the claims for the exercise of reason and positively they will encourage belief in the existence of the world of the supra-rational, including forces and powers which religion alone can claim to control.

In the history of religious belief in Europe it would seem such currents can be traced for the last three hundred years. C. C. J. Webb and others have pointed out how in the eighteenth century the idea of God was that of a transcendent Being having a separate existence from the Universe and from man, and standing over sharply against man as the Creator of omnipotent and omniscient power. With the change which the scientists initiated in the idea that cosmic process was to be viewed in terms of evolution rather than of creation, came also the idea of God as immanent, a Being permanently pervading the Universe and in a sense an integral part of the life of the world and man. It was not out of the question that God for the accomplishment of His own purposes was prepared to limit Himself in both power and knowledge, and to participate through His world substance in the evolutionary process. Man, as a semi-autonomous creature, could take part, so to speak, in working out the designs of God. Salvation and human happiness could be sought in the world which represented the evolution of the Great Design. As time has passed, the early glories of the industrial revolution have begun to fade, first one, and then another great war has shaken the fabric of civilization, and all established social order has been challenged to its roots by the Marxist state. Correspondingly the tendency to seek religious values within civilization has begun once again to be regarded as fallacious. The sense of otherworldliness has once more come to be looked upon by many as fundamental in religion. Reinforced by arguments based upon the primacy of feeling, the value of irrationality, and the claims of mystical experience to a validity apart from their subject, this may be described as the new transcendentalism.[42]

What is to be the anthropological attitude towards this development? Must we look forward to see our science remade in the light of this approach which, novel in some of its formulations, carries nevertheless the kernel of age-old argument? I suggest that, as before, the anthropologist can only take man as the centre of his study. Emotion, unreason, belief, intuitive knowledge and mystical perception, may all be regarded as modes or bases of action for the individuals to whom they seem appropriate in given circumstances. But they must be regarded as essentially modes of personal adjustment and not as scientific instruments. The rational dispassionate analysis which the anthropologist applies to religious phenomena and in which his own position as the analyst is reduced to a minimum, even though it cannot be eliminated, must still remain our guide.

If this be so it appears to me that the range of phenomena we have been discussing can find an explanation not inconsistent with the point of view which I presented at the beginning.

These phenomena – views on theism, theodicy, and progressive revelation; theo-symbolism and its inversion; belief in the insufficiency of scientific knowledge and in the integral character of the new humanism – are not all aspects of reality beyond the scientist's perception. They are modes of grappling with a reality which is open to observation though by no means adequately measurable by scientific knowledge – at least in the present state of our technique. What is this reality? It is the individual human being himself, in relation to the physical world of which he has cognizance and the society of which he is a member. Man has to face the reality of his own mental make-up, with all its conflicting desires, emotions, intellectual drives and moral sentiments. He prefers to do so in a mirror.

The value of religious belief to him is in meeting his own personal wants. It provides him with a means of reacting in a range of social situations where without it he would be severely hampered. His belief supplies him also with a principle of order – order in his relation to his fellows, including the moral norms he follows, and order in his conception of the universe. This search for an external order in events and things demands that their relationships to one another can be recognized as intelligible and not merely fortuitous association. The principle of order deals with time as well as space; it can compromise even eternity. In the view of such universalistic religion it is this which makes the eternal order authentic. But it is not merely order, it is the assurance that we know where to find guidance upon that order that is desired. Religious belief supplies also a principle of authority or certitude upon which indecision and the need for resolution can seize. The relation of son to father, believer to Church, man to God all exemplify the operation of this principle, in which wisdom is believed to reside in a superior, into whose hands the inferior resigns the decision.

Religious belief also provides objects of attachment for sentiments of dependence and affection. Belief is a comforter in time of trouble. It can also serve as a vehicle for the transports of ecstatic love. This involves not merely self-expression in the sense of ability to give vent to creative interests. It also involves opportunity to exercise those self-regarding sentiments which are part of the personal constitution. There must be outlet, too, for what we may call the 'other regarding' sentiments, of which there must be at least a minimal exercise for any social existence. All this gives occasion for emphasis upon individuality. The relation of the mystic to the divine with which he seeks union may seem to negate this stress. Yet in all such cases there is emphasis upon the uniqueness of the experience, the particularity of it, as being incapable of being grasped by another person – except perhaps a mystic who has attained the same state. A heightened consciousness of personality in social matters then is correlated with the claim to a merging of personality on the supra-rational plane. It is precisely by that capacity of being united with the Divine essence, of grasping reality direct, that the mystic feels he is singled out from his fellows. Over the whole range of religious belief, stress upon the personal relation of God to man is a marked feature. It helps to satisfy that desire for personal recognition and personal assertion which is germinal in every one of us. It can serve also those attitudes which, springing from an enlightened self-regarding sentiment, demand the application of principles of equity and justice to the results of conduct. Religious belief usually embodies some concepts whereby behaviour is related to a scheme of consequents, whether or not these are interpreted in terms of moral approbation or disapprobation, and of reward or punishment. Religious belief also offers a prospect for those curious for truth. Many things which science and com-monsense knowledge cannot provide, religion offers as certainties. If one cannot know the truth by reason one must know it by faith. Certitude, rest from the internal dialectical battle, from the effort of grappling with inconsistencies and half-answers, is undoubtedly one of the great attractions in religious belief. One can always painfully build up one's own ideas, but a framework already put up makes the work much easier. This has always been recognized. Reason and the delights of logical argument, too, find their place in religious belief. There may be disagreement about the extent to which the assumptions from which the analysis starts are data ascertained by experience. But the highest philosophical and dialectical skill can be developed whatever the basis. The intellect can thus be satisfied by the intricacies of formulating and defending religious belief even while it professes to rely on and find truth in other instruments.

This analysis is not an argument in metaphysics nor an essay in the scholarship of comparative religion. It treats some charac-teristic types of beliefs in a variety of religious systems as modes of adaptation. This is not to deny Durkheim's contribution in relating religious symbols to social forms, nor that of Max Weber in showing how different personal solutions of an integrative kind are to be found in different systems of religious thought.[43] But it is important to show how religious belief can be related to the structure of personality, not merely to social structure. It is an instrument in the maintenance of personal integration, not simply of social integration. And, to get the stamp of conviction, belief must fit somehow into a personal intellectual system, not only into an emotional system. Denying reason with one breath, faith seeks with the next to produce the final compelling reason to justify its own primacy.

In all this, every individual has his own adjustment-points, every belief its own adustment-values. To a Tyrolese peasant what appeals is God as a simple family Father of a patriarchal, some-what overbearing type, with the Madonna as a kindly protectress and intercessor, to be represented, as in one homely image, with a cosmic umbrella sheltering herself and the Child, while their suppliants pay their devotions. Not for the peasant the concep-tions that meet the intellectual needs of a professor of electrical engineering, with God as the supreme expression of the laws of mechanics, as the research mind *in excelsis*. The more highly elaborate the social organization the greater the diversity of situations open to individuals for resolution, and the greater possible range of adjustment-points. The diversity of religious belief tends to increase as science develops. The logico-empirical system of scientific thought can destroy belief – but it can also develop it, stimulate it to erect new variants to buttress itself.

Understanding of these processes is essential in the study of how change in religious belief comes about. New facts are always being presented to individual experience, and new interpretations of experience are always being suggested. There is the impact of the behaviour of fresh personalities, or of known personalities in new situations. New verbalizations of experience are always being demanded. A refusal to make adjustment may lead to heightened emphasis on the customary expressions of belief. But fresh defences are also built up. Wittingly or unwittingly these become substantial alterations to the corpus of belief in the individual religious armoury.

With diversification of the types of situation to be met by an individual, so is there diversification of expression in belief. The anthropologist's concept of a specific belief is a summation of individual views, an abstraction of time-place expressions. The beliefs of even the most simple religious system are always mobile, sensitive to changes in external circumstances or in social composition. 'Primitive' religion, contrary to a common view,[44] is not devoid of sceptics, heretics, and other unorthodox who have had to meet a personal intellectual or emotional challenge by individual formulations which diverge from the community norm. When a tribal religion is met by Christianity or by Islam, each with a new social and economic system, it is not only fear and respect for the new God, the perception of a higher morality, or the principles of comparative economic advantage that move to conversion. A more complex set of factors is responsible, involving delicate adjustment in more personal terms. Social relations with community members, the sense of communion itself, the appeal of the new beliefs in a universe of greater scope than hitherto imagined, intellectual conviction of the fitness of the new ideas to explain situations difficult to comprehend, acceptance of the necessity of a new value system – all have weight.[45]

But the demands on the new beliefs may be different from what was at first envisaged. Hence still newer beliefs arise, attempts at more complete adjustment. We are familiar with the variety of new cults that have sprung up in Africa, North America, New Guinea and elsewhere as congeners of or offshoots from Christianity. They have been termed 'nativistic' cults, but they might almost be termed 'adjustment-cults'. The amount of native reversion in them is very variable, while it is their quality of adjustment that is outstanding. They are an attempt to provide an aetiology for new situations of which the implications are but dimly grasped. Something has 'gone wrong' with the process of change – the people have adopted Christianity or other Western culture forms, yet the things of the European have not accrued to them. Traditional forms alone are incompatible with new demands, yet they still meet some wants. The beliefs of the new cult, whatever be their precise content, are attempted adjustment to these anomalies. The greater the anomalies, the more fantastic the beliefs – that all Europeans will vanish, leaving their goods behind; that the spirits of the dead will all return to an earthly Elysium; that if there is fighting for the new cult all the faithful are invulnerable. Faith in many of these cults has smashed on reality, when belief in immediate miracle has failed to redeem its promise. But belief has often been plastic enough to make a fresh adjustment, by buttress rather than by complete modification (see pp. 79–80).

I do not deny the value of Malinowski's theory of religion as satisfying basic human needs, especially that for personal continuity – 'building out heaven beyond the grave', in William James's expression. But this theory needs reformulation. It does not explain why change of belief takes place, how conversion, heresy and apostasy can occur. The views of Radcliffe-Brown need qualification in the same way. The function of ritual, he argues, is in the perpetuation of sentiments – especially the prime one of dependence – on which the maintenance of society depends. But if an ancestral cult, for instance, expresses this, why does it not continue, no matter what be the change in external events? The ancestors do not change; in time of stress, then, why not appeal even more to them, and cling to them? Emile Nolly has given in his novel *La Barque Annamite* a skilful analysis of the desperate attachment of an old man to his ancestral cult in the face of the new forces of civilization. But this fails to satisfy the hopes, thwarted passions and new interests of his dearest kin. The basic human needs in such a case are still there; the response is inadequate, fails to satisfy intellectually as well as emotionally the demands of the individual in the changed environment. The Tikopia, among whom I worked when Christianity and some Western cultural items had already gained a foothold, are a case in point. Christian and heathen all still had a sense of dependence on their ancestors, and all participated in some minimal ancestral rites. But differential reaction to the new wants and opportunities emerged not only in conversions, but also in modification of the beliefs of different heathen. Some defended their ancient faith stoutly, others placed God in the native deity system. Some assigned supernatural powers to the Bishop and other Europeans, and some produced versions of myths which accounted for the distribution of iron between Tikopia and European (Firth 1970: chs 11–15).

Such new developments of belief show adjustment in terms of rational logical thought as well as of emotional reaction. So trenchant was the attack of Durkheim, Marett and others on the early anthropologists for over-intellectualization of religion, that emphasis has tended to be placed almost entirely on the elements of feeling and emotion in belief. Reason, it is claimed, cannot destroy faith. I would argue that it can. Faith buttresses itself. But what may be termed the covert atheism of large numbers of putative Christians is evidence of some rational inference as to the incompatibility between traditional religion and contemporary social and economic circumstances.

I think that the implications of what I have said necessitate some change in the emphases of current anthropological views on religion. Clearly, religion is much more than a sentiment-carrier for society. The hypothesis that religion is an integrating force is more closely applicable to the simpler than to the more highly complex societies. With social and economic differentiation religion often becomes a banner for sectionalism. Society is split, not welded together by religious development. Individual interpretations of accepted religious truths find backing from others whose personal adjustment-points they meet, and emerge in modifications of dogma and rite. Temperamental differences are reflected there too. The history of schism, sectarianism, heresy, of conservative and modernist movements, of ascetic groups and those to whom austerity has no appeal all give evidence of such tendencies. The establishment of a religious organization may rend the society by the creation of monopoly or strong vested interests in social and economic affairs. Religious enterprise may drive the social order into specific channels – as the role of monastic institutions in commerce affected the development of capitalism in Western Europe.

Religion may also perform an important social role in providing an outlet for individual sentiments, where other institutions in the society may be inadequate. Individual desires for prestige and advancement, incapable of finding temporal channels, turn to religion as a vent. I am not thinking here only of the worldly clerics, like those cardinals displayed in the plays of Webster and James Shirley, with their 'purple pride that wants to govern all', the reflection of a long line of priest-politicians. I have in mind rather those who through dogmatic assertion and conviction of righteousness find their imagined level of superiority over their fellows. Social relations may be embittered rather than improved thereby. If social integration be promoted by such behaviour, it is integration by catharsis.

A cathartic function of a more creative kind is given by the way in which religion provides a powerful vehicle for aesthetic expression. A conventional way of regarding the relation of religion to art is to point to the manner in which religious emotion provides the stimulus to artistic creation. To my mind the reverse is more often the case – religion provides the medium. This is a point of view admirably examined in detail by Yrjö Hirn who has demonstrated how much of Catholic doctrine results from speculation directed by aesthetic aspirations.[46] In general, in a society where religious institutions occupy an important part of their total field, religion may be a recognized means of canalization for aesthetic impulses. The trappings of the religion are embellished, the imagery elaborately worked out. Religious belief is externalized as part of the process of a personal adjustment in art. I suspect that Michelangelo's Sistine Chapel designs, Bach's cantatas and passion music are good art not because they were inspired by religion; they are religious in theme because when they were created religion was one of the most effective channels and media for the production of good art. The poverty of good religious art at the present time is probably the result less of a decline in religious sentiments of inspiration than of the existence of many other avenues for the expression of the artist's creative urge. Similarly religion attempts to provide a framework and supervised outlet for metaphysical and allied speculations. For nearly a thousand years Christendom controlled in Western

Europe the intellectual forces which would otherwise have rebounded on society. It thus acted as a shock-absorber for thought. It would seem indeed that as societies develop, technologically and economically, institutions other than religion must arise to allow of the exercise of the creative imagination. Otherwise this might burst religion itself apart.

This study of religious belief has stressed its importance in the action systems of individuals. It has shown also how essential is this consideration for an understanding of religious change. But what of the ultimate content of belief? This question, though not the subject of inquiry by science, stands behind many of the inquiries made. If there be an external reality, transcendent, providing its own cause, author of the moral order, and illuminant of the life of man, this would be a significant assumption behind our theories. There is a common belief that God is real since the effects attributed to Him are real. Whether man exists only in the mind of God, or God exists only in the mind of man, seems to me unproven, and as far as I can judge, unprovable. The evidence produced for a supra-human mind and will is I think of the same order – though on a high plane – as other anthropological data concerning belief. A preferable and more economical assumption, offering what to me is a greater degree of probability, is that this is all part of man's attempt to make the supreme, final and unique but really unattainable adjustment – the search after the complete formula for the synthesis of human conduct.

Chapter 3

Spiritual aroma?
Religion and politics

Anthropologists have thrown much light on the variety of religious forms throughout the world. They have studied belief and ritual, the expressive and the symbolic character of religious ideas, and their relation to modes of production and to social institutions. There has been controversy. Different assumptions about the validity of religion and the nature of religious knowledge have divided anthropologists more deeply than have any other positions, even though in public they have been politely reticent about this. Notwithstanding these divisions, they have followed the tradition of their profession in not being afraid to tackle difficult questions about humanity in their several probing ways. So, collectively, though some analyses of religion may have been defensively obscure, we now understand many aspects of religion much better than we did sixty years ago – when I first began my own study of the subject.

In my own early experience, on the personal side, from a nonconformist Christian churchgoing background I moved by an intellectual route to a skeptical humanism which still left me with a great curiosity about the role of the nonrational and mystical in human thinking and activity. Then as an anthropologist I studied religion firsthand. In Tikopia I was able to make participant-observation of a very complex ritual cycle latched into an elaborate political structure. For a synoptic, more abstract analysis of the whole Tikopia religious system, I studied not only the traditional religion but also the processes involved in the change from a pagan fusion of chiefs and priests to a Christian separation of political from religious leadership. In Malaysia I studied aspects of rural Islam, with particular reference to the relation between this and non-Islamic elements in the culture. On more general theoretical issues I focused on the nature of religious communication, personal adjustments in religion, mysticism, offering, and sacrifice. I mention this personal history because it has been argued that a 'conversion experience' is necessary to get a revealing knowledge of religious processes. I could claim that a 'deconversion experience' too can give a special insight and a useful parallel standpoint for examining religion.

Religions are basically concerned with problems of meaning and problems of power. Anthropologists have been recently much occupied with meaning problems – systems of thought and belief, classification of world view, concepts of spirit and deity, image and apparition, cultic and symbolic communion. Committed believers, mainly Christians, have contributed much to our understanding of such themes. I admire their analyses without having to endorse either their assumptions or their conclusions. But many issues in the power relations of religious affiliation are still not clear. So in the course of my own thinking I have been led to try to sort out my ideas about the political implications of religion, a subject of grave practical as well as theoretical significance through the course of human history.

CONCEPTUAL OPPOSITION, PRAGMATIC INTERACTION

The relations of religion to politics are complex and paradoxical. Both try to secure and maintain power. But they differentiate by contrasts in the aims and values they set upon power, and by a radical divergence in their conceptions of the nature and source of power. At an abstract level, the religious and the political tend to be conceptual opposites. The basic power envisaged in politics is secular, of this world; that envisaged in religion, whether immanent or transcendental, is of another quality, from another world. Both politics and religion imply awareness of social relationships, and emphasize integration – politics in its concern for order in society and religion in its concern for congregational bonds. But whereas politics is focused on relations of people with other people, religion is more oriented to relations of people with gods or other spiritually conceived forces. Religion deals with the sacred, politics with the profane. Religion and politics both use calculation and appeal to emotion, but religion is grounded in revelation while politics tries to keep within the bounds of reason.

With reference to value, religion operates in the name of a principle of truth, while politics often makes do with canons of expediency. In a hierarchy of social activities, religion commonly stands at a peak of evaluation (paralleled in some contexts by art, science, or philosophy); by comparison, politics may be rated low in the scale of public esteem. Such everyday contrasts are commonplace, and long-standing. As Edmund Burke put it 200 years ago (1790: 14) in his reflections on the role of religion in revolutionary France, 'politics and the pulpit are terms that have little agreement'. Indeed, they have often been in conflict – a struggle commonly epitomized in the contrasting ideas of church and state.

Long ago (Firth 1971: 241–50) I argued that religion is really a form of human art, a symbolic product of human anxiety, desire, and imagination expressed in a social milieu. Like any art, religion is a product of tension – between the ideal and the actual, between the individual and the mass, between the urge to satisfaction and life, and recognition of the inevitability of suffering and death. A religion is distinguished from other arts by three main criteria. Its most effective expressions are generated, as in all arts, by individual creative effort, but they depend more than other arts upon tradition and membership of a community. Again, while every art has its forms and ceremonies to guard its practice, the rituals of religion tend to be so frequent, elaborate, evocative and mandatory that they provide very strong guidelines for faith. Then, the rules of religious interpretation and conduct, unlike those of science and philosophy or the visual arts, are given a legitimacy of ultimate authority which is regarded as absolute and unchallengeable by those who subscribe to them. Now politics has been variously described as the art of the possible, or the art of the plausible. However this may be, one basic character of religion is clear – after a certain point it becomes the art of the implausible, in the sense of resting upon postulates which are nonempirical, which claim an inner rather than an outer appearance of truth, since they may run counter to what are ordinarily thought of as natural laws. In this promise to provide explanations which go beyond the world of sensory experience lies much of the appeal of religion.

But the conceptual opposition between religion and politics, especially when expressed in practical terms by the idea of separation of church and state, must be looked at historically. It is largely a Western abstraction, and relatively modern at that. In fact, the three great religions which claim to be universal in scope and in one sense nonpolitical, have been historically centred and massed in geopolitical terms – Christianity in the West, Buddhism in the East, and Islam in the belt between; and each has split again into major sections on what are largely regional, even national, lines.

At the practical level, despite claims of religion to uniqueness and autonomy, in the West as elsewhere, the religious is apt to be constrained by the political. In its political form, the state, a community may support or suppress religious activity, may differentiate between religions by having an established church, or may define religion by giving constitutional guarantees of freedom of worship to what are specified as religious groups. The state may also prescribe the duties of a citizen in such a way that they present a religious person with unpalatable choices of a moral order. The resistance of some religious bodies to conscription of their members for military service illustrates how insistence upon religious obligations can lead to judicial penalties. Even a democratic compromise of the 'conscientious objector' type may mean a legal definition of a person's religious rights in terms of the political duties of a citizen (Wilson 1961: 89). In the West, even the most tolerant states have sometimes been stirred to intervene if the activities of an extreme religious cult have seemed to put undue pressure upon, or cause undue suffering to individuals or to be offensive to public order. A well-documented study with a strong anthropological component has shown the dilemma of the Canadian government in regard to the Doukhobors, especially when provoked by the nudism and other demonstration acts by a subgroup, the Sons of Freedom (Hawthorn 1955).

But by contrast a religion may circumscribe, define, or qualify political activity or institutions. Penetration of the broad political field by organized religious interests is common in a Western democracy. In Britain, recent examples include expressions of hostility by the Lord's Day Observance Society to any parliamentary proposals to weaken laws against Sunday trading, or by various Catholic organizations to the use of public funds under the National Health Service for contraception and abortion services. In both Australia and the United States the longtime concern of indigenous inhabitants for conservation of their sacred religious sites has at last produced some political action to inhibit some kinds of commercial development. Notable illustrations of the complex ways whereby religious interests may seek political power occur in electoral systems where a national party has had explicitly religious aims and composition. Such are Christian Democrats in Italy or Germany; Islamic Union (Sarekat Islam) and Indonesian Muslim Party (Partai Muslimin Indonesia) in prewar and postwar Indonesia respectively; Pan-Malayan Islamic Association (Persatuan Islam Sa-Tanah Melayu, now Partai Islam) in present-day Malaysia; or the Islamic Republican Party in Iran. A striking Buddhist example is that of Sōka Gakkai, a huge vertically organized association of Japanese religious laymen, with a militant nationalist ancestry going back to the thirteenth century, but with fiercely modern protestations of peace and clean government expressed in new political party form. How acute can be political effects of action based ostensibly on religious premises is illustrated, as we know, by the persistent settlement of some Jewish groups in parts of biblical Israel on the ground that the territory was divinely allocated to them some 2000 years ago – despite the bitter challenge offered by their occupation to the resident Arab population. How massive can be the constriction of political advantage by opposed religious interests, and how far-reaching can be the results of religious intransigence has been tragically illustrated in the separation of Pakistan from India in 1947.

But anthropologists well know how religion may have a supportive role for some broad aspects of the overall political system. Even in a relatively secular state, a religious validation of general political institutions or activity can be important. Most Western countries, including Britain and the United States, demonstrate what I call a 'canopy syndrome' of religious operations.[1] Despite the diverse religious composition of their peoples, on basic public occasions political leaders invoke a postulate of an Almighty God to confer blessing and guidance on the nation, and this may be intensified in time of crisis. Such periodic public prayer is supported by more enduring, if vaguer, forms of religious statement. Even a state's monetary issues have been drawn into the communication of religious messages. Visitors to the United States observe that all currency in this country now bears the solemn affirmation 'In God We trust', a comforting if somewhat ambiguous notion if the solvency of the dollar should ever be called into question. In Britain the authorities are less pious or more cautious. British coinage, now in effect all of base metal, bears the head of our Sovereign Elizabeth II, with the legend 'D.G.Reg.F.D.', the abbreviated form of a Latin statement meaning 'By the Grace of God, Queen, Defender of the Faith'. Most British people probably think that the faith referred to is either the Church of England (of which the Queen is head) or Christianity generally. But the better informed know that historically it refers to a Catholic title awarded to Henry VIII by the Pope for a polemic Henry wrote against Martin Luther's attack on the sacraments before Henry broke away from the Roman church; and that our Protestant sovereigns have kept the title ever since (Moorman 1967: 163). But the assertion that the Queen is sovereign 'by the Grace of God' is far broader. It encapsulates more than 1000 years of ritual sanction in which English monarchs received the crown in a religious as well as a political commitment (Carpenter 1966: 406–8). Here the pious formula, going back to coins of Edward I in the late thirteenth century, represents a historical mystical engagement of strong emotional and moral significance. But our British coinage alone bears the religious message. Our paper currency, of much higher value but a recent creation, bears only a portrait of the Queen without any reference to the Almighty, and is guaranteed for solvency quite prosaically by the Bank of England alone. The point of such 'canopy syndromes' is presumably to provide a kind of umbrella formula for general social action, whereby the religious commitment of large numbers of citizens can be expressed symbolically in broad terms which will not offend any specific sectarian interests. But in another form of 'canopy syndrome', religious leaders may endorse more specific secular values of the society, with obvious political implications. A noteworthy example is the statement of Pope John XXIII in his message *Mater et Magistra*, declaring that a right to private property is a part of the natural order (Davis, Thomas and Crehan 1971: 256).

RELIGION IN FORMS OF GOVERNANCE

Among the political concomitants of religion, I want to consider particularly the relation between forms of religious governance and of political governance. I am not offering any formal definitions or typologies. And while structures are important I will be dealing mainly with organizational processes. I take two major types of relationship: where the religious and political forms of control are amalgamated in the traditional god-king or other divinely endowed ruler; and where religious and political leadership are separate but an ecclesiastical, clerical, or analogous organization attempts to control the body politic.

A functional division between ritual and executive leadership has been common in many types of society. But familiar also to anthropological literature is the fusion of political and religious leadership in variants of the divine-king or priest-king theme, where religious sanctions give peculiar weight to the controller or leader of the political system. More than a century ago the historian and proto-anthropologist Fustel de Coulanges (1873) revealed the close relation between ancient Greek and Italian religious ideas and their rules of private law, and between the rites of the ancients and their political institutions. Not only did he emphasize the sacerdotal role of kings and family heads, he also supplied a theory of change, of gradual separation of religious from political leadership which, even if idealized, did set out many of the basic issues still before us. But in anthropology we have drawn more from Frazer than from Fustel. Even if we do not take literally Frazer's (1890) *Golden Bough* thesis of homicidal succession to the sacred priest-kingship, his general ideas of a mystic association between the vigour of a ruler, the fertility of nature, and the prosperity of a people have been well attested.[2] Yet with the diversity of cultures, the divine has been conceived as related to the human political agent in a great variety of ways. The ruler may be worshipped as a living god, may be revered as always divinely inspired or as only an occasional medium for the words of the god, or may be thought of as simply under divine protection or legitimacy (Firth 1979a: 154–6). From a political point of view, the significance of any such religious sanction for the position of a ruler is clear. Even if the religious convictions of the people are not strong, the periodic rituals help to buttress the legitimacy of the ruler, and provide a positive force for maintaining order and conformity to demands by authority.

Less well understood, perhaps, have been the connections between religious sanction, political leadership, and administrative efficiency (Firth 1964: 75–80). How far is the acceptance of a religiously framed polity contingent upon some minimum of fulfillment of expectation of benefit and of orderliness of the

society in mundane affairs? This is a question which anthropologists have not been very well equipped to tackle, since criteria
of efficiency are not easy to define, and in any case answers call
for considerable historical perspective. Historically, a people's
threshold of tolerance of weakness, error, and failure in their
rulers who have been protected by ritual sanctions has seemed
to be quite high, as the record of the sovereigns of Europe or of
the papacy reveals. And yet, the course of events in Western
countries, for example, has demonstrated a broadening of the
basis of recognition of human frailty of rulers, and a denudation
of the ritual sanctions surrounding them. Corresponding to this
has been either a growing belief in their personal accountability
as rulers, or a marked reduction in the political powers allocated
to them. The conception of the divine right of kings, for which the
scholarly James I of England – 'the wisest fool in Christendom' –
argued so strongly, now seems the most fusty kind of anachron-
ism. Granted that some of the magical aura of kings and queens
has survived, most of these monarchs themselves have vanished,
and where they still exist they have tended to become cultural
symbols rather than religious officiants or executive leaders.

These matters of Western hisotry are not my field. But my
experience of Tikopia over more than fifty years allows me to
give an anthropological comment on a limited case of relations
between the religious and the political (Firth 1959: 254–84; 1965:
187–236; 1967a: 19–21; 1969; 1970: 402–18; 1979a).

Tikopia chiefs have not been considered as divine in their
lifetimes, but traditionally were elevated to positions of great
power in the spiritual hierarchy after their deaths. The traditional
pagan religious system came to an end nearly forty years ago,
after I had seen it in operation in two periods. In this system the
chiefs were the major priests for the society, intermediaries
between the gods and the people, responsible for the formulae
of appeal for welfare and prosperity and the elaborate sets of
ritual offering to the gods and commemoration of their mythic
deeds. But the major rituals of the seasonal cycle were performed
as much for the sake of the society as for that of religion. The
chiefs were also the ultimate source of economic and political
authority in the Tikopia community, with powers of life and death
over offenders, administered sometimes harshly but usually in
flexible and sensitive ways. Pagan chiefs were credited with mystic
power. When they spoke ritually, their words were believed to

yield crops, fish, and the health of their people. They were also held to be sacred, with their persons protected by rules against bodily contact, menial tasks, and slighting language. They were prime examples of the classical anthropological categories of *mana* and taboo. Now a most interesting fact is that though the pagan religious system has been abandoned, and the ancient gods are no longer worshipped or revered, in Tikopia belief the chiefs still retain most of their authority and some measure of their sacredness and mystic powers. From a Tikopia point of view the change in religious allegiance has meant an alternative extra-human framework for the operations of their chiefs – a transfer of the validation of any mystic powers with which they may still be credited to the Christian God. It might be argued from this that for these Polynesians the concept of chiefly authority in itself conjures up notions of esoteric force, which they will justify by any religious device to hand. Certainly in the Tikopia political system the election of a new chief is held to effect a transmutation: he who was a common man without sacredness or occult power now as chief has suddenly become sacred, and has the potentiality of proving himself to be endowed with a special form of efficacy. But the process is automatic to only a limited degree. Attribution of mystic power, like that of qualities of character, is personalized and depends upon an accumulated material evidence. Moreover, such attribution is politicized in that while the Tikopia are very willing to credit their own chiefs with power qualities beyond the normal, they seem much less certain about the potentialities of European secular leaders to produce mystical results.

The essence of my argument here is that religious validation of political office can be subtle, complex, flexible, much more than a one-to-one relationship. I argue too that public interest, however defined, will ultimately seep through. Anthropological statements about the breakdown of political authority when traditional religious sanctions are removed – and I myself have sometimes made such statements (cf. Firth 1965: 236) – must therefore be looked at with care. It is important to specify the conditions in which changes take place and the alternatives that are open. In Tikopia chieftainship the cultural demography is very relevant. The Tikopia are a small Polynesian community of limited resources among a vastly greater Melanesian population by whom they could be submerged, economically and politically.

Their religion has now lost its local identification; they have become part of a great Anglican Church of Melanesia (in which, however, there is already a Tikopia bishop). Economically, they are being partially absorbed into a modern wage-earning and salaried system. Administratively, though for about fifty years their chiefs were treated by the government of the Solomon islands as the prime representatives and decision-makers for their people, that role was increasingly being threatened by planned advances in local self-government. Now that the Solomon Islands have become an independent nation, the political future of the Tikopia and their chiefs is even more in question. It makes sense, I think, to see the qualities the Tikopia attribute to their chiefs as not simply a perpetuation of traditional values, but also as a positive adaptive part of the symbolic defence of their culture. So far, even the most skeptical of their educated secular prominent men seem ready to accept at least the feasibility of this modern adaptation of ancient beliefs. How long before sophistication of Western influence leads to a divorce of mystical from pragmatic judgments about the operations of Tikopia chiefs I cannot say. But preservation of belief in the mystical powers of the chiefs, in my view, will be helped by any retention of authority and administrative leadership which they can manage in the modern economic and political situation.

This Tikopia example suggests an important theoretical point. In any society there is a fairly constant demand for viable administrative measures for economic and cultural control and maintenance. Here a religious commitment can provide a powerful spur. But while theoretically supplying invariant values, religious ideas may have to be fairly flexible in action. To argue that the parameters of politics may be less adaptable than those of religion may seem paradoxical. It may also seem to accord to some extent with Karl Marx's position on religion. But as I will show later, my ideas go along rather different lines.

In more complex types of situation than Tikopia, where religious and political leadership have long been differentiated, religious leaders have often tended to stand for a system of moral and spiritual values – to represent as it were the conscience of the people over against the manoeuvres and expediency of their rulers. But such situations are rarely simple and have great potential for tension.

A guiding theme of all the 'religions of the Book' has been

their holism – what may be called the alpha and omega view of religion. The religious canons are believed to contain within themselves all the rules necessary for the life and salvation of the believer, including all provisions for his political behaviour. The scriptures or allied sources of religious authority, sacred and unalterable, are the beginning and end of the guidance of man through life. In theory, both Judaism and Christianity recognize such an interpretation, but only intermittently have their leaders tried to insist upon it as a working principle.[3] Indeed, in periods when Christianity undertook a fusion of spiritual and temporal power, the results were disturbing rather than harmonious, as the medieval and Renaissance papacy showed. There were times when, as Machiavelli put it in 1513, the 'ambitions of prelates' led to much discord and tumult in Rome (1903: 46; cf. also Burckhardt 1945: 64–79). And, in the alleged promotion of spiritual interests, religion often became an idiom of political expression. As historians tell us, when, after the Reformation German princes espoused the cause of Protestantism, religion became part of the ammunition with which they bombarded their political opponents. When Jesuits became confessors to the sovereigns of Europe, the Catholic religion became part of the state machinery for maintaining the system of government (Foss 1969: 62–3, 281).

The fullest and most overt expression of the alpha and omega view of religion is to be found in Islam – as the example of Iran has lately forcefully reminded us. The main argument of Islam must be well known, but I restate it briefly.[4] Islam is a religion of stark monotheism – to 'give God a partner', as in the Christian Trinity, is an extreme heresy. Islam is also a religion of austerity. To make images of God, as in the Christian faith, is blasphemous, and even to shape the forms of living beings in painting or sculpture is to run the risk of usurping the role of the Creator. It is true that the theological purists were often disregarded, both domestically and at the Muslim courts, and even the Prophet himself is said by tradition to have allowed a little latitude in his household (Arnold 1928: 7). But from the central postulate of God as the supreme, ultimate, blinding reality come propositions about man as the servant of God, about nature as symbols reflecting the divine reality, and about the law (*Shari'a*) as expressing the will of God and covering all aspects of human life. It is a neat and logical faith. For Muslims there is no ultimate distinction between divine law, natural law, and human law. So every act, including every political act, has a religious dimension and should have a demonstrable religious sanction. This field of sanctions is the sphere of the religious scholars ('*Ulama*). For Muhammad was the Seal of the prophets, the mouthpiece of God's last revelation to man. Hence innovation in doctrine is error, even heresy; all that is permissible is interpretation. Hence comes the role of the scholars as jurists, not laying down the law but pronouncing on what is lawful. It can be a role of great power.

But Islam, like all religions, faces some hard problems: the frailties of men; the stubbornness of local custom; the dangerous probings of mystics; the technical, economic, and social processes of a changing world. The sacred writings are complex and apt to be obscure; they are often difficult to apply to modern conditions. As a Malay once said about Muslim rules for division of property, Muhammad was thinking about camels, not fishing boats or rice lands. So the interpretation industry of the religious scholars is kept busy with opinions on the propriety for Muslims of conduct ranging from dancing ritually or keeping dogs as pets to accepting corneal and other body grafts in medicine or investing religious council monies in hotel development. And despite their formal setting, the opinions of Muslim jurists, like those of lawyers anywhere, have by no means always coincided (see Muhammad Salleh 1974: 157–61; cf. Firth 1971: 148–52).

In most modern Muslim countries movements in what have been variously called reformist, fundamentalist, scripturalist, or puritan directions have become especially strong in recent years. This is partly a reaction to Western pressures. It is a conviction widely shared by Muslim reformers of today that however they may have borrowed from the West in the past, the Western countries have now lost their spiritual traditions, have a secular theory of law, have an illusory notion of freedom through excessive individual self-expression, and debase humanity with a vulgar immoral consumption technology – including a deplorable use of the drug alcohol (see Nasr 1975). So wishing to revive Islamic ideals as a working theory of society, many Muslim leaders oppose what they regard as Western influences in dress, diet, conduct of women, and other modern adaptations. Here an accusation of 'unIslamic behaviour' levelled at anyone who does not toe the orthodox line is a very powerful weapon to induce conformity.[5] Fanaticism is no excuse for blackmail. But the advance of Muslim fundamentalists into diverse areas of public conduct, and their opposition to many Western customs, even if at times unpalatable, are intelligible reactions of a religion seeing itself threatened by antithetical values. Resort to extreme political action in efforts to redress its position is another matter – in part a sign of the frustration of the faithful in finding that faith alone without the appropriate technology is unable to move mountains.

Yet, historically, Muslims, like followers of other religions, have adapted to external pressures, to changing consumption standards, and to the requirements of administrative efficiency. While a religion may claim responsibility for the civil law, it cannot necessarily guarantee the civil law. As Clive Kessler has shown in an admirable study of religion and politics in Kelantan, the Islamic social vision has remained important not because it has reflected social reality but because it has not carried this reflection (1978: 209). Clifford Geertz too has pointed out how the explicit Muslim claim to possess a comprehensive social theory did not match up to the inescapable facts of political life, as chroniclers of the early days of Islam have made clear (1960: 121–61). It does much less so nowadays, as the varied responses of Muslim countries to the complexities of the modern international scene demonstrate. Hence the tendency to operate the ideal at the level of ritual and of statement of belief, and to accept the pragmatic discrepancies as merely temporary divergences.

The problem has taken on a special form where Muslims have had to live under alien political rule. The Shi'a solution is of special interest as a form of adaptation. In Shi'a theory, in the absence of the Hidden Imam (last of the historic successors to the Prophet, having disappeared over 1000 years ago) no ruler, even if he is a Muslim, can be fully legitimate in his own right; though he may be granted partial legitimacy if, recognizing Imāmic doctrine, he is good and just. But Shi'ite cooperation with any secular power can be allowable if done with intent to save life or property, or to support the rights of believers. As one metaphorical statement has put it, 'the atonement for working for the government consists in taking care of the needs of the brethren' (Madelung 1980: 29)[6] – a view with which many Western academics may feel some sympathy.

The internal structure of a religious system may also present political problems of another kind.

AUTHORITY A CRITICAL ISSUE

If politics be regarded not simply as a discrete segment of social relationships (Bailey 1973: 185) but a pervasive aspect of social relationships, a field for the exercise of power in determining actions and statements, then a religious body has political problems in the management of its own affairs. To put it provocatively, I would contend that for any religion to operate as a viable social movement of any significance it must develop its own political dimension. Central to this is the issue of authority. This arises in the allocation and control of resources, most obviously in the management of property, but most important in the direction of peoples' activities and expressions of opinion.

As far as property is concerned, what have been described as 'the temptations of power and prosperity' have entered religious organizations at all levels. Historically, in the United States, contention of essentially secular order over the financial as well as the moral implications of slave owning before the Civil War was responsible for lasting divisions in two leading churches (Mead 1956: 31, 149). In Britain recently a comparable though less destructive issue has been the propriety for religious bodies of investing their funds in companies with economic interests in South Africa, before the abolition of apartheid.

A fertile field for political manoeuvre is that of succession to leadership, bringing with it problems of alignment of supporters and focus of their energies. The history of the major religions is full of examples. Even in the early years of Islam, for instance, when the religious influence of the Prophet was fresh, the bitter violent struggle over his succession was decided much more on dynastic grounds, claims of precedence and status, local loyalties, and other secular considerations than by spiritual principles. Very revealing in parallel context is Michael Mendelson's remark in his penetrating study of Buddhist sects and the state in Burma, that he might have been wiser to have spoken of factions rather than of sects (1975: 28).

The political dimension of a religion may emerge when questions of authority over the minds or at least the expressed opinions of adherents arise. How far can individual variation of doctrinal views be permitted without imperilling the religious tradition, the purity of the faith? In both Christianity and Islam the illumination of the mystic has often been judged to border on heresy (Firth 1964: 302–6). In Judaism, the euphoric mystical heresy of Sabbatai Zevi and his prophet Nathan of Gaza has been magnificently illuminated in the profound study by Gershom Scholem (1955: 287–324). Any antinomian element in mysticism, any tendency to treat the moral law enunciated in religious terms as not binding on the mystic, must obviously be offensive to those who propound the orthodox doctrine. But anthropologists may also guess that protection of the doctrine is almost certainly mixed with protection of power centres, of the right to control the allegiance of the faithful in practical as well as in theoretical matters. When variations of doctrine have led to schism in a religious body, the interest of the schismatic in maintaining his own power base among believers seems often likewise to have been an impelling force – as, for example, anthropologists familiar with Bengt Sundkler's classis study of Bantu prophets (1948) are well aware. In the diverse Christian churches of today the issue of ultimate authority to prescribe doctrine and ritual is probably the toughest obstacle to ecumenical reunion.

Protection of political interests of a religious body in the main-tenance of its own authority system may be involved even in what appear as cases of religious martyrdom. 'Martyr' basically means a witness. On this score Thomas Hobbes, in his seventeenth-century *Leviathan*, had some sharp things to say of alleged Christian martyrs who do not bear witness to the risen Christ but 'die for every tenet that serveth the ambition, or profit of the Clergy' (1904: 368). We know that men can die equally for a political as for a religious cause. And in terms of an old saying, Hobbes held that it's not the death of the witness but the testi-mony itself that makes the martyr. Properly speaking, he argued, Christian martyrs should die for the conversion of infidels and not in a struggle against the civil authority. This issue has been much debated. Indeed, Hobbes was an interested upholder of royal authority – though not of the divine right of kings. But from the point of view of Hobbes's pertinent comment, saints such as Thomas Becket, whose martyrdom has been given an impressive and moving analysis by Victor Turner, died more for a political than for a religious principle. As medieval historians have indicated, issues of feudal loyalties of propertied bishops, and autonomy of ecclesiastical courts in judgment of 'criminous clerks', fortified by papal temporal claims such as that of the English Pope Hadrian IV over England, all entered into the defence of Roman pontifical authority which was the basis of Becket's defiance of Henry II (Turner 1974: 65–9; Mann 1925: 254 *et seq.*; Moorman 1967: 76–80; Southern 1970: 252). As Gobineau pointed out more than a century ago, political necessity often speaks in the name of religious doctrine (1933: 32).

What I have been saying about the significance of religion for civil government reaches far back into the history of ideas, from Fustel de Coulanges and Sir James Frazer through Giambattista Vico and Thomas Hobbes to the Greek philosophers. If only in a fleeting way I hope to have shown how an anthropological approach rubs shoulders with those from other disciplines in the exploration of an eternal question, the relation of principle to expediency in public life.

RELIGION AS POLITICAL IDEOLOGY?

So far I have tended to suggest that despite its political entanglements, a religion can supply some of the most positive, innovative, overriding moral values of a society, the leaven of the spirit which redeems the sins of the flesh, the ideals to which political behaviour should aspire, whatever be its earthly shortcomings. An ultimate sanction of force in politics, it might be argued, has as a dialectical type of response an ultimate sanction, if not of nonresistance, at least of moral superiority to the exercise of physical power. Yet another view is in radical contrast to this. The title of this chapter, as many students of the political literature know, embodies a reference to an opinion by Karl Marx.

Marx saw religion as a human construct, not an individual creation but a social product, arising from man's immersion in society. This was a theme which Durkheim was to elaborate half a century later (Firth 1974). A product of man's participation in the real world, religion, said Marx, is the general theory of this world, its logic in popular form, its moral sanction, the consolation for the miseries and injustices of the world. Religion is the spiritual aroma of the world ('jene Welt, deren geistiges Aroma die Religion ist' – Marx 1927: 607, cf. 1963: 41). 'Spiritual aroma' is a vivid metaphor, even if somewhat enigmatic, in line with some of Marx's other sensuous imagery for social relationships. But it was ironic. It was intended probably not to suggest the smell of corruption, but rather an aesthetic fragrance which concealed the rotting condition beneath. For certainly it was meant to convey Marx's idea of religion as a manifestation of the inverted world of capitalist society, a fantasy of alienated man.

Marx's analysis of religion, a product of his early years, had characteristically involved a criticism of two men whose ideas he admired – Hegel, whose dialectic he adopted and transformed, and Feuerbach, one of the few thinkers he considered to have advanced from Hegel. Marx, an atheist, criticized Hegel for his compromise with religion, but as a socialist he criticized Feuerbach for attacking religion directly rather than the state of society which produced religion. Marx's ideas about religion have often been misrepresented. He saw religion as providing an illusory happiness, concealing the conditions of exploitation in the real world; but the actual enemy was the structure of society in which religion operated. For Marx, religion was not a monstrous thing. 'Religious suffering is at the same time an expression of real suffering and a protest against real suffering. Religion is the sign of the oppressed creature, the feeling of a heartless world and the soul of soulless circumstances.' These words, though immediately followed by the well-known metaphor of religion as the 'opium of the people' (McLellan 1973b: 88–9) show Marx as not just deriding religion. He was like a doctor who, seeing a false sense of security and euphoria produced in his patient by a drug, does not let his compassion overcome his perception of truth. Since religion is an illusory form of social consciousness, the conditions which require and foster it should be radically changed.

Marx did not seem to have been interested very deeply in religion.[7] In incidental references he criticized priests for pushing God into the background, and he grew indignant at the way Christian leaders in England had loaded predatory officials in India with titles and honours. Prophetically, if cynically, he pointed out how worship of the holy places in Jerusalem had become a series of desperate rows that concealed a profane battle of nations and of races, one of the phases of the Oriental question incessantly reproduced and never solved (Marx 1976: 92, 907n; Aveneri 1969: 86, 151). But Marx hardly went beyond such brief empirical comments. In fact Marx's message about the palliative or sedative instrumental significance of religion was not unique. Apart from the skeptical views of Plato and Aristotle down to those of Edward Gibbon, there was in Marx's own time an explicit opinion, as in Britain, that religion was part of the exploitative machinery of society. Charles Kingsley, a Christian Socialist, in a letter to the Chartists in 1848 wrote that many working men believed the Bible to be the invention of kings and prelates – 'to pretend God's sanction for superstition and tyranny' – though in fact, Kingsley argued, it was written to keep the rich rather than the poor in order. Though he may not have read Marx, Kingsley even used the narcotic analogy – 'we have used the Bible as if it was . . . an opium-dose for keeping beasts of burden patient while they were being overloaded' (1848: 58–9). What was essentially Marx's own contribution was the clarity and analytical force of his assertion that the 'earthly roots' of religion were its place in an ideological system determined by the relations of production.

Marx's challenging arguments did have some historical plausibility. The Western Christian church (and Marx seems to have thought of little else under the head of religion), by its alliance with the propertied classes for much of the growth of industrialization in Europe, had supported unequal distribution of wealth and ignored social ills. When the evangelical call came for spiritual regeneration on a personal basis, this tended to distract attention from the root cause of social evils. While it may not be true that Methodism in the eighteenth century saved England from revolution, it seems clear that renewed hope given by religion did serve as some alternative to political action.

Perhaps most galling to religious believers was Marx's political definition of religion, a denial of its autonomy even more slighting than his call for its direction abolition would have been. Among theologians, opposition to his propositions, generally reduced to an 'opiate of the people' formula, was predictable. No one likes to be accused of intellectual drug-peddling. An orthodox counterattack, arguing that Marxism itself is a rival form of millenarianism, can be found even among anthropologists and sociologists – 'all the fervour and potency of a religion without its ultimate concepts' as the anthropologist and cleric E. O. James put it (1940: 220, 297; cf. Yinger 1970: 107, 196–9; and Macintyre 1969: 113; also critique by McLellan 1973b: 89, regarding this as confusing the issue).

But if one disregards transcendental assumptions and shares Marx's view of religion as a form of social consciousness, an essentially human creation – as I do – I think there are still other grounds for criticism of his position and that of many Marxist anthropologists. One basic caveat has been stated crisply by Bryan Wilson: 'A rigorous economic determinism is insufficiently

subtle to explain religious phenomena' (1961: 5).[8] Religion is by
no means always a simple reflection of current relations of production or a historical expression of earlier material conditions.
Even in a capitalist society it is not merely supportive of the
ruling class, disguising the exploitative state.

Undoubtedly, religious phenomena in any society are shaped
and constrained by certain material parameters – the forces or
powers and relations of production. In ideas of offering and
sacrifice, for example, central to so many religions, not only the
material apparatus of wine, or coconut milk, bread, cattle, or pigs,
but also the whole system of thinking about and managing such
goods in a scheme of relations of production becomes manifest
(see chapter 5). But this does not mean that the role of religion
is confined to a symbolic expression of power relations in a given
mode of production, and symbolic compensation for them. So
far, Marx might have agreed. He might even have allowed a
proposition that religion is not merely a means of coping with
a given mode of production but is one traditional way for an
individual to cope with society itself. The human mind as a social
product, he could argue, can take all kinds of liberties with its
contact with the real world, including the problems of the inescapable cooperation and competition with other members of society.

But that the conventional Marxian view falls short of an
adequate understanding of religion, even from a humanist standpoint in anthropology, emerges in at least two types of situation.

Religion can be a very powerful political instrument. But the
strength of conviction of its followers, their certainty of the legitimacy of their premises, can lead to innovative action, to political
challenge instead of political support. If in a broad way we can
divide religious followers into moderates and extremists, it is
among the moderates that Marx's propositions about religion as
the ideology of the capitalist political system have historically
applied. Among the extremists, the zealots, and the fanatics, God
and Caesar are either unified or irreconcilable. A religion can
then offer a revolutionary alternative to an established political
system such as that which would define the relative powers of
church and state. More generally, it might be argued that some
of the most important religious movements, at their beginning,
have been as much challenges to the established political and
economic order as escapes from it.

Predisposing conditions for the development of a religion into a preoccupation with political power tend to exist where mass forms of political expression are denied to a people. Development may take the form of trying to build a kingdom of God within the secular state, to maintain an authority system not answerable to the civil power. But it may take the form of more direct attack. Historically, a religion has often provided a spearhead for nascent nationalism, as its role in many former European colonial territories demonstrated. Forces of religious protest can then assume not just palliative or reforming shape but a revolutionary dynamism that reflects a mode of production by opposition, not endorsement. Drawing together the threads of much historical and anthropological work on millenarian movements, Yonina Talmon, for example, showed how a millennial view of salvation is revolutionary and catastrophic, often in active revolt against the established order (Talmon 1966).[9] Some revolutionary movements in Islam and some aspects of the theology of liberation in Latin America, whether they acknowledge Marxist inspiration or not, seem to show an independent critical force in their reaction to particular economic and social structures. And Victor Turner's account of the Mexican Revolution of Independence in 1810 shows how religious symbols served as supreme mobilizing factors in the insurrection (Turner 1974: 151–4). Indeed, some recent Marxist theoretical work seems able to accept a liberating compo nent in religious experience (Birnbaum 1971: 125), as some Christian theologians have found relief in Marxism from the conservatism of their churches in regard to the inequalities of the social order.[10] But revolution does not of itself construct a new order of society. To get a hard edge on to solutions for economic and political problems needs a sophistication and practical competence not necessarily found in religious leaders. So theocracies of any kind, whether innovative or conservative, are apt to be short-lived, often dissolving on the death of a charismatic leader.

A second type of situation which raises doubts about Marx's view of religion as just political ideology is the position of religion in socialist countries. Marx too easily assumed that products of the human imagination such as mythology would vanish if material conditions altered (McLellan 1973a: 56). But when the mode of production and the shape of society have been radically changed, religion and its associated myths do not necessarily wither away. They may be abandoned by large sections of the people, but by others they may be retained in adapted form. Some socialist countries have actively discouraged religious organizations, turned churches and temples into museums, laicized religious personnel, destroyed religious sacra, or converted them into art treasures. As I myself have recently seen in the Peoples' Republic of China, this has had a powerful effect in secularizing the religious field. But in such countries religious allegiance, though often muted, has continued in some measure, according to historical circumstances. In Poland the position of the Catholic Church as a historic defender of national liberties – victim and hero, as it has been said – has given it a strong resistant base for withstanding political pressures. Despite its ties with an external spiritual authority, the Polish Church remains an outstanding national symbol, operating as we have recently seen in some ways as an alternative to the political establishment. In China, after the repressions of the Cultural Revolution, Christianity has once again become a permissible allegiance, provided it is in conformity with national and socialist aspirations. It is a careful Christianity, anxious to make clear its willingness to work for the common good of the Peoples' Republic. It is also showing a nice discrimination in its attitude to external Christianity. While fraternal relations with the West are sought, any suggestion of policy direction from the West is firmly set aside. No longer do Chinese Christians see any need for Western missionaries – they believe they can manage their own proselytization, in a temperate style. There is the Protestant Three-Self Movement, based on the principles of self-government, self-support, and self-propagation. There is the Patriotic Catholic Association, which provides for the consecration of its own bishops without reference to the Vatican and recognizes the Pope simply as a spiritual equal, the bishop of Rome. Such are signs that the Christian churches in the Peoples' Republic have been coming to terms with political realities. Intriguing possibilities of doctrinal modification of traditional religious forms appear. For example, a Chinese Christian notion that creation, a primary process in their theology, need not always be serene and evolutionary, but can have been violent and revolutionary, has obvious political implications.[11]

How does this relate to Marx's thesis? It is significant that religion has survived, even in such limited degree, and not withered away. But more significant is the point that if it survives in accommodation with a socialist regime, religion cannot be simply a political ideology of a capitalist society. Is it then part of the ideology of a socialist society, helping to conceal from the masses the reality of their condition, and to compensate them for the sufferings they endure along the freedom road? Was Marx more accurate than he knew, and is indeed religion one form of expression of the soul of a soulless society? Does it express the difficulties and malaise of living in *any* type of society, especially one where the demands of economic efficiency and orderly government lead to the creation of an administrative bureaucracy from which the ordinary citizen feels alienated? Or did Marx overlook some important considerations about religion? Even if it does provide some ideological cover for a political system, does it still have other functions of quite a different kind? An anthropological answer, conventional but I think still largely valid, could be that religion can provide three kinds of service which Marx ignored. The religion of a people, both in belief and in ritual, can symbolize their group identity irrespective of the particular structure of government and economy. A religious organization can also provide a counterpoise to the authority of the state, a rallying point for people against unpopular decisions or stressful conditions imposed by those in control. And last, perhaps most vital, a religion can serve its adherents in personal crises. It can form part of the explanation of the vagaries of human existence, from abstract opinions on theodicy to a rationale for individual concrete misfortune, suffering, and death. Even Engels's 'tedious notion of personal immortality', as he called it (Marx and Engels 1970: 594) need not necessarily be extinguished by a socialist revolution in the mode of production.

A central problem in the accommodation between major religious systems and newly emerging radical political groups controlling many modern states is where shall be the locus of religious authority. In the perennial struggle for power over the minds of men, as well as over their actions – a struggle which goes on in any form of society – can a religious body continue to strive for autonomous direction of its affairs in the face of a comprehensive socialist policy? All the great religions have attached crucial significance to the legitimacy of their scriptures, their traditions, their teachers, and to the control of these. But to preserve their viability as meaningful guides to their adherents, will the world religions begin to localize their message? Will they dissolve their universalist pretensions and structure, fragment as authority systems, and admit a political component into their direction? Will they create not merely local autonomous administrations but also indigenous doctrine and canons of inter-pretation? To put it brutally, will the forces of localization already demonstrated in, say, aspects of African, Melanesian, or Chinese Christianity so develop in the radically changing conditions of the modern world that Christianity will divide into a series of national cults? Whether this will be so or not, in this field of religious operation in radically changing political systems I see fascinating problems for anthropologists.

CONCLUSION

Religion is a name for some of man's most audacious attempts to give meaning to his world, by giving his constructions a symbolic transcendental referent. In its mundane relations a religion can operate as a system of political manoeuvre. In a more enlightened role it can be a powerhouse for aesthetic creation and moral endeavour. It can help to translate individual interest into that common public interest necessary for the success of a political community. It can give standards for individual conduct and be a support for individual fortitude. Religion is not alone in these fields, but it can be very important.

But a religion faces a basic dilemma. Religion is an art of making sense out of experience, and like any other such art, say, poetry, it must be taken symbolically, not literally. Many of its imaginative constructs express in very moving terms elements of the human condition which it is not easy to formulate otherwise. But there is a problem for sophisticated religious thinkers in deciding what in these images is a symbolic expression of human values and what belongs to an ultimate intrinsic truth. The corri-dors of the history of religion are littered with the broken images of dead gods and forgotten rituals, each in its day purporting to hold the key to the human mystery. What are the odds against any contemporary religion being able to sustain its claim to unique relationship with an eternal verity?

Yet the capacity of some religions to endure, to adapt, to throw up defence mechanisms and to survive, has been notable. By contrast with political values and their deference to expediency, part of the appeal of religion lies in its offer of certainty of ultimate standards against the flux of constantly changing conditions of social life. Yet by itself religion cannot control these conditions and must adapt to them in order to operate. Its roots lie in imaginative and emotional responses to the human condition, in suggesting solutions to the basic problems of human existence. But being a human construct, a religious organization must come to terms with the human condition. Purporting to be not of this world, it cannot escape the world. The strength of its convictions gives it a unique force for social and political action. But its conclusions often lack the validity which its postulates affirm. Whatever be its promise of salvation in the next world, it cannot give complete freedom in this world. So its compromises with politics are not just the weaknesses of the flesh. They are an inevitable result of the incompatibility between art and life – or between the life of art and the art of living. As technological developments tend to give more facilities for political control, a central problem for the leaders of any religious system is to adapt with as little loss of freedom as possible, so that their religion does not become what Marx thought it was, a mere spiritual aroma of a given economic and political system.

Chapter 4

Gods and God
Monotheism and polytheism

Anthropologists are accustomed to looking at religious systems in a relatively neutralist way, as social analysts. Some do so while committed to some variety of religious belief, which predisposes them to the assumption of an ultimate reality of a more or less mystical order behind all the social behaviour which they register and examine. Others, probably the majority, regard all religious ideas and institutions as explicable solely in human, social terms. They look upon assumptions of extra-human entities or powers at work in the universe as so much additional material, for consideration in the same terms of social inquiry. But anthropologists of either frame of mind have rarely looked directly at Western religious beliefs in the way in which they are used to examine 'primitive' religions. This chapter indicates my own standpoint in such analysis from a comparative point of view.

Anthropologists have been respectful of God, even without a capital letter. Ever since the days of Edward Burnett Tylor more than a century ago, we have recognized that there is no society, as we ordinarily define it, which is without some form of religion. But the conceptual forms by reference to which the religion is described, manifested, impelled to action and validated, are of an immense range. Tylor encapsulated them for his 'minimum definition' of religion under the general head of 'spiritual beings'. But to this was soon added a concept of impersonal mystical forces far removed from any idea of voluntary action such as a spirit being might be thought to engage in.

In all the societies they have studied modern social anthropologists have been led to perceive what may be called the essential human drama. People everywhere, in all kinds of technical and social conditions, have been preoccupied with the ultimate problems of living: relation to nature and to one another; reason for variation in skill and endeavour; competing claims of loyalty and self-interest, generosity and greed, love and hate, self-denial and ambition; the anguish of pain, suffering and fear of death; ideas of the definition of the self and the relation between initiative and the operations of chance or fate. Every human society has had answers to the questions so posed, or at least has worked out ways of alleviating or preventing the worst misfortunes and promoting success. In myths, creeds and rituals people in all societies try to locate responsibility for human affairs to some degree outside the human sphere. But major themes such as the creation of the world, of man and human institutions, the source of knowledge, the moral law, of good and evil in the life of man, are very differently envisaged in different societies. An essential attribute of divinity is power – extra-human, extra-physical power, and associated with this is some notion of the sacred. When power and sacred are interpreted at ultimate or utmost level, especially in personalized terms, then divinity is God. Many societies have no image of God as such a unique ultimate Being. While a monotheist might see here a fragmented conception of Divinity, adherents of other religious systems see their own pantheon or analogous set of concepts as positively fitted to their problems.

In exposing religious ideas held in a range of societies, the modern anthropologist has set out a vast array of formulations about guardian spirits, powers, gods, deities, creator beings, demiurges, culture heroes. And since inferences about belief are derived from study of non-verbal rites and practices as well as from speech, an anthropologist's account of a religion can be deeply infused with analysis of worship, offering, libation, sacrifice, consecration, prayer, communion, prophecy, divination, spirit mediumship. Problems familiar to us from the classical Greek philosophers appear in exotic context. When I investigated notions of the fate of the soul in so-called 'primitive' communities I found that while the health of the soul in life was a matter of critical interest, the future of the soul after death of the body was not a matter of deep concern to many peoples. They rarely believed the soul to be immortal, they often had no belief in its dependence upon any God. On the other hand, their eschatology has been more dynamic than ours. The souls of the dead are believed to be in frequent social intercourse with one another, the ancestors and the living. In Western belief, by contrast, the souls of the dead have very little to do and have almost no volition. The problem of the relation of impersonal fate to personal responsibility was examined by the late Meyer Fortes, in a striking essay entitled 'Oedipus and Job' (1959), analysing beliefs of a West African people, the Tallensi. Fortes pointed out that the Tallensi in their traditional beliefs handled the idea of man's fate as a combination of two elements of Destiny, an initial endowment and a subsequent protective supervision by ancestral spirit guardians. These represented symbolically innate disposition and concrete parental upbringing on the one hand, and the more abstract forces of society on the other. The extent of a man's success in life was then a figurative expression of his ability to control his innate drives by the proper performance of ritual to his ancestors. Any failure – including his eventual death – was interpreted as a result of his unwitting neglect of obligation. Such religious conceptions are closely linked with basic ideas of family structure and kinship ties. They are given a sacred value, but this does not derive from any idea of God. In such context, the outcomer of any divine will is highly socialized, and seen in definitely personal human terms.

The recurrent problem of evil has also received anthropological attention. In a recent collection of essays edited by David Parkin it is suggested that there is something inherently ambiguous in many peoples' understanding of evil. Accordingly there is great diversity in the reasons given for the existence of evil, and in the classification of what actions and persons may be labelled under this head.

In theistic systems, where evil may be isolated as a principle, even personified, anthropologists recognize distinctions already made by theologians. In some Hindu and Sufi Muslim systems, evil becomes an aspect of God. In the Semitic religions there is a qualified semi-dualism, with God opposed by Satan but capable of mastering him and willing to help mortals in their struggle against evil. And full dualistic systems such as Manichaeism recognize good and evil as two opposed cosmic principles, eternally in antagonism. But for anthropologists the religious problem is not just one of theodicy in any narrow sense. Studies of Buddhism show that while there may be no belief in God, the concept of evil occurs at a folk level, though in a relatively weak form, consonant with the idea that the roots of wrongdoing lie within the individual himself. In many 'pagan' religions both man and his gods are conceived as naturally embodying a range of impulses which may lead to good or evil actions, judged by their results. In such a pagan system creation is commonly believed to have been devoid of moral purpose and evil is accepted as part of the constitution of the world. The problem is the power of evil, not its ultimate origin. Much effort may be spent, as in divination or spirit mediumship, to ascertain an immediate source of evil – as in witchcraft. But the controlling powers of the religious system may be neutral or indifferent unless stirred to intervention by propitiatory offering or sacrifice. In revealing the variations in the concept of evil in many societies, anthropologists have emphasized its human, pragmatic dimensions in a social context, and by implication have reinforced ideas of theodicy as a still open question.

Where anthropologists have dealt explicitly with the expression 'God', three important points should be borne in mind. The first is that God is rarely figured as a universal concept, with abstract connotation such as theologians commonly use. In an anthropological analysis God is culturally located, and described in terms which translate what the people of a given society say and do in His regard. Secondly, while an anthropologist may occasionally state propositions about God as arising from his own beliefs, in general he/she is citing the opinions of other people, produced in an alien society, and so is making a report, an interpretation at some remove from the actual experience referred to. (The exact status of a theologian's assertions about God raises some interesting questions for anthropologists, about evidence and authority.) Thirdly, anthropological statements about God are essentially heuristic and exploratory. They are not concerned primarily with questions of truth or falsity or with moral qualities, but with the understanding of social concepts and relationshps, with the way in which ideas of symbolic value relate to the structures of societies and the operations of men in them.

Ethnographically, interpretations of what may be thought to be specific apprehensions or images of God, among peoples of different cultures, fall into three broad categories. Colloquially these may be seen as God among the 'pagans', God in the mainstream theistic religions, and God in the offshoot cults.

Of high significance in the first category are the findings of anthropologists in some – though not many – African societies, where a spiritual entity of supreme quality has been recognized. A classic example is that given by Jomo Kenyatta in his anthropological study of his own people, the Gikuyu, in his book *Facing Mount Kenya*. Kenyatta stated 'The Gikuyu believe in one God, Ngai, the creator and giver of all things'. He went on to say that Ngai had no father, mother or companion of any kind, lived in the sky but had temporary homes on earth, in the mountains, where he might rest when he brought blessings and punishments to the people. In prayers and sacrifices the Gikuyu turn towards Mount Kenya, which is believed to be Ngai's official residence and is accordingly known as 'mountain of brightness' and thought to be holy. Ngai, invisible to ordinary mortal eyes, is called upon at the birth, initiation, marriage and death of a person. He is thus plausibly described as God from his combination of supreme qualities. But Ngai is a distant Being and takes but little interest in people in their daily walk of life and must never be pestered by frequent appeal. And he is not accessible to individual prayer. Only a family group with the father at its head may supplicate him, that is, he is God for social units, not for persons. It may be asked whether Kenyatta, in his desire to represent the Gikuyu with dignity in the face of Western pressure and proselytization, did not exaggerate the role of Ngai as God. But Kenyatta's position is supported by comparable evidence from other African peoples – from Evans-Pritchard on Nuer, Nadel on Nupe, Godfrey Lienhardt on Dinka and Middleton on Lugbara.

The picture of a Supreme Being thus presented is not a conventional Western one. It is a deist rather than a theist picture, that is, the Supreme Being is regarded as the ultimate source of reality, including humanity and human institutions, but does not often intervene in natural and human processes by way of voluntary acts of care and salvation. God may be the ground of moral value, but there is no general expression equivalent to 'God is love'. God is either otiose and indifferent or has a general benevolence which must be sharpened into supportive action for men, not by right thoughts but by rituals of propitiation. The location of God is vague. He is usually thought to be not in the terrestrial world. However, Lugbara speak of a transcendent God in the sky and an immanent other half on earth, with wives and many children, responsible for the inspiration of diviners, for the power of rainmakers and for all death.

Even God's personality is in question. Most accounts give Him as anthropomorphic, but the syntax of some African languages, being genderless, leaves it open whether God is being referred to as 'He', 'She', or 'It'. Such a problem may not disturb modern Western theologians, for whom a concept of 'modes of being' may cater for such difficulties. But a semantic problem remains over God's name. In an African context, what is presented as a 'pagan' religious concept may have been influenced by ideas from Islam – as with the Nupe. Then an anthropologist's own experience may have predisposed him to accept a theistic labelling – as perhaps Evans-Pritchard, a professed Catholic, did with the Nuer *kwoth*. But the issue is a delicate one. Godfrey Lienhardt, a sensitive interpreter of African religious thought, has described how the Dinka of the Sudan claim to encounter spirits of various kinds, which he glossed as 'powers'. A common Dinka term *nhialic* is used in some contexts where Lienhardt says it could be suitably translated as God, with reference to prayers and sacrifices offered to a father and creator. Yet the connotation *nhialic* is much wider than this, embracing notions of the sky above, and of a collectivity of spirits. So Lienhardt concluded that to use the word God for such Dinka concepts would raise difficult metaphysical and semantic problems for which there is no Dinka parallel. His solution in his major study was to use the term Divinity. He argued that this, with a capital initial letter, can convey the idea not only of a Being but also of a nature and existence with less personal meaning.

The ambiguity of gender in some African concepts of divinity is paralleled by recent developments in the modernization of the Christian concept of God. Attempts have been made to broaden the conventional gender ascription of God as masculine. Even if no longer conceptualized as an old man with a long white beard, as in early European paintings, God has been regularly spoken of as He in the history of the church. Now a report from the Faith and Order Committee of the Methodist Church argues that God is 'beyond gender', that the use of exclusively male language to describe God is a patriarchal reinforcement of the subordination of women, and that God may be referred to as 'She' and addressed as 'mother'. Such 'inclusive' language, it is said, should be strongly encouraged in all official Methodist publications. Such use of female imagery for God is regarded as striking a truer balance in a believer's thinking about God. (*The Times* 21.5.92; cf. also *The Times* 13.7.94. for a Church of England general synod view.) To an anthropologist, this is obviously a concession to modern feminist pressure. But it seems that Christianity by this is coming closer to the depersonalised genderless concepts of god among the African pagan peoples mentioned! The new liberalization of gendering for God seems however to pose a dilemma for those who recognize the status of the Virgin Mary as the Mother of Jesus, more colloquially as the Mother of God. If God is to be addressed as 'Father and Mother of us all', as one version of the Lord's Prayer would have it, what becomes of the role of the Mother of Jesus?

Orthodox Christian theologians have tended to concentrate mainly on questions about the nature of God and His relation to man. Some have examined the question whether God exists or not – concluding usually that the evidence for His existence is acceptable. The question of *why* there should be belief in God is not commonly raised. This is a question which to a humanist anthropologist seems obvious and to which rational answers can be found.

So anthropologists have shown growing boldness in tackling the concept of God in the mainstream theistic religions. Their studies have tended to refer to the Divine in three ways: how concepts of God are formulated at the folk level rather than at the level of scholarly exegesis; how the pragmatic experience of a congregational worshipper relates to the ideal theological pattern of ideas; and why such beliefs should come into being at all. Yet anthropological contributions to an understanding of the idea of God in the Christian faith have been fairly restricted. Long ago a path-breaking study of Christian myth and ritual was made by E. O. James, who was both an anthropologist and in holy orders as a professor of the philosophy and history of religion. Recently, as well as studies of Christian congregations in various parts of the world, there have been intriguing studies of pilgrimage as a means of securing a closer relation to God's grace. And going to the roots of assertions about the divine, there has been anthropological enquiry into what is meant by such expressions as 'I believe . . .'. But direct analysis of the concept of God has been rare.

In the Islamic field, anthropologists have reflected upon the way in which a pious Muslim must try to lead a virtuous life in an imperfect world. The religious obligations of the Faithful to Allah, as interpreted with finality by the Prophet, are mandatory and all-embracing. They involve a tussle between the faculty of reason implanted by Allah and the passions and interests which animate every man and woman. Anthropologists have explored the varying interpretations of the notion of God's will in relation to the actions of men, and the meaning of prayer as an aid to carrying out God's will. To a pious Muslim villager, prayer is not the means of making ritual requests to God, but a sacred duty, and an instrument of self control in the battle of reason against passion in the desired 'surrender to God'.

A marked feature of religious movement during the last four centuries or so has been the spread of major 'universal' faiths through much of a 'pagan' world. Anthropologists have seen this not as a simple conversion from darkness to light, the replacement of gods by God, but as a complex process of transfer of belief and ritual. They have studied strategies of the transfer, why people convert, how the new doctrines relate to the old, and what changes in the social structure are associated with an acknowledgement of a new divine Father and Lord. The anthropology of folk religion presents a kaleidoscope picture of many different combinations of ideas of God and indigenous beliefs, when the data are interpreted in sociological rather than in theological terms.

Particularly striking have been the many anthropological studies of religious cults outside the established mainstream churches – cults called not too accurately chiliastic or millenarian. These range from the independent Bantu churches of South Africa to the voodoo cults of the Caribbean and the 'cargo cults' of Melanesia. Such cults are often marked by a theological tolerance in which God is assisted by local spirits of varying power. They interpret the divine very closely in terms of personal experience in dreams, ecstasy, glossolalia. Social parameters of the cults are very much in evidence. There are European and Asian analogies, but in Africa, the Caribbean and Melanesia the congregations are black, they retain many indigenous elements in their ritual, such as dancing or healing techniques, and traditional values such as the propriety of polygamy may still remain. Essentially, these cults are asserting a cultural appropriation of God. Their members can feel God personally – sometimes their prophet leader claims to *be* God. 'Jehovah is ours, our very own' has been one cry. Long before the recognition of a 'black liberation theology', as the poet Countee Cullen wrote of the 'Black Christ', so these cults were presenting God in a new light. He was not the God of the Europeans, with their economic and political domination, but a God who could help the repressed people to an independent life of their own. (Analogies with the rise of Christianity are not far to seek.) Shot through with racial tension, the 'cargo cults' in particular have been presented by some anthropologists, perhaps over-dramatically, as incipient revolutionary movements. On the other hand, they have sometimes seemed to be trying to seek, by cultic means, to get what they could not achieve on the pragmatic economic and political plane. But what in effect the cults have been saying is that self-help is an essential part of the salvation process. Even if it means a radical reinterpretation of God's nature and role, theological notions give way to pragmatic interests.

DEATH OF GOD

Many years ago, it is reported, a judge in a Maori Land Court in New Zealand was hearing a case in which control by spirit beings was adduced as evidence for long-standing ownership of a piece of land. The court showed no surprise at hearing gods cited to support a claim in the case. But when the name of one god was mentioned a witness said, 'That god is dead'. The court demurred, 'Gods do not die'. The witness replied, 'Gods die when people cease to believe in them'.

We may commend the robust commonsense of the Maori witness, a quasi-anthropologist who had seen the passing of his ancient religion. And yet at the back of our minds may linger a memory of early social conditioning, that a god as a spiritual being cannot be subject to the laws of mortality. If in the Western idiom we think of monotheism and write God with a capital initial it is inconceivable to most people that God could die. If people cease to believe in him, we are apt to think that nevertheless He continues to exist for them, even though unrecognized. Even if, putatively, all people in the world cease to believe in Him, on the conventional Christian view he would still be there, invisible, holy, omniscient, omnipotent, ever-loving – though presumably sorrowing. When in the Christian faith God did die, to take upon Himself the sins of the world, it was His human semblance that died – God the Son; God the Father continued to reign supreme.

Yet a relatively modern 'Death-of-God' movement in Christian theology has argued that the traditional idea of a transcendent God no longer obtains in a secular world; that the Judaeo-Christian idea of a personal provident God has been superseded by a search for a deity of different attributes, such as a Christ of love. In a dialectical view, an absolute primordial transcendent God has annihilated himself, has died in Jesus Christ so that a new spiritual entity may appear (Bent 1967).

Such rather fanciful theological arguments have not received much support. But among peoples all over the world anthropologists have seen or had reports of the death of gods. Religious proselytization, as by Muslims in Africa, by Hindus in India, by various sects of Christians the world over, has destroyed pagan cults, has converted polytheists into monotheists or has restricted the range and altered the labelling of the spirit entities worshipped in the traditional systems. Such spirit personalities have been denied as false, and, their names forgotten, have passed into oblivion. In similar style historians have noted the disappearance, the 'death' of many gods once current in the world of classical antiquity – Attis, associated with death and resurrection, with fertility and the annual renewal of spring vegetation; Isis, queen of heaven, mistress of the elements, associated with rites of purification; Mithra, linked with sacrifice, with the dualism of good and evil and doctrines of rewards and punishments in the afterworld.

Yet what is meant by the death of a god? With a human individual we have a fairly clear-cut index of death, the cessation of the functioning of the physical body. Even here the criteria are not as final as used to be thought, with the advent of new modes of resuscitation. Granted that the confusion is merely semantic, and that cessation of the beating of the heart is best described as suspended animation, which becomes death only if the heart is not revived. Still, however, something of the person survives. Genetically, some portion of his substance, infinitesimal maybe, continues in his descendants. Ideationally, his personality lives on in the memory of his family and friends, and, if he has been a productive scholar or artist, in the transmitted materials of his writings, paintings or other works. So, even if there be no belief in a survival of his soul after his bodily death, as a person and not simply as a physical individual, he cannot be said to have completely died.

Something analogous occurs in the death of a god, or indeed in the history of any concept given a personalized form. For the prime fact about a god or God is that he/she/it is a quality or set of qualities conceptualized as a person. Equivalent to the physical death of a human individual, a god can have a material dissolution. This likewise can occur in two forms, cessation of behavioural function and physical decay. At intervals over a period of nearly forty years I have observed this process in a small, remote Polynesian community in the Western Pacific, on the island of Tikopia. Half pagans, half Christians when I visited them first, the lives of them all were deeply affected by the pagan cult with its elaborate cycle of ritual performances of worship with offering and prayer. Later, as proselytization became keener, the number of pagans declined, the offerings became fewer, the rites curtailed.

In 1966, when I returned for the third time, all the people had been Christian for a decade, the ancient temples were in ruins, the wooden symbols of the gods in decay, the traditional rites completely abandoned. Physically, the gods were dead. What the people called their 'bodies', their material embodiments, had rotted away; their 'doings', that is, the ritual which recognized, honoured and perpetuated their names and attributes, had perished and begun to be forgotten.

As an anthropologist, this is what I class as religious conversion, the change of people from one religious system of observances to another. The major indices of conversion are of overt commitment – alteration in style and rhythm of ritual behaviour, and alteration in name of the extra-human entities to whom the behaviour is oriented. Believers regard this as a change from darkness to light, laying prime emphasis on change in belief. But the belief situation may not follow such a simple pattern.

It may be the worship of a god which dies, while belief in his existence still remains. On this island of Tikopia, a generation ago, it was the belief of many people that the traditional gods were not dead but in limbo. The worship of them had been abandoned, for what seemed good reasons. These gods stood for the principles of fertility in vegetation, prolificity of fish, health and welfare of man, as well as for sex complementarity and differentiation, cultural invention and other major social interests. In the public view, as circumstances changed the gods had failed in their major tasks. They had proved to be relatively inefficient in confrontation with the modern external world. Though they had on occasion demonstrated their power by striking sacrilegious trespassers with illness, and though they had provided their worshippers with fish and vegetable food with which to sustain themselves and continue religious rites, these gods in drought, famine and epidemic had appeared to provide a less effective defence than that provided by the Christian God. Moreover, the concept of the Christian God, an import from overseas by a Mission whose representatives were highly respected, seemed to be in broad conformity with the beliefs of white men whose command of resources and political power were increasingly attractive and dominating. To the Tikopia pagans, then, who like the rest of their community wanted to take advantage of the facilities of the modern world, it seemed only reasonable to convert to the Christian system. As far as I could judge, they had changed their religious affiliation sincerely; they now believed that the One God was supreme.

But this did not mean that they felt they had to disbelieve in their old gods. These gods were regarded as still existing, but no longer summoned to concern themselves with the affairs of men, they stayed in their spirit abodes, quiescent. Indeed, they had been specifically despatched there by the thoughtful Tikopia. The priests, chiefs and ritual leaders of their people, took care to celebrate final rites in which the traditional gods were called upon, given a last feast and dismissed with placatory words which explained why they could be no longer asked to return. The new day had dawned, the One God had taken over, and they were no longer needed.

In this sense, then, the traditional gods are physically dead, but ideationally they live on, at least in the minds of the older people. A conventional view of religious conversion is that the new God is admitted as true, the old god as false. But falseness may mean only inaccuracy in prediction, and inaccuracy is not equivalent to non-existence. For people who have deserted them, pagan gods may stand for impotent and inefficient beings, not figments of the imagination. This position is reinforced by the association between traditional gods and ancestor-spirits. The line between these two categories of super-natural beings has often been tenuous. Many 'primitive' religions, like Christianity, have had concepts of god becoming man, and man becoming god. If, as most religions proclaim, the spirit of a person survives after his bodily death, then the spirits of people's relatives and ancestors must still be extant somewhere. And if the spirits of ancestors, why not those of allied spiritual beings, the traditional gods, still surviving in some conceptual dwelling place which does not challenge the moral destination of the faithful? For a people such as the Christian Tikopia, there is analogy too with beliefs in saints, admitted in Christian hagiology to be sometimes mythical personages, whose essential character lies in a combination of human individuality and demonstration of extra-human powers; and who are regarded as still sentient. Treated by the Tikopia as 'sacred men', and as responsive to the appeals of the faithful, saints are equivalent to traditional gods who have got on the right side of the religious fence.

It is not in memory alone that the gods survive. Presumably after a generation or so away from paganism knowledge of names and attributes of the traditional gods fades. But the themes which have given shape to the conceptualizations of the gods still may live on, in another form. In the European classical field, many of the qualities of the classical gods were absorbed into newer representations of the divine. The death and resurrection of Attis reappeared in that of Jesus; the queen of heaven, Isis, had her parallel in Mary the Mother of God. So also in a simpler pagan religion such as that of the Tikopia. Their principal god, known by such titles as the Sacred Chief, the Fear-making God, according to the accepted story had been a human being, an ancestral chief, some fifteen generations or so ago, who made his reputation as a culture hero by stabilizing relations between man and nature and instituting the major customs practised by the community. Killed by a competitor in a struggle for land, he abjured revenge and claimed supremacy in the spirit world. Death as man, rise to power as spirit, is therefore a theme which pagan Tikopia could continue to recognize and perpetuate in the story of Jesus. Of female deities the Tikopia had several, regarded as highly power-ful, especially concerned with the affairs of women, and apt to be malevolent towards men, for whom they epitomized the darker forces of sex. A female deity – for such the Mother of God must be pragmatically – of benevolent habit must have been a great relief for newly converted Christian Tikopia men! Western Chris-tian apologists have gone to great lengths to demonstrate the lack of connection, especially in the classical field, between such anterior religious themes and the more modern presentations in the form of God, Jesus, Mary and the saints. But historically, there need be no direct connection between the various named entities of the pagan and the Christian world. What is relevant, and what seems to emerge very clearly from the evidence, as many scholars from Cumont to Bultmann have shown, is the repetition of similar themes of individual and social concern at different periods of human history. What is also relevant is how these themes – 'great universal ideas', as Hirn has called them – become modified and re-formulated with the passage of time, as social conditions change.

One of the most striking modifications in the religious system of ideas of the Western world was the Christian conception of God as Love. As Bultmann has put it, the basic proclamation of Jesus was that God demands the whole man, inner commitment as well as external conformity, and the demand is for love. Love had entered the religious field before Christianity but not in such selfless form, not in such highly personalized even domestic family imagery, and not with such direct and intimate application. Symbolism of the domestic family circle had been part of the pantheon of earlier religions, but with Christianity idealization of its qualities reached a new height. In the Holy Family, at a relatively earthly level, St Joseph is not much more than a kindly step-parent head of household. But at a more elevated spiritual level God the Father is not only creator and judge, he is also loving parent. Jesus, the moral analyst, teacher and ideal, personifies humanity with its imperfections and demand for understanding, forgiveness and comfort. Mary the Mother of God is the principle of womanhood and maternity, that unique sympathetic bond which, even allowing for Freudian interpretations, tradition has hallowed into the ideal of selfless affection.

GOD AND HUMANITY

In all this the Christian faith has been able to utilize some of the most powerful moral stimuli to social action. But in so doing Christianity has been saddled with two pronouncements which serve as sanctions within its bounds but, comparatively viewed, are distinct liabilities. These are the assertion of the divinity of Jesus and, backing this up, the assertion of the virginity of the mother of Jesus. The first, looked at anthropologically, is only a symbolic statement, but taken literally becomes a major sanction in giving absolute value to what are represented to be the words and ideas of the prophet and teacher, Jesus. The second is an ancillary sanction in that if Jesus is not divine his mother's virginity would be meaningless embroidery. Biologically and historically it is nonsense. But symbolically it is a statement about the supernatural quality and especially the purity of Jesus. Dogmatically its major importance is perhaps that it serves as a critical index in a test of faith.

The assertion of the divinity of Jesus is a prime stumbling block in the way of closer rapport of Christianity with its parent religion, Judaism, and its younger sibling, Islam. For orthodox Jews, conceiving of the coming of the Messiah as part of the development of God's personality, already laid down like the inevitable course of history, Jesus is a false prophet. Of more than ordinary effrontery in the personal claims made by him or on his behalf, he remains a teacher and interpreter of practical and mystical doctrines, by no means the last 'suffering servant' to see himself as the Messiah, the Christ, the Lord's Anointed. For the orthodox Muslim, assertion of the divinity of Jesus is plain heresy, an attempt to 'give God a partner' which the Koran expressly forbids. But in Islam Jesus is venerated as a major prophet, who was given clear proofs of his mission by God, strengthened by the holy spirit, and furnished with the Evangel as confirmatory of the earlier law. But just as his mission confirmed that of Moses and added to it, so that of Muhammed confirmed that of Jesus, but was final and complete. Muhammed, a man like Jesus and Moses, was the seal of the prophets and the completion of revelation. Ascription of some superhuman attributes to the messenger of good tidings, the bearer of a new revelation, is common enough in the religious field. But the concept of a prophet as God the Son, as a personal Redeemer, a Saviour who has encapsulated the divinity he proclaims, is a very odd phenomenon among the more successful religious systems, though it occurs among messianic cults in Africa and elsewhere.

The assertion of the virginity of the mother of Jesus is odder still. Mother goddesses are common in many religions, and so also are miraculous conceptions of gods. But mother goddesses normally are regarded as having gone through the physical processes leading to motherhood, while miraculous conceptions are treated as commonly followed by normal births. In neither case is virginity of the mother thought to have been preserved. The idea of a virgin giving birth to a god is spectacular, and is a flaunting of faith in the face of nature's laws, a dogmatic challenge which is intelligible as symbol, but hard indeed to accept as true of an historical person. If one believes in the birth of God from a mortal woman, there is no more reason why one should boggle at his being born of a virgin than of one whose hymen has been perforated. But it does add one step more to the height of the credibility threshold. It seems indeed that in the early centuries of the Church this concept of virgin birth caused some difficulty but was dealt with in terms of the penetrative powers of light and analogous symbolisms. But, as Yrjö Hirn has pointed out, what the successful maintenance of this dogma has done has been to present in one person the idealization of important, yet contradictory, attributes: virginity and motherhood; humanity and godhead. Moreover, the dogma of the Assumption and representations of the Coronation of the Virgin, following on her sorrowing for her Son, provide the ideal type of maternal grief and joy, as well as the sorrows of death followed by triumph over the grave. So the Madonna can serve as symbol of womanhood in all her aspects.

Judaism and Islam are monotheistic religions. Christianity is ordinarily called such, but at the level of popular faith it is very doubtful if this categorization can hold. God the Father, God the Son and Mary the Mother of God are separable conceptual entities. Leaving aside God the Holy Ghost, whose relationships are somewhat obscure to the non-theologically inclined, the other three have their parallels. It may be objected that Mary should not find place in this trio; she was human, not divine. But if the subtleties of theological defence be set aside, the Bodily Assumption of Mary and the role assigned to her in the heavenly world (including such earthly interventions as those in 1830 of ordering the striking of a Miraculous Medal) entitle her to honours equivalent to divinity. It may also be argued that God the Father and God the Son are but different facets, different symbolizations of the same unitary Being. But while this may be so at the theological level, in practical worship they are apt to be treated separately. Moreover, the phenomenon of syncretism is common in many religious systems. Christianity in this respect is like many religions which are polytheistic at the popular level but whose more sophisticated adherents, especially priests, describe them in syncretistic monotheist terms.

When we turn to the more sophisticated Christian circles, a very interesting situation is seen. The Catholic Church may be still, as it was described fifty years ago, the Middle Ages in the twentieth century. But its more intellectual representatives, with the more advanced theologians of other Christian faiths, have been earnestly exploring the ways of adapting the tenets of the Church to modern thought and social changes.

Among the multifarious ways in which this has been occurring, two trends are of particular interest to me as an anthropologist. They are to a large extent alternatives. One is to emphasize the human aspects of religion, to show its relevance to the concerns of man, and hence to stress its up-to-dateness, its role in promoting social justice and the development of the individual personality. The worker-priests, the tentatives of Catholics and Marxists to find common ground in such subjects as workers' control of industry, or Marx's concept of alienation, illustrate this. Advocates of such points of view are apt to find dissent in their own camp, and to be marked by impatience with traditional authority. Coming to terms with the present-day problems of society means jettisoning some of the traditional attitudes towards the problems of the past – hence the pressure from within the Christian body itself for more liberal Church attitudes towards divorce, birth control and marriage of priests where celibacy has been hitherto the rule, and the yielding of authority on such matters as replacement of service of the Mass in Latin by the vernacular. In a more abstract, analytical framework of ideas attempt is made to separate the institutional trappings of religion from its essential belief core. Naturally, opinion among the faithful differs on what are the essentials.

Stripping of the accretions of past centuries may be intended, however, for an alternative end, not to bring religion closer to man, but to allow him to realize more clearly its other-worldly character. The demand made upon religious belief is not then to be in terms of making the relevance of the superhuman depend upon that of the human order, but of giving credence to a superhuman order for which the human being is satellite, not focus. Hence the emphasis upon the Christian gospel as revelation; on the nonlogical character of belief in virgin birth and resurrection; on the notion of commitment; on the transcendence of God, who is not in the world even though he may be immanent in all of us.

Anthropologically speaking, the character of the idea-construct

'God' is comfortable with the diverse social and intellectual currents of our time. If one regards the concept of the divine in every society as a reponse to social and personal needs, then one may expect such a double reaction by believers, against the challenge of modern secularist thought.

One type of reaction is to emphasize man's insufficiency and dependence on forces outside his personal control: the uncertainties of scientific generalizations; the irrational elements in human thinking; problems of the genesis of value within the human field and of cosmic origins outside it. Man alone, so the argument runs, cannot pretend to supply answers here; the only answer must be Deity. At a more concrete level the analogues with the religious concepts of pagan people here are close. They too have conceptualized and answered the problems of origins of the world and of man, the unpredictability of natural forces, the dark impulses of sex and aggression, with symbols of blood and death. But pagan peoples, confronted by external economic and political power, have for the most part conceded the temporary, contingent nature of their conceptualizations. They have acknowledged the more effective moral and intellectual scope of an alien religious ideology – even if in many cases they have re-formulated this later in terms of 'cargo cults', 'separatist churches' or other messianic movements which seem to them to fit their needs more personally and more appropriately.

Another type of reaction, perhaps more lofty, the apophatic retreat into the assertion of transcendence, has not been conceived with the aim of stifling argument, but does inhibit discussion from any contrary position. For if God *is*, but is not of this world, is not fully knowable by man even with special techniques of approach, it can always be held that objectors speak from only partial apprehension of what so far has been made available to man. Pagan peoples have not gone in much for transcendence in their characterization of their gods; they have liked the gods removed in space but ready to come when called, and accessible to some kind of approach, even to the point of providing substantial evidence of their own existence, through dream, vision and miracle.

A whole series of logical developments is linked with this assumption of transcendence, or run parallel with it. There is the flat affirmation, directly contrary to the assertion of the Maori witness years ago, that God exists, whether men believe in him or not. Belief is essential for the full existence of man, not that of God, and religious belief is idealized as the most complete form of belief, allowing man to realize his own potentialities to the highest degree. Satisfaction for the individual concerned may be explicitly rejected as the keynote here; belief may be the counsel of despair; for human dejection and ineffectiveness there may be no other resort. But to the external observer such belief does clearly represent a kind of fulfilment for the believer, if not in security, at least in hope.

A position in some ways closer to that of an anthropologist, is that God is to be looked for not in the conventional notions of Creator who made the world, tutelary of the Jews, spouse to the Virgin, Real Presence in the Mass, and other personifications, but in the faculties or propensities giving rise to these notions. God is not as depicted in the myths and images, but is exemplified in what lies behind them, the creative strivings of mystic and poet, and of ordinary people, to express the ineffable, to portray in figurative, aesthetic ways the essence of human relationships. In one fashion of speaking, then, God is communication. In another, a Durkheimian retrospection, God is society divinized. Advanced theologians, speculating on what is left 'after the death of god', tend to find it in the forces of inspiration, love, imagination, for which, they argue, secularism can supply no rationale and which therefore are a fit subject for religious postulate.

To me all this offers a rich, fascinating field for anthropological enquiry. The content and structure of Jewish and Christian myths await the social analyst who will focus not upon problems of historical relationship but upon the basic themes the myths display – family, sex, status involvement, aggression, sacrifice, suffering – and upon the structural principles upon which they have been built up. One line of inquiry leads to the consideration of the particular types of social institutions and social conditions to which the myths have corresponded, at various historical periods, and the changes which they have undergone in conformity with social changes. (Where now, in popular belief, is hell?) Another line of inquiry can concentrate especially on theological exposition, and the social correlates of the different kinds of interpretation put forward of key questions of ritual and belief. Of special interest here could be an examination of theology in England before 1914; then after the First World War when neither religious ideas nor political ideas could ever be quite the same;

and after the last war, which gave a new impetus to theological speculation. The trends in biblical theology, the swings away from and back towards the notion of God as truly personal – personal in himself and personal in his relations with the humanity he created – could be well set against secular intellectual movements in the natural sciences, psychology and sociology, from Darwinian evolution to communication theory. Especially interesting here is the persistence of the symbolism of the Mass – that chthonic preoccupation with ideas of victim, sacrifice, death, blood and anthropophagy, and their sacramental value.

Superficially minor, but actually far-reaching in their implications, are problems of the theory of transubstantiation in the Mass, including the distinction between the doctrine of Real Presence as veritable body and blood of Christ, who died once and for all upon the Cross, and that of the Presence as exhibiting the renewal and actual repetition of the death of Christ. This is a good instance of the intellectual compromise made between the implications of two significant but potentially dangerous principles – of commemoration and of re-enactment. Simple commemoration of the Last Supper and the death of Christ might tend, as Catholic theologians hold, to impoverish the Christian bodies which follow this plain symbolic interpretation of the Eucharist. Hence the doctrine of the Real Presence, which engages the emotional attention of the faithful. But to argue (in a 'heretical' interpretation) that the conversion of bread and wine into body and blood at the moment of elevation means that the victim is actually slain afresh strikes at the root of the notion of the uniqueness of the sacrifice of the Crucifixion – it implies that the original sacrifice was insufficient in its saving grace. Hence, rather incongruously, the elements of the sacrifice must keep on reappearing, but the act itself must not. Looked at as a total system of belief and practice, set in an elaborate institutional framework, such doctrinal controversies can be seen to have their place as regulatory mechanisms for the religious body.

In the kind of analysis I have been giving here the prime aim is not to try and demonstrate the falsity of religious belief and the superfluousness of religious ritual. It is rather to try and understand their complexity, their rationale within their own basic assumptions, their correspondence with or divergence from their own internal structure of control and the social conditions of their time. In such study, as I see it, assumptions of extra-human entities or powers are unnecessary. There are alternative and perhaps more economical assumptions – that the search for ways of coping with man's ignorance and irrationality has got to be conducted in human terms. If one accepts inadequacy, aggression, evil, suffering, as part of the endowment of man, then why should one not regard imagination, creative effort, aesthetic inspiration, love, as also part of human constitution? On such a sceptical foundation, to theo-logy succeeds anthropo-logy – the study of God is included in the study of man.

Chapter 5

Offering and sacrifice
Problems of organization[1]

Offering in some form appears to occur in nearly all religious systems. The custom of making religious offering is part of a vast series of actions involving conceptions of transfer of good or service from one person to another person, or to a putative entity, without direct and immediate counter-transfer of any visible equivalent. An offering is a species of gift. This means: (*a*) that the thing given is *personal* to the giver, his own property, or something over which he has rights of alienation; (*b*) that the thing transferred must have some *value* for the person who hands it over; and, (*c*) that it is transferred with some degree of *voluntary initiative* – it is not given by compulsion nor does it occur as a technical part of a series of actions dictated by some generally planned end. What distinguishes an offering from a gift – though the two terms are often used synonymously – is that an offering implies an asymmetrical *status relationship*, an inferiority on the part of the person making the offering and superiority on the part of the recipient. A gift may also involve a status relationship if not between equals, but this relationship tends to be created by the act of giving and receiving, not acknowledged or partially resolved by such an act. (A subject in a kingdom may make an offering to his Sovereign, but the Sovereign does not make an offering to the subject; he makes a gift.) The effect of gift and offering may be directly opposite in social terms. A gift may put the recipient in a state of social inferiority and indeed emphasize that inferiority. An offering emphasizes that it is the giver who is inferior and that the recipient is in a state of social superiority. *De facto*, the manner of transfer, the words and actions employed, may determine which terminology is most appropriately used in classification.

The concept of offering may carry other qualities. Linked with the notion of status difference is that of *uncertainty* – decision as to the acceptability of the transfer of value may be thought to rest with the person designated as recipient, who may refuse it. So also with a gift, but this concept carries with it a more positive idea of handing-over as a *fait accompli*. Another quality often attached especially to an offering is the suggestion of an *emotional element*. A gift may be emotionally neutral; an offering carries with it the notion of some outgoing sentiment of respect.

This brief semantic discussion is only in a very general sense, since neither gift nor offering are precise terms. I do not want to overdrive their meaning, especially since in common usage they shade into each other. But for analytical purposes it is useful to draw attention to such elements which frequently, though not necessarily always, occur implicitly in the usage of these terms, since they enter into an understanding of much religious practice and belief.

A religious offering or oblation embodies these ideas more definitely. Status difference, volitional aspect of acceptance, emotional attitudes of offerer – all are recognizable, and often present to a marked degree. They are correlated with the special notion of the recipient being an extra-human, supernormal being.

The concept of sacrifice includes a further element. As Gusdorf has pointed out, gift is a first approximation to sacrifice (1948: 17). Sacrifice is a species of offering or oblation, but implies a relation between what is offered and the *availability of resources*. Offering indicates an allocation or transfer of resources, but implies nothing about the degree or quality of allocation in relation to the total resources at the command of the giver. 'Sacrifice' implies that the degree or quality is significant – that the resources are limited, that there are alternative uses for them, and that there is some abstention from an alternative use in making the offering. The sacrifice is giving up something at a cost. This is indicated in dictionary equivalents – that sacrifice means 'the loss entailed by devotion to some other interest', or 'the destruction or surrender of something valued or desired for the sake of something having a higher or more pressing claim'.

The notion that a sacrifice is involved in the diversion of some valued object from one end to another which is regarded as more pressing, raises the question of alternative response or equivalents to be expected according to the end served. When a gift is made from one person to another, later reciprocity in the form of counter-gift or counter-service is common. If there is no such reciprocity, presumably the giver regards himself as compensated by the satisfaction arising from the knowledge of the effects of the gift or by the moral virtue attaching to the act of giving itself. Such vicarious action is characteristic of most forms of sacrifice. When in the religious sphere offering or sacrifice is made, no direct counter-gift of a material kind is normally expected, although ensuring material benefits – in the form of fertility of crops or health of persons maintained or restored – are frequently regarded as its outcome. But even where no such material benefit is thought to arise, religious offering and sacrifice have other compensatory functions. These may be generalized as benefits arising from belief in the establishment of appropriate relations between the offerer or sacrificer and some spirit entity or extra-human power. Commonly, too, the performance of sacrifice in particular is regarded as inducing or marking a change in the spiritual constitution of the sacrificer, renewing or intensifying his moral qualities. But sometimes the concept of sacrifice involves the ideal of a dual loss, to the victim as well as to the sacrificer. The issue is then not always clear from the moral point of view, as when Agamemnon sacrificed Iphigenia to his political loyalties and ambitions.

In a religious sense sacrifice is one of the most critical acts. In its Western etymology it is akin to the notion of consecration, of removal from secular to sacred sphere. It has been called 'a peculiarly religious term' and to many people it expresses more than almost any other concept the heart of a religious system.

In the religious field various meanings have been given to the term. But the most common is that sacrifice is a voluntary act whereby, through the slaughter of an animal, an offering of food or other substance is made to a spiritual being. Sacrifice then ordinarily implies immolation, a living victim, e.g. the *zebah*, animal-offering or 'bloody oblation' of the Hebrews (Danby 1933: 468–90). At the same time most anthropologists would probably be prepared to agree with Robertson Smith (1907: 214) and with Hubert and Mauss (1899: 39) that the notion of sacrifice can properly include even a vegetal offering, provided that some portion of it is destroyed with intent in the act. The element, if not of destruction, at least of transformation or transmutation of what is sacrificed is basic to the concept. It is related to what Hubert and Mauss and others have referred to as the aspect of abnegation, the denial of something to the self, which does seem to be involved in every sacrificial action. In the doctrines of many religions a concept of legitimacy is also strong; a sacrifice is valid only when offered by an authorized officiant or minister.

The theme of sacrifice in religion has provided copious literature, from William Outram and John Davison through Robertson Smith and Alfred Loisy to H. C. Trumbull, E. O. James, and R. K. Yerkes, and it has received special attention in much Africanist anthropology. There has been a spate of theories to account for the origins of sacrifice and to describe its functions. The gift theory, the homage theory, the abnegation theory, are all in Tylor's writings, with the idea of development of one from another. The communion theory and the piacular theory of Robertson Smith have stimulated many later writers. The rejuvenation theory and the cathartic theory of Sir James Frazer, the intermediary theory of Hubert and Mauss, the symbolic parricide theory of Freud and Money-Kyrle, help to round out the interpretations. As Evans-Pritchard (1954: 29) has shown, elements of many of these may be discerned in the sacrificial system of any one community.

The treatment of sacrifice in recent general anthropological studies of religion has been very uneven, though Goode (1951) has some significant observations.[2] Apparent lack of interest in sacrifice as a feature of primitive religions may be partly because the view has been taken, as by Howells, that sacrifices are special forms of ritual and not of first signficance in general religious development. Ethnographic accounts, however, as by Evans-Pritchard, Middleton, and G. Lienhardt, have brought out in a most penetrating way the religious meaning of sacrifice, its relation to concepts of divinity and of human personality, its symbolic force, and its sociological significance.

But considering that sacrifice normally involves the use of material resources, often important ones, how much reference is there in the older or in the more recent literature to the means of mobilizing these resources, to the social problems posed by the procurement of sacrifices and to the implications of the solutions for the ideology of sacrifice itself?

When is the decision to make a sacrifice made? Which animal shall be sacrificed? These are unorthodox but relevant questions.

In studies of sacrifice, preoccupation has been with the concrete ritual procedures and with the underlying beliefs; the organization of the sacrifice has been neglected. From Robertson Smith, Lord Almoner's Professor of Arabic in the University of Cambridge or from Royden Keith Yerkes, a professional theologian, this is natural enough. But it is surprising to find how this aspect of the subject has been largely passed over by social anthropologists. Studies of African peoples, embodying several hundred references to sacrifices, give a good deal of interesting data on who provides the sacrifice and who attends it, together with occasional information about types and numbers of beasts furnished. But when one asks, what do the sacrifices represent in terms of proportionate loss to the people who make them? there is no adequate answer obtainable. These frontal problems, the drain upon the owner's resources which the sacrifice represents, the calculations involved in deciding what particular animals are to be sacrificed and when, and the relation of the sacrificial activities to other economic activities, are hardly ever studied. This is the more notable because, in theory at least, the necessity for such calculations may have some bearing upon the central ideology of the sacrificial act.

Briefly put, the problem may be expressed in this way. When people are said to make sacrifices, does this mean simply that they kill animals ritually? What is the relation of what they sacrifice to what they possess? What loss do they suffer? How can they afford this loss? What social movements do they go through in order to be able to make sacrifices? In case of illness, for example, do they make sacrifices even when they cannot 'afford' them? How do they manage in such event? If they can afford sacrifices, what is the relation of religious dictate to personal initiative? Has this anything to do with the frequency and style of the sacrifices they do make?

Of course even bare information about numbers of available stock allows us to make some inferences. Evans-Pritchard gives some data about the average number of livestock in a Nuer byre in the early 1930s (1940: 20) and Middleton gives data about livestock and about the number of sacrifices performed during a period of about a year in a Lugbara compound (1960: 127 seq.) But though Lienhardt has given a most impressive account of the significance of cattle to the Dinka, he seems to have taken their economic importance for granted, and one can therefore not find any details of the number of livestock at the command of a family or larger social group and the relation of those sacrifices to the group resources. (The Dinka dislike numbering their herds, but did this debar the anthropologist from counting? See Lienhardt 1961: 22.) We are told that the Dinka prefer in theory to sacrifice strong beasts (as a reflection of their own prowess) but 'must often make the best of what they think they can afford' (Lienhardt 1961: 293). But what *do* they think they can afford? And if they must compromise, how do they explain it to themselves?

If one wished to be challenging, one might put forward as a hypothesis that, in default of information to the contrary, the frequency, amount, and quality of sacrifices in a given community are determined primarily not by the type of social structure, nor by the specifically religious ideology, nor by the chance events demanding resolution, but by the availability of material resources of the domestic animal population. (I use the term 'domestic' because, as Robertson Smith has shown by implication, the sacrifice of wild animals which can be regarded as the free gift of nature is rarely allowable or efficient.[3] The sacrifice must be something of the operator's own or his community's. The offering must be detached from himself.)

That sacrifices are the result not of ritual actions but of economic actions has some plausibility if one considers the utilization of the meat for food. Among many peoples, e.g. Dinka, Nuer, and Lugbara, livestock (or at least cattle), it is stated, should not be killed primarily for meat, but kept for sacrifice. But if cattle are very plentiful, then there need be no real problem in securing meat. Provided that the occasion can be found for a sacrifice – and it is usually simple – enough cattle could be sacrificed to provide a frequent meat supply. On the other hand, where cattle are not plentiful, sacrifices simply cannot be very frequent. But the number of them in a stated period, and their spacing, may reflect the relation between cattle supply and meat demand as well as the intensity of ritual obligations. The relation between sacrifice and ritual slaughter is also at times close. Sacrifice is presumably a killing which is not in the immediate food interest of the slaughterer, but of some more general obligation. But if each beast that is killed must, according to the dictates of the religion, be slaughtered according to a set ritual form, the line between killing for meat according to rules laid down by God, announcing the killing to God, and offering the slain beast to God must be very tenuous. As a reverse proposition to the local statement one might put it that implicitly cattle are killed for meat and only explicitly or nominally offered for sacrifice.

But in the crude form that sacrifice is a reflex of economic resources the hypothesis cannot of course be sustained. We remember at once that in many religious systems there are specific obligations to perform a sacrifice, irrespective of the economic situation. There may be a requirement for a regular annual or other periodic sacrifice: the Pawnee 'Morning Star' sacrifice (Lowie 1936: 173); the 'year-minding' of the Beduin for their deceased male kin and ancestors (Doughty [1921] 1926, I: 442, 451–2; II: 252, etc.); the Ketsá and other rituals of the Kede to secure the welfare of the people on the Niger River (Nadel 1940: 190–1); or the sacrifices of the Tallensi at sowing and harvest (Fortes 1940: 254). There are also the irregular but recurrent human contingencies to deal with: the sacrifice at the installation of a new chief as among the Ashanti (Rattray 1923: 137); to rectify a homicide, as among the Tallensi (Fortes 1940. 261) and Nuer (Evans-Pritchard 1940: 152); to cure illness or avert accident as among the Swazi (Kuper 1947: 189, 192) and Nuer (Evans-Pritchard 1940: 156, 165); or after it as with the Lugbara (Middleton 1960: 87); to expiate incest as among the Ashanti (Rattray 1923: 138) and Dinka (Lienhardt 1961: 284–5); or to expiate fighting at some very sacred rites, as among the Owele Ibo (Meek 1937: 27). There are also the sacrifices to avert disasters of nature, as when the Lovedu try to secure rain (Krige and Krige 1943: 278). In all such cases the regular religious need, to establish communication with the god or with the spirit world, or in whatever other terms the sacrifice be defined, would seem to be pressing and primary. 'Afford it or not,' the attitude might seem to be, 'we must offer up our cow, our goat, our chicken.' There may be also implicit reasons of sociological pressure. A sacrifice may be necessary to seal a man's assumption of office; a sacrifice may be needed as a symbol of the restoration of threatened social relations between kin. Here too sanctions for a sacrifice may be so strong that postponement of it is inconceivable.

Yet this merely pushes the problem a stage further back. If indeed there are some types of sacrifice which are obligatory and immediate, brooking no omission or delay, then how are they effected? Some organizational devices in the economic sphere must come into play in order that the ritual need may be satisfied. If the would-be sacrificer has the resources at hand, how has he managed this: has he ample for all his wants, or has he had to practise prudent husbandry by careful anticipation, or has he just had luck? How will he fare afterwards if a further unanticipated sacrifice is necessary? How well can he sustain a 'run on the sacrifice-bank' if a series of misfortunes demanding the attention of gods and ancestors should strike him and his family? If he has not the resources at hand, to what shifts is he put to mobilize them? Does he forego sacrifice and risk the anger of the unseen world? Does he resort to makeshift devices or substitutes, and if he does, what is their validity for him and his belief in the views of his ancestors and gods? In particular, what additional social relations are entailed thereby, and with whom? Does he contract credit obligations, mortgaging his future income against his present demand? Does the system ever break down? If something has to go, some sacrifice to be omitted, which one? Some indication of the nature of the problem is given by the case of the Lugbara father reported by Middleton who, when his son was sick, waited and did not sacrifice a goat, having it in mind presumably that his son was not *very* sick. Here may be a test of the relative importance of values. In modern conditions of social change and of conflict between traditional and Western values, competing demands may well make these organizational issues of high significance.

In the ethnographic record, relatively thin in this matter as it is, there are enough examples of the prudent handling of resources to show that sacrifice does seem to be a matter of some economic calculation as well as ritual obligation. Goode (1951: 92 seq.) notes that the religious goal of establishing one's ancestral dead by worship and sacrifice causes a decrease in immediate consumption and may necessitate prior saving. What he terms the 'economic burden on the distributive system of the collectivity' should not be ignored. It is fairly common in the literature to state that sacrifices are performed in proportion to the issue at stake (e.g. Herskovits 1938, II: 49; Evans-Pritchard 1940: 26). This involves the concept that the less important the issue the less valuable the object sacrificed. But it leaves untouched another side of the question – granted that the issue was of major importance, how then were resources handled, and in particular were they so organized as to reduce as far as possible the economic loss? Evans-Pritchard has reported that normally (in the early 1930s) the Nuer killed stock only for ritual purposes, not for food. Yet according to him they got thereby (apart from the odd cattle which died) enough meat to satisfy their craving. But the balance would seem to have been not altogether easy, and care to have been exercised lest the stock be unduly depleted. The 'proper' Nuer sacrifice was an ox. But on minor occasions or 'more usually' (including piacular sacrifices to God, who did not require larger beasts) sheep or goats were sacrificed by the Nuer rather than oxen because they were of less value. Again, a barren cow was sacrificed rather than a fertile one, which was immolated only in mortuary rites. Then again a cucumber might be presented instead of an ox, a point which I discuss again later. Moreover, the Nuer held that some men, in their desire for meat, sacrificed 'without due cause'. Yet there is inconsistency here, since on their own showing there were always spirits and ghosts to whom sacrifice would be appropriate and such sacrifices were often said to be long overdue (Evans-Pritchard 1940: 26; 1953: 194; 1956: 263).

The implication from all this is that the occasions for sacrifice have a strong economic control. Evans-Pritchard does mention the relevance of the smallness of their herds and says that 'doubtless their high value is an important consideration'. But he implies that religious intention, tradition, and convention are the prime factors involved in sacrifice, and that the requirements of the spirit are relevant rather than the prudent calculations of men. Yet the significance of the latter is reinforced when one remembers that Evans-Pritchard estimated the average stock at the time he worked with the Nuer to be only about ten head of cattle and five goats and sheep to a byre, the related personnel being about eight people (1940: 20). Cows probably composed about two-thirds of the cattle, which were fairly evenly distributed. Therefore, allowing for natural increase, these figures would seem to imply that, if the livestock average was to be maintained, not much more than one or two sacrifices a month per byre could occur. This does not seem to have allowed a very heavy meat diet, though the system of meat distribution presumably meant that the people of the byre shared in the flesh from other animals sacrificed elsewhere.

The general conclusion that frequency and quality of sacrifice are affected by economic position is supported by further evidence. In the general summary list of factors which Fortes gives as responsible for the selection of animals among the Tallensi, he mentions: importance of the shrine; importance of the occasion; and status of the suppliant or his group. He does not include reference to the *resources* of the person or group as being in any way significant. Yet he does note in a few cases a direct relation between the size of the sacrifice and the wealth of the person making it. He also gives examples of the postponement of sacrifice on apparently economic grounds (1945: 98; 1949: 147, 180). Likewise Nadel who, in general, does not deal with this aspect of the subject, notes that the Muslim Nupe sacrifice of a fattened ram at the 'Id festival takes place 'in every household that can afford it'. He also gives a little information about the relative infrequency of Nupe sacrifice to ancestors which suggest that these, at least, occur so rarely as to present a small economic problem (1954: 25, 109, 240). That sacrifices are related to command of resources by the Ibo is made very clear by Meek. He records the view that stumbling or being bitten by a snake is interpreted by Ibo as possibly due to a man's personal genius being annoyed at the sacrifice of a chicken when the man could easily have afforded a goat (which indicates some prudent calculation somewhere). He notes also the ingenious mechanism whereby a diviner, it is alleged, thinking that a patient will die, prescribes as a sacrifice to save him one that is far beyond the means of the kinsman who consults him. In addition, he gives examples of the sharing of the expense of a sacrifice, as by dividing equally the cost of the sacrificial animal among the segments of relevant kinsfolk or, for public sacrifices, deciding at a general meeting the manner of earning the necesary funds (1937: 27, 35, 120, 146, 169, 201).

Incidentally, the fact noted by Hubert and Mauss and others that the species, sex, colour, and other markings of the sacrifical animal are often laid down by traditional rule, divination or other ritual procedures has an organizational implication that is usually overlooked, the problem of finding one which will conform to specification. That this is not a purely academic question is indicated by instances given by Kuper and by Krige and Krige, showing the delay and difficulties that can result from such a ritual specification. Only where livestock are particularly abundant, as appears to be the case among the Dinka, can such prescriptions not be particularly onerous.[4] Such economic control can be applied directly in two obvious ways, by spacing out at wider intervals the sacrifices it is deemed necessary to make, or by selecting among the possible recipients of sacrifices only those gods and ancestors deemed to be of primary importance. Social anthropologists have stressed the importance of the operation of selective mechanisms in the record of genealogies. It could be that considerations of such an economic kind have played some part in the reduction of spirit entities in communities which offer animals as sacrifice, and thereby have affected the structural character of the genealogical record.

But apart from its possible effect on the frequency of sacrifices, economic controls may affect their quality. R. K. Yerkes, who was not directly concerned with this problem, nevertheless stressed that for the ancient religions of the Near East sacrifices were always as large as possible, and that the larger they were the more joyful the occasion, and contrasted this with the 'unworthy modern view' that a sacrifice is a loss and a misfortune, and that the outgo should be minimal (Yerkes 1953: 4). Robertson Smith, too, seems to have frowned on the notion that a sacrifice might be a matter of prudent calculation. He rejected, probably with justice, the allegation that the sacrifice of very young animals at the annual piacular rites of the ancient Semites was getting rid of a sacred obligation at the very cheapest rate. But in another context he said that 'the introduction of ideas of property into the relation between men and their gods seems to have been one of the most fatal aberrations in the development of ancient religions', which looks as if he had had some inkling of an economic problem and was antipathetic to it (1907: 376, 388). An anthropologist might surmise that this property idea was not an aberration but was in fact basic in the relationship.

Some writers not concerned with the more abstract aspects of the theory of sacrifice have seen the situation empirically and more clearly. C. M. Doughty, living among the Beduin in the nineteenth century, pointed out that sacrifices were performed according to ability, and gave examples. A suckling camel calf was killed, he noted, despite protestations that it was a female and that a sheep or goat should be slain instead. In reply to these arguments the answer was very sensibly, 'she refuses the teat and we have determined to kill her.' He noted again that Beduin did not use a cow camel as a sacrifice to the dead because the households were so indigent, and it was impossible to cut off this 'womb of the stock'. In its place the Beduin bought, for three or four sheep or goats, a decrepit old camel that had lost its front teeth and was past bearing, and released it from work for several months to fatten it up (1926 I: 451-2). Thus the Beduin got meat as well as the credit for the religious act.

But variation in the quality of the sacrifice and use of low-grade animals on occasion is not just a matter of economic organization. It involves an interpretation of the ideology of the sacrifice.

A procedure of collective sacrifice involves concepts both of economy and of religious ideology. The collectivity of a sacrifice is commonly regarded as a symbol of group unity – the members of a descent group or a neighbourhood, by sharing in the common ritual act, give overt expression to social bonds which are significant for them, and strengthen the value of the sacrifice for an individual particularly concerned. But a collective sacrifice often means not only a common presentation of a victim, but also a lightening of the economic burden upon each participant. Collective sacrifices may be of various types. In one the sacrifice specifically represents an offering not by an individual who is the foremost participant but by the lineage or other group he represents. In another type no descent group as such may be involved, but some members of the community may in free association pool their contributions. Such a sacrifice is that of a bull or cow offered by Kelantan Malays in celebration of the annual pilgrimage in Mecca. The animal is usually bought by subscription from several people, the price always being made up in seven shares. Over a period of years, by accumulation of shares so contributed, a person may acquire as it were a complete sacrificial animal for himself and so secure the appropriate merit (Firth 1943: 203). Such collective acts of immolation of an animal may not necessarily reduce the number of sacrifices performed in a community, but they spread the cost and the benefits. They also usually allow people with few resources to take advantage of the relative wealth of others, so that the ideology of charity may be subjoined to that of sacrifice. Again, the emphasis upon the ritual unity of the sacrificing group may be a virtue which is closely allied to necessity.

Another way of meeting the problem of resources in sacrifice which raises important questions of meaning is the use of permissible substitutes or surrogates. Robertson Smith mentioned this subject briefly, though he did not examine it. He regarded such substitution, as that of a sheep for a stag in a certain Roman rite if a stag could not be procured, as an evasion. (He called it bluntly a fraud.) Only in passing did he admit that otherwise the ceremony might fall through (1907: 364, 421). More sophisticated discussion of this whole question is given by modern social anthropologists. Evans-Pritchard's argument takes the form that ultimately the sacrifice of an ox by the Nuer is a surrogate for the sacrifice of a man, and that man and ox are symbolic equivalents. For the Nuer, oxen are the appropriate sacrifice *par excellence*. If there were enough oxen a man might always sacrifice an ox; but there are not enough. Hence, a Nuer will sacrifice a lesser number of livestock or even in some circumstances will bisect a wild cucumber in sacrificial manner (1956: 146, 184, 298). Such a wild cucumber is a symbolic equivalent to an ox. For the Nuer, a cucumber is equivalent to an ox in respect to God who they think accepts it in the place of an ox. Ideologically the position here is very interesting. When a cucumber is so used as a 'sacrificial victim' the Nuer speak of it as *yang*, 'cow' i.e. normally an ox. Sometimes they appear to regard it as only a temporary substitute, an anticipatory offering in terms of an ox to be sacrificed later on. At other times they appear to regard it as a final substitute (Evans-Pritchard 1954: 27; 1956: 203, 205). It is spoken of as an ox and, for ritual purposes, an ox it is. The conception of a wild cucumber as an acceptable substitute for an ox involves an attribution to the cucumber of a quality not proper to it in any material sense.

A significant point to an anthropologist, though whether the Nuer clearly perceive it is not brought out, is that a wild cucumber is a most *economical* way of meeting one's *ritual* obligations. In order that what seems to be an expenditure of minimal resources shall be ritually valid, the Nuer have had to enlarge their sacrificial ideology and attribute to the cucumber an arbitrary religious quality. It is not clear from the evidence just how much trouble a person has to take in order to secure a cucumber for sacrifice, but the inference is that it is not too difficult to find one. It may be suspected that this readiness of the Nuer to compromise in the sacrificial field, and to clothe cucumbers with the attributes of oxen for ritual purposes, is to some degree a reflex of their economic position – in particular their scarcity of oxen – perhaps by reference to their neighbours the Dinka. That in a somewhat

analogous situation such a solution does not find favour is seen
by the views of the Lugbara, who were incredulous when told of
the Nuer practice, and obviously were not prepared to cheat the
spirits by such worthless surrogates (Middleton 1960: 88). The
complexity of Nuer thought on this surrogate is indicated by the
statement that the Nuer say that a man must make invocation
'in truth' and if the sacrifice is to be effective what is said must
be true (Evans-Pritchard 1956: 211). How they square this with
calling a cucumber an ox is not apparent. The Dinka, who also
split sacred cucumbers, use them specifically as temporary substitutes for animal victims and as an earnest of intention to provide
such a victim when possible (Lienhardt 1961: 257).

An interesting variant of this principle of substitution is the
Swazi practice of the *licabi*. This is a particularly fine beast which
every family priest dedicates to his ancestors. If a sacrifice is to
be made the *licabi* animal is driven into the byre with the other
cattle and the real victim is shepherded near it to acquire something of its ritual qualities, 'so that by proxy the best goes to the
dead'. But the *licabi* itself serves the role many times; it is not
killed until it becomes too old to serve as the display animal. By
this practice clearly the proxy which is actually slain can be an
inferior animal, thus conserving family resources (Kuper 1947:
192).

The ideology of symbolic equivalents of things which may be
offered in sacrifice may therefore be directly correlated with the
problem of allocation of scarce resources. In the last resort
the greatest surrogate of all is the sacrifice of the mind and
heart, the abnegation of individual judgement and desire in
favour of devotion to more general moral ends. Such a substitution is in line with very general trends of ethical and religious
interpretation, and the material sacrifices are often regarded as
one early developmental phase in a long line of substitutions.
One ancient Rabbi is said to have held that the Mosaic laws
appertaining to animal sacrifices were primarily designed for the
generation of the desert; that burnt offerings were but time-
conditioned ways of doing honour to God; that at a later time the
sacrifices of righteousness would have precedence over offerings
upon the altar (Mattuck 1954: 27). This view is clearly compatible
with our modern attitudes towards human personality, but one
need not overlook entirely that removal of the notion of sacrifice
from the material to the immaterial plane does away with an

awkward problem of organization. Readers of Max Weber and of R. H. Tawney do not need to be reminded how an ethical view can emerge side by side with a convenient economic doctrine.

If the elasticity of a surrogate is not possible, then other alternatives may be found. One method is to borrow for a sacrifice. But as Wagner has shown for the Logoli (1940: 232) and Evans-Pritchard for the Nuer (1940: 165), this may lead to social difficulties for the borrower. In other words, though obligation is translated from the ritual to the social sphere the economic problem is apt to remain.

Again, the material of a sacrifice can be treated in either of two main ways: by complete destruction or by reservation. In destruction, if solid it can be consumed by fire, by water, or by exposure; if liquid it can be poured away. In reservation, it can be offered to god or spirit and then withdrawn for the consumption of the worshippers. Empirically, this latter seems to be by far the most usual course. Interest in the meat or other ingredients, as much ethnographic evidence shows, may be at least as important an element in attendance at the occasion as interest in the religious aspect of the sacrifice itself. While the sharing of sacrificial food may be a significant ritual act, it is very frequently nothing more than ordinary commensality.

The legitimization of such an economic rebate has very important implications for the practice and the theory of sacrifice. On the one hand it allows the sacrifice to be performed with much greater frequency than would certainly be the case if the sacrificial material was always destroyed. On the other hand it necessitates special beliefs about the manner in which the gods or spirits take their fill. Either they must be satisfied with the killing and display of the sacrificed object, or they must be satisfied to consume its least valuable portions, or to absorb some immaterial aspect or equivalent of it. In other words, the practice of reservation of the sacrificial material for the human participants almost inevitably demands some theory of essences, representations or symbols. Such, for example, is the theory of the Tikopia, who regard all their offerings as having an immaterial, invisible counterpart. They describe the immaterial counterpart in some detail, linking it with analogous spirit counterparts in man, and give it various names according to circumstances. This whole set of notions is part of an integral system of ideas about the meaning of ritual behaviour. When food offerings are set out it is this counterpart, invisible to men, that is thought to be taken away by the gods and spirits, and presumably consumed by them. The Tikopia describe in terms of such spirit action the wilting of fresh vegetable plants such as taro, set up on a grave as an offering to the spirit of the dead. But they are relatively uninterested in the process by which this abstraction of immaterial counterpart is believed to be done. They describe it as being 'after the manner of spirits' and leave the subject there.

The point I wish to make here is this. From our Western angle of approach, like Robertson Smith, we probably regard the notion that it is the essence and not the substance of a sacrifice that is consumed by the god or spirit as a more refined idea than the crass belief that the god or spirit actually eats the material bread or meat or drinks the material beer. It may be so. But it is not only more refined; it is also more economical. The point was made essentially by Tylor many years ago. 'Through the history of sacrifice it has occurred to many nations that cost may be economised without impairing efficiency. The result is seen in ingenious devices to lighten the burden on the worshipper by substituting something less valuable than what he ought to offer, or pretends to' (1873, II: 399).

I think that one is entitled to say then that even at the heart of primitive religious ideology in such a basically important phenomenon as sacrifice, notions of rationality and prudent calculation enter. In other words, the concepts of sacrifice held by any people must be understood in relation to their notions about control of resources. I want to stress that it is not my argument that concepts of sacrifice can simply be reduced to rational, economic terms. Sacrifice is essentially a symbolic act of grave significance to human personality, and normally has important social components. But my basic point of view here is that, to understand the operations of a religious system even in such a highly symbolic rite as sacrifice, we must consider the implications of organization in men, material and timing of procedures. Much of the effect of these organizational concomitants is seen only in the magnitude and the style of the rites, but their quality, their content and their ideology can also be affected.

I conclude as follows: sacrifice is ultimately a personal act, a giving of the self or a part of the self. The self is represented or symbolized by various types of material object. Such a material object must have social significance or value, or the implication

will be that the self is trivial or worthless. Part of the theory of
sacrifice then is the giving of a valued object involving some
immediate personal loss. In this giving of a valued object there
are elements of rational calculation, or organization, of matching
material loss against command of material resources, as well as
against immaterial or spiritual gain. This element of rational calculation may condition the value or the quality of the object
offered. It may also condition the mode of offering, for example
by withdrawal of material once offered with the explanation that
its essence has been taken. But rational calculation may also
condition the ideology of the sacrifice, which may be elaborated
in explanation of the particular operation of the offering. Into
this field of ideas comes the notion of the surrogate, of a ram
instead of a human being, of a cucumber instead of an ox. These
are physical substitutes, but they are often offered instead of a
man not only as a physical substitute but also as a moral substitute. This notion interpreted conventionally is that it is not the
thing itself but the spirit of the gift that is important. It is the act
of giving rather than the gift that matters, that is, the expendi
ture of time and energy is significant, and beyond this the
expenditure of thought and of emotion. But sacrifice as a moral
act is a conception at a different level from sacrifice as a material
loss.

All this implies that the value of the thing offered is attributed
to it only conventionally by virtue of its being selected for
offering. This is distinct from the value of the thing in ordinary
economic transactions. Granting this, nevertheless one function
of such beliefs is that they may allow the retention of objects of
economic value. One may serve God without losing touch with
Mammon. In the last resort, then, sacrifice in primitive religions
is the action of giving up something to which has been allotted
an arbitrary or specially circumscribed attribution of value.
Communal objects of the highest economic value are regarded
as most appropriate for sacrifice. But the use of them represents
an equation of decision, the result of the effects of a number of
variables in respect of the value put on the self and on its various
properties in a specific social milieu. Sacrifice is a critical act for
a human personality, but it is an act performed in terms laid
down by the evaluations of the society.

Chapter 6

Ritual and drama in Malay spirit mediumship

Most studies of universalistic religions have focused primarily upon their theological constructs of belief, and assume a uniformity of ritual and practice in the followers. Anthropological studies by contrast tend to be concerned with the actual behaviour of the people, with discrepancy between their religious ideals and their religious conduct, and their range of commitment to religious norms. Local factors of an historical kind, of a social, economic and political order, enter into the situation. So it has been in the Malay state of Kelantan.[1]

Moreover, in Kelantan the formal tenets of Islam have been supplemented by an antecedent set of folk beliefs of more local Indian and Indonesian origin, involving spirits known generically as *hantu*. Belief in these spirits has varied considerably in different strata of the population, but it was not an alternative to Islam. Every Kelantan Malay has been a good Muslim, believing in the overall operation of the will and bounty of Allah. But Allah is remote and the religious functionaries oriented to ritual duties rather than to the daily concern of the ordinary villager. So in the earlier years of this century (the situation may now have changed) Kelantan rice farmers and fishermen and their womenfolk tended to invoke local spirit forces in time of crisis, such as sickness in the family or economic misfortune.

This chapter and the following chapter accordingly describe aspects of Kelantan folk belief and the way in which, while fully accepting Islam, they added in ritual terms what they considered to be the help of local spirits to resolve their immediate problems or distress. These are illustrations of religion in action. They indicate how closely religion and what may be called magic may be related. They also show how concepts such as those of soul and spirit, and personification of natural forces can be inextricably linked with mundane ideas and practices of daily life in such peasant communities.

CULTS OF ECSTASY

Phenomena identified as spirit mediumship seem to be world wide and to be recognizable from an early period in human society. Attention has been paid to them by writers on classical antiquity of whom, from an anthropological point of view, Jane Harrison was one of the most noteworthy. Influenced by Durkheim and by Rivers, she recognized the importance of collective elements in religion and of the need for a knowledge of the social structure to gain an understanding of any particular cult. Robustly she argued, 'What a people *does* in relation to its gods must always be one clue, and perhaps the safest, to what it thinks.' Knowing that her attempt to build a bridge between anthropology and the classics was viewed sceptically in some quarters, she countered trenchantly 'It is only a *little* anthropology that is a dangerous thing' (1903: 7; 1912: 22).

Particularly interesting to an anthropologist in Jane Harrison's treatment of religion was her exploration of the significance of Dionysiac and Orphic cults. Emphasizing ecstasy, abandonment of the self and identification with God, these cults ran parallel to the more orthodox practices of Greek religion. With its emphasis upon the significance of what she referred to as 'potencies' (*daimones*) rather than personal gods, and of emotion rather than reason, Jane Harrison's work may appeal once again to modern anthropological students of religion. Study of the relation of a religious system of beliefs and practices to the social structure of communities is by now a well-worn theme. Where we are much less at home, and where some of the most interesting problems seem to lie, is in the relation of religious belief and practice and of ritual more generally to the complex, non-rational elements in personality. Anthropologists are concerned primarily not with the more purely individual aspects of this problem, but with the way in which, generated and conditioned by society, individuals in relation to one another express their thoughts, beliefs and values.

The type of behaviour which I have taken for consideration here falls under the general heading of what Greek scholars have discussed as ecstasy (*ekstasis*), a standing outside oneself, perhaps

a dissociation of the personality, interpreted by the person concerned and by others as *enthusiasmos*, possession by a god or
spirit (Guthrie 1955: 149; Harrison 1903: 388–9, 424–5, 568 *et
seq.*). This phenomenon, in that form which I would class conventionally as spirit mediumship (Firth 1964: 247–8), I shall discuss
in particular from my observations in the state of Kelantan in
Malaysia.[2] These spirit medium procedures can vary considerably.
But characteristic of the more complex are elements of dance,
even of drama, as well of ritual. It is the relation between these
elements that I wish to examine.

Jane Harrison, like most anthropologists of her day, was concerned very much with questions of origin and development –
how one type of social behaviour, pantomimic dance, provided
the base, 'the root inchoate' material, out of which both ritual
and art, at least in the form of drama, developed. Modern anthropologists, at least those outside the classical field, have been
conventionally much less interested in such questions. But later
I consider if this problem has any relevance for anthropology
today.

What is clearly of concern here is the problem of the relation
of personality to society, as exemplified symbolically in the
theme of human struggle. We may interpret in a different sense
from Jane Harrison her view that pantomimic dancing was a
ritual bridge between actual life, and those representations of life
which we call art. But when a man as a spirit medium goes into
a trance, claims to be a god and dances in the name of the god,
while a sick person lies before him on the floor, we too must try
to understand what is represented. For whom is the dance really
performed; what is the character of what Jane Harrison has
termed the 'enactment'? When art and ritual are so conjoined,
in what proportion are they welded, are they separable in intent
or in effect, and what is the function of either in a situation of
human suffering?

A MALAY SPIRIT MEDIUM PERFORMANCE

Let me first describe an actual example from northeastern Malaya
which my wife and I observed late in 1963. These rural Malays
have some faith in Western medicine and also a little of their
own folk pharmacology.[3] But they tend to think that any illness
which is of a refractory kind must have a supernatural cause.

In this case a man had been ill for about two weeks, and a spirit medium performance took place in order to diagnose his illness and to attempt to cure him. The performance began at about nine o'clock at night at the sick man's house. A special shelter was erected outside the house by stretching a sail over a bamboo frame. In one corner of the shelter gongs were hung, and pandanus mats were laid down thickly on the ground as floor covering. The performing team arrived and were given a meal inside the house. These were mundane preparations.

But from the outset it was clear that extra-human powers were expected to be involved. Offerings were prepared to the spirits. A plate of rice with an egg on it was hung up for the spirit patron of the performance (Dewa Betara Guru, classically identified as Shiva). A tray with parched rice, betel materials, scented oil and other ritual elements was arranged for the spirits as a whole. A most important figure was the master of ceremonies, known as the Mindok, a specialist in the magical lore of healing and in the control of spirits. He opened the proceedings by perfuming the offerings with incense and pronouncing formulae of invocation to the gods and spirits, announcing to them the name of the patient and the purpose of the performance. After a ritual dedication of the orchestral instruments, of which fiddle and gongs were the chief representatives, the master of ceremonies began to play his fiddle in a wailing melody and to chant, with the orchestra following and supporting him. Each stage of the performance has its own melodic and rhythmic indicator or 'signature tune'.

These were preliminaries. Now the spirit medium performance was about to begin. One of the drummers left his instrument, and bare to the waist put on a new yellow kilt, and purified himself by ritual performances with incense, scented oil and parched rice. By this time the orchestra was playing in quick rhythm, and the master of ceremonies was singing vigorously. He was calling loudly in formal terms, with many honorifics, on the spirits. These, generally termed *hantu*, included a range of entities of various status – Arabic jinn, Hindu and Indonesian gods (Dewa) and local sprites. Some have elaborate titles: Sheikh Triumphant Ruler, Grandsire Earth Jinn; Grandsire White Jinn; Grandsire Conqueror Glowing Light. It must be emphasised that the invocation is not a pagan affair; the master of ceremonies places himself, and the performance, under the protection of Allah, and cites putative leading Muslim figures – four Sheikhs, seven Saints, four Archangels – in support of his procedures.

By now the performer had his eyes half closed and was beginning to sway his head and shoulders round and round counter-clockwise. He was sitting cross-legged; the fingers of his left hand resting on his right foot began to quiver rapidly. His right hand too began to quiver. Quicker and quicker he rotated the upper part of his body, his head now nodding rapidly in response to the rhythm of the drums, his hands raised alternately and then clapped. He gave a shriek of '*Ais*', and threw out parched rice around him as a ritual gesture. He turned one by one to the four quarters, the east, the west, the north and the south, in ritual acknowledgement, and then began a dialogue with the master of ceremonies.

This introduced the main business of the evening. The patient sitting nearby reclined against a long pillow. The central performer, now believed to be possessed by his ancestral spirit influence, began to dance. His movements, though without the refinement with which we are familiar in Indian classical dancing, did have a certain rhythmic grace of their own, and were marked particularly by delicate symbolic gestures of the fingers. He danced for about a quarter of an hour in the small, central space of the shelter. Then to a rally of music, with his head nodding rapidly in time to the rhythm, he went into a kind of paroxysm which suddenly stopped as the music ended. Then began the diagnosis of the patient's illness. The medium, representing a visiting spirit, undertook a rather aggressive interchange of comments with the master of ceremonies, who replied in quiet but firm tones. The medium then spread some grains of parched rice on a little cushion, and began a diagnosis of the source of the patient's illness by an elimination technique rather like our own childhood 'ickle ockle black bottle' formula. Here the reference was to a system of 'temperaments' or humours: earth, air, fire, water, somewhat akin to European medieval doctrines. The broad, preliminary diagnosis was established in terms of one of the major elements, air and water being relatively benign, earth and fire relatively malignant. The medium turned to the patient, gave him parched rice to eat and chanted over him; then re-knotted a yellow scarf around his own waist and again danced. He and the master of ceremonies chanted alternately over the patient, addressing the ills in him in spirit form to emerge and so relieve him. The medium went through a 'laying on of hands' on the patient, including a kind of pursuit along the length of the patient's body, ending with a wild shaking of his feet in a last attempt to drive out the afflicting spirit. Dialogue between master of ceremonies and medium was pursued, the purpose of the master of ceremonies being to identify the particular spirit responsible for the patient's illness, and to induce it to acknowledge responsibility, leave his body and return to its own abode. Sometimes the afflicting spirit was quiescent, sometimes he resisted violently and had to be argued into submission. From time to time the medium was possessed with violent seizures as the spirit within him or acting through him was pressed more closely by the master of ceremonies. All the time the orchestra was playing. As the night wore on people had begun to assemble around the shelter; some quietly talking, most intently watching and listening. By about midnight nearly a hundred people were present, about half of them adults; in a village affair of this kind there are always plenty of children, so they get socialized at an early age.

At last the patient himself, ill as he was, rose and danced in the middle of the floor, the medium encouraging him and as it were instructing him. This was the sign that benign influences had come to him and that he would be better. After the patient, looking rather exhausted, sat down again the medium and the master of ceremonies alternately sang of these benign influences. Then the patient himself joined in the song, wailing out in high chant his spiritual agreement and rapprochement. Finally, after some gentle massage from shoulder to waist by the medium, the patient himself went into a brief trance state from which he was relieved by a ritual scattering of parched rice. This was for him the final rite, the 'release', as the Malays themselves express it, and he turned away, dismissed as it were from the scene. The audience began to drift away. For them the performance was over. All that was left was for the medium to recover himself and perform his final ritual obeisances, with gestures to head, face, shoulders and breast, with the orchestra giving a final rally while he unwound the yellow scarf, a symbol of his status, from around his waist.

INTERPRETATION AT THE LOCAL LEVEL

What is the meaning of these complex proceedings? There are several levels of interpretation. In essence, the local interpretation is that at least four kinds of spiritual powers are involved. First there is the patient's own soul (*semangat*) which has been attacked. Then there are the afflicting spirits (*hantu*): jinn, sprites, sea or earth spirits, one of which has found lodgement in the patient's body. The type and identity of spirit responsible for the illness can be found most effectively through the agency of the medium in trance, a state which he can assume because of his own peculiar ancestral endowment, a hereditary disposition or humour, known by the same word as for wind (*angin*). This congenital propensity to trance behaviour is a spiritual force rather than a spirit entity. But another type of spirit is the medium's own familiar. Sometimes this tutelary is described as a tiny spirit of a dead person – not an ancestor – known as *penggawa* (leader); it is fostered by the medium by being given periodic offerings, as of eggs. *Penggawa* are superior to *hantu*, who are afraid of them, and so they can be used to expel *hantu*. Finally there are the most powerful spirits of all, the *Dewa*, a term of Hindu origin. It is they, frequently, whom the medium represents when he dances, each of them – there are seven – shown by different gestures. *Dewa*, unlike most other spirits, are not thought to enter the body of the medium – he would die; they repose at the back of his neck and on his shoulders, and influence his actions. *Dewa* are usually benign, assist medium and patient and provide the clarifying influence which restores serenity after violence. Their function is to make the patient at ease after the exorcism. But I must point out that many of these spirits have no particular moral character; they are neither good nor evil in themselves. They act according to circumstances, and if not treated with proper deference can turn against a man instead of working for him. If I were writing in another context, indeed, I should emphasize how these various spirit forms can be taken by us to represent in a rather amorphous symbolic way, exterior projections of various aspects of human personality. In a sense *Dewa* represent existence, memory, thought, etc. If not used rightly, these aspects are destructive to the person concerned.

But in Malay eyes the spirit medium performance, with its

trance and seance, was in essence a struggle for the spirit and body of the sick man, to lure out and expel the alien spirit afflicting him. When the afflicting spirit has departed the sick man is left 'with his illness alone' as the Malays say. His spiritual disability has been removed; it is only the physical disability that is left, and the man will respond to medicine or get better of himself.

In the present case, enquiry revealed that the afflicting spirit (*Hantu Dewa Muda*), who was very powerful, had stricken the man because of neglect. The reason given seems trivial to us – an ancestor of the man had not made the spirit a present of a small *kĕris* dagger which he had admired. But the weight of the excuse seems never to be called in question. What is important is that a reason *is* given. Moreover, the spirit reproached the patient and his relatives through the spirit medium for not having had a mediumistic performance much sooner. The spirit was angry – why did they allow the man to be ill so long without any attempt to find the cause? The relatives replied to the medium that they didn't know that he, the spirit, had been actually residing in the man and causing the illness. They asked would the patient recover soon or would he be ill for long? The spirit, through the medium, replied that the patient would recover quite quickly provided he complied with instructions, which included a gift of atonement, called a *balai*. In the context of a spirit medium performance this term means a frame of bamboo which simulates a royal palace or hall of audience and which serves as a stage, a few feet high, upon which offerings to the spirits can be exposed. The spirit specified also that he wanted offerings of sea creatures, sharks, stingray, and so on, made and put upon the *balai*. These, as was customary, would be made of wheaten paste, crude little models which represented the objects asked for. This stage would be constructed either by the man himself when he recovered or by his relatives, and with its offerings carried to a piece of waste land or the side of a stream near his house. This propitiation of the spirit was accompanied by a payment to the performers of the evening, but neither the cost of the propitiatory offering or of the remuneration to the performers was very high. As it turned out, the sick man did in fact recover quite soon.

COMMUNICATION AND CONTROL:
INTERPRETATION AT THE EXTERNAL LEVEL

Now for interpretation by the external observer. We are clearly dealing here with procedures at a symbolic level. Dispositions and forces are manifest in which individual characteristics are closely related to social relationships, norms and pressures. This is exemplified by the chants of the master of ceremonies, which embody a number of references to senses, orifices, parts of the body in metaphorical form and even symbolize them as spirit titles. This implies the relation of man to the external world, and to religious structure. Each of the Archangels, or of the Companions of the Prophet, controls an orifice and an organ of the body. Even the *rebab*, the Arab-type fiddle, was explained to me by one expert as a simulacrum of the human body. The scroll is the head of man, the pegs for tuning are equivalent to human ears, the strings to veins and muscles, and so on. In a way we are given a homocentric symbolic system. Symbolically, what has occurred to the patient has been an establishment of public concern in his illness, and a diagnosis of it in terms of conflict of elements in his personality. The illness has been given an aetiology not of blind fate but of human error, and certainty has been given where before was ignorance and anxiety. There is now a basis for action, and a demand for offering of atonement which can be thought to cleanse the man from guilt.

Let us focus here on the behaviour and situation of the medium. The medium in this performance is obviously a kind of bridge between the ideas, emotions and behaviour of the sick person, and those of the people who surround him. What he does, among other things, is to take the brakes off the speech conventions of ordinary social discourse. Instead of conventional expressions of concern for the sick person, in his trance state the medium can allow his ideas about responsibility or feelings of frustration, anger and aggression to come to the surface. But the words that he utters are regarded as not his own, but those of a being apart from and for the most part more powerful than he. Since he is thought not to be able to help himself, but to be merely a vehicle of communication for the spirits, any praise or blame which he may attribute to the patient, to the patient's relatives or to persons outside is not treated as rebounding upon him. In a sense, indeed, the words he utters may not entirely be his own; they are his rendering of what he feels other people's attitudes force him to express. Through the medium in trance then there comes to the surface what ordinary people think and feel about the case in question. The medium's utterances can serve as a very useful safety valve for collective and individual attitudes.

But to understand the significance of this phenomenon more fully we must lay stress upon its importance as a means of *communication* between individual and society about a problem of concern. This is where I think in the past some studies of spirit possession and allied phenomena have failed to be quite clear. In many societies various forms of craziness have been interpreted as possessions by spirits. But the only forms which are socially utilizable are those where the relation between society and the individual concerned can operate in some mutually intelligible way. Let me illustrate this further from the Kelantan Malay field. Among the forms of mental disorder recognized by Malays, there are four which can be fairly simply distinguished by different terms. They are:

1 The classical *amok*. This is a state in which a man goes into a homicidal paroxysm, killing or wounding all whom he may meet, and prepared to devote himself to death in so doing. The ostensible basis for such conduct has been to wipe out some deep affront. *Amok* seems to have been a condition to which men only were prone, and to have occurred particularly among gentry and warriors, for whom insult and honour have high significance, and for whom resort to arms was no novelty. Although well-known in the literature, *amok* has apparently had a markedly declining incidence in Malaya since changes in the politico/legal structure began to be effected in the latter part of last century. Even in 1939 to 1940 I personally never knew nor heard of an actual case of *amok* at that time, although in the past apparently it was fairly frequent.

2 *Latah*. This is a specific reaction produced by sudden psychological shock in a naïve, undeveloped or poorly endowed personality.[4] The person afflicted can be thrown into this state by any sudden movement or sudden loud noise which startles him. The result is that the person must then engage in some form of compulsive imitation – echolalia, repeating any words uttered to him; echokinesis, imitating, it may be to an extreme,

any gesture seen, as pulling a glowing coal from the fire when someone makes the appropriate gesture. Sometimes the state is characterized not by imitation but by a compulsive excess, going beyond all the normal social bounds, as by coprolalia, when a normally refined, composed Malay bursts forth with obscene phrases. *Latah*, a condition which may occur among men or women, seems to persist nowadays, and I have known of several local examples, in Kelantan.

3 *Gila*. This is a state of madness or 'craziness' characterized by such socially odd behaviour as muttering or shrieking without apparent cause, depressive apathy, maniac attacks. Such conditions can occur among men or women, and have a number of colloquial terms given to them, such as the Kelantan vernacular term *gong*.[5]

4 *Lupa*. This term, which means literally forgetting, is applied to a condition of trance in which an individual, man or woman, takes on another personality, speaking and behaving in another guise.

Now it is important to note that of these four general categories of mental disorder recognized by Malays, only one, the last, is, as it were, convertible to social utility. *Amok*, equivalent to going berserk, may have been socially useful at an earlier stage of Malay society when nobles and their retainers might fight each other, but the condition would seem to have been too unpredictable and too much out of control to be of much value to others. Similarly, neither *latah* or *gila* conditions are sufficiently controllable nor yield sufficiently intelligible communication to be socially useful. Out of the entire field of mental disorders only that of *lupa*, trance, can be put to social use. In this type a person who is of sufficient sensitivity, and liable to such a change of state, can induce trance in himself (auto-hypnosis) or be aided to induce it without great difficulty when required, and when in such a state is commonly capable of consistent, intelligible conversation. What is particularly striking about this condition is that in many societies it has been incorporated into a system of therapeutic aid. Because the condition allows of a freedom beyond the ordinary social conventions, and is regarded as ritually sanctioned, it can be used as a means of symbolic expression in a relation between a sick person and the community.

I have spoken so far of trance, implying by this a blurring of consciousness of the individual concerned such that the full controls of ordinary life are not operative. But it would seem that the state may also commonly be described as one of dissociation, in that the personality of the individual appears to have altered or a different facet of the personality is presented than ordinarily appears in social life. Sometimes these conditions appear to be simulated, and the social recognition and evaluation of this offers an interesting field for interpretation. But from ordinary observation of the physical effects involved and the after-reactions it would appear that 'genuine' phenomena are common, and it is only those which I am considering here. Moreover, I wish to make it clear that I am not concerned with the physiological or medical aspects of the phenomena, but with their institutional functions and effects, including the interplay of social and individual elements in the relationship.

I regard the aspect of *control* as very important here. For social utilization the mediumistic state must be able to be induced and not simply have to rely on spontaneous generation. Mediums must be able to go into trance when people are ill. Here the external stimuli such as music and ritualized gestures such as head swing and rhythmic alternation of arm quiver are important aids. But there must also be a mechanism for focusing the attention of the person in trance upon the matter in hand. Here the master of ceremonies, the attendant crowd, the phased climax and relaxation of the performer's movements are significant. Finally, there must be a mechanism for helping the person in trance to return to normal when the matter has been satisfactorily disposed of. This is necessary in the interests of the person himself as well as those of his companions. There is little doubt that in some respects the trance state is looked upon as a burdensome condition, and may have attached to it unpleasant physical consequences. Yet to some degree also it provides an escape mechanism from the trammels of ordinary life. In trance the medium speaks with a different tone of voice, often much rougher and more aggressive, expresses opinions by no means complimentary to others present, is the centre of the stage and possessed of authority in dictating what a sick person must do to get well. He assumes to some degree another personality of greater power and freedom. Hence there may be satisfactions in this state and he may have to be assisted to leave it and to return to his ordinary one.

In all societies where spirit mediumship obtains, there is some form of control in each of these spheres, though these controls differ from one society to another. One may assume for instance that every spirit medium has some form of internal control by which he is enabled to return from his state of dissociation to his ordinary condition. In each case this internal control has its given symbolic form. For example, in one community in which I have worked, Tikopia, each medium in the local view serves as the vehicle for several spirits, some ancestral, some not. One of these, usually the spirit of a dead father or brother, is regarded as being a 'familiar' who controls the other spirits, and who may 'jump into' the medium at a certain point to break the chain of spirits and so relieve the medium of their burden. This is a kind of built-in mechanism which allows the medium to emerge from his dissociated state.

The external controls in this society are unformalized. Other members of the household, neighbours, kinsfolk, sit around and by their behaviour help to channel the medium's expressions and acts in the desired direction. By their questions and comments they help to intimate when they are satisfied and so when a seance can conveniently end, but none of them is in ritual charge of the proceedings. Among the Kelantan Malays there is also the 'familiar' spirit, the *penggawa*, part of whose job is to protect the medium. But here, however, as we have seen, the external control is formalized, and personally identified with ritual sanction. The master of ceremonies plays a leading part in questioning the medium, interpreting what he says, and by his control of the musical accompaniment stimulates and guides the medium's actions. For the most part he adopts a quiet, rather neutral position in the verbal exchanges, agreeing with the putative spirit or commenting rather drily in a kind of 'so, indeed' fashion. Sometimes, however, he will cross-question the spirit closely and argue with him. Throughout he is recognized as the person having prime authority in the proceedings; at the symbolic level he is the 'master of spirits', a shaman in the strict sense of the word.

DRAMATIC ELEMENTS

So far I have discussed this performance primarily as a therapeutic measure designed in the Malay view to elucidate the cause

of an illness and produce relief or cure. A similar kind of performance sometimes takes place to exorcise evil spirits generally
(*jamuan hantu*) from a village or other place where people con-
gregate. In all cases the performance is highly ritualized, that is,
regular series of actions are performed in systematic sequence,
each having its validity in terms of the whole cycle, conceived as
basically operative in spiritual rather than human terms. It is
also a mode of communication between different social elements,
especially kin and neighbours, though the communication is
phrased in symbolic terms of spirit behaviour, not human actions
and feelings.

But the performance is not only ritual, it has also elements of
drama. It is symptomatic here that the performance is regarded
by the Malays themselves from one angle as a form of recreation.
In Kelantan terms it is known as *main puteri*,[6] which means that
in general classification it is grouped together with other *main* –
games, amusements, plays – including the shadow play (*wayang
kulit*) known in Kelantan as *main royang*. Moreover, the links
with the shadow play are more specific. Some of the puppet
characters in the shadow play, such as Arjuna, may appear as
powerful spirits in a spirit medium performance. Conversely, a
shadow play is a ritual performance, with incense and offerings
to the spirits symbolized by the puppet characters.[7] Sometimes
there is also a mediumistic performance in the dawn at the end
of the shadow play, with the puppet master possessed by the
spirits of some of his puppets. Night after night he has manipu-
lated them; in compensation as it were before they are shut away
again they manipulate him. So violent may one or two of them
become that the puppet master as I have seen may have to be
restrained by his companions from devouring the offerings in the
name of the spirits.

Obvious elements in which the spirit medium performance
enters the recreational field are the dancing and the singing of
the person in trance. That the dancing is of considerable significance in the whole performance is seen by the fact that Jeanne
Cuisinier, who has given us the best analysis to date of the spirit
medium performances of Kelantan, includes it under the general
title of magical *dances*. In my experience, the dancing certainly
attracts attention. But on the whole it seems to be considered as
of less importance by the spectators than the *singing* of the
medium. When a spirit medium performance is to take place, and

it is known that a celebrated medium will be taking part, people may come from villages several miles away across the rice fields. What they comment upon primarily, however, is not the medium's dancing but his singing, and they compare and criticize mediums according to whether they do or do not have *suara molek*, fine, agreeable voices. But the whole situation is complex, with side issues. The performance is often long drawn, lasting commonly for three nights. On the second night, around midnight or later if the performance goes on till dawn, when interest may be flagging, the medium, clearly in a fairly light state of trance, may take on a comic character. He may pull his waist cloth up over his chest and purport to be a female spirit. He engages in gross badinage with the spectators, may demand bananas to eat, may comment critically on the poor hospitality offered or on the lack of proper decoration to the cloth canopy – the 'sky' – over his head. In such ways, by complaint and by humour, the interest of the audience is kept alive and exchanges of chaff often take place between them and the medium.

But there is another element of greater importance, though not given such overt weight. This is the dramatic tension that exists and mounts during the course of the performance until towards the end it is resolved. The performance begins on a quiet note, a little instrumentation, a long chanted invocation. The early spirit representations of the medium are relatively quiet also. But as the night wears on, especially if the illness is severe, stronger – one might say darker – forces begin to emerge. The medium may present himself as opponent of a fierce demon or the dreaded tiger spirit (*hantu rimau*). As antagonist to the demon, he may grunt and growl, spring from side to side on all fours, worry at the body of the patient and generally behave in a violent manner. This is the performance known to the Malays as *main kuat*, playing in a powerful way. The onset of such a mode is usually anticipated well in advance. If the performance lasts three nights, it is usually known that on the last night there will be violent struggles with spirits. The performer who is to play this part is usually well prepared. I remember one occasion on which he borrowed a pair of long trousers so that, if he engaged in violent contortions and exposed himself more than usual, he would be decently covered. Sometimes in such scenes the forces controlling the medium seem to take charge completely and, unknowing of what he does, he is hurled to and fro, as it were in the grip of powers unseen. On one occasion I saw a medium, in such a condition, roll over and over in a ball along the floor of the house, down on to the platform near the doorway; unless he had been seized by the bystanders he would have shot right out on to the ground six feet below. In such scenes is great dramatic effect, heightened by the audience's view that what they are seeing is not just a man exhibiting aspects of his own psyche, but a spirit, aggressive and powerful, struggling either to express itself or to be free. This is where the function of the *mindok*, as controller, comes to the fore. By comment, by formula and by ritual actions such as pelting with parched rice, he acts as it were as a spirit daunter, calming, subduing and guiding it into more socially acceptable channels. From the Malay point of view he is performing his job as a master of spirits. From our point of view he is a master of men, using traditional techniques to facilitate and control the expression of forces which, uncontrolled, might damage physically and psychologically the personality of a man. For this violence has in a way its own rationale. On the one hand it releases forces in the medium which have been stirred up by his passing into a state of dissociation and the subsequent searching and challenging of mental and emotional issues. On the other hand it serves as a visible expression to patient and to audience of the gravity of these issues and of the affliction from which the sick person is suffering. It is a cathartic mechanism.

There is drama then to be seen in the interrelation between the different facets of the medium's personality, in the relation between the medium and his human controller, and in the bringing to the surface issues in the life and behaviour of a patient which may relate to his illness. In all this tension is first laid bare, indeed generated, then brought to a crisis and a resolution achieved. The patient is led to elicit the reason for his own condition and is given a means, however simple and crude it may seem, of doing something to relieve it.

RITUAL AND DRAMA

I think that to understand spirit mediumship we must examine more generally the human dilemma which lies behind these performances. What dilemma? That of the logic of human action as compared with the arbitrariness of external events. We are accustomed for the most part to conceive these external events as the development of uncontrolled movements in the physical world, for example the behaviour of bacteria in generating illness. What the Malay or other spirit medium performance does is to identify them as the uncontrolled movement (initially at least) of spiritual powers. But the spirit medium performance, though lacking in medical knowledge and skills, is not simply to acknowledge defeat but to exercise control and to assign responsibility nearer home. The arbitrariness of the external world is translated into terms of the logic of human acts or relations, though these are expressed in metaphorical form.

From all these angles, then, one can see how a ritual performance can also be a dramatic spectacle. In a strict sense, of course, all this is not drama, it is dramatic material in the raw. Not that it lacks so much the vision and imagination or the tension of art; nor indeed are elements of patterned handling of action absent. But it is still ritual rather than drama. By ritual I mean a formal set of procedures of a symbolic kind, involving social communication, and believed to possess an efficacy of themselves in *changing* the technical or social conditions of the performers or other participants. Spirit medium performances aim to change rather than represent a situation in aesthetic and moral form, which is what I take it drama primarily attempts to do.

Now I am going to ask a rather unorthodox question for a modern social anthropologist. What would be needed to convert this ritual performance into dramatic art? I would say two qualities, which are present only in embryo in the spirit medium performance as it stands – a sense of general statement about human experience and the human condition; and a more deliberate focus on the development and unity of the form of statement. The content of the spirit medium performance has dramatic potential. Its aesthetic development would demand more attention to the patterning of relationships between the various elements, including a more economical use of time as well as of other resources.

The Malay spirit medium performance as spectacle lacks some of the characteristics of drama in the more specialized or strict sense in which we are accustomed to think of this art form. Drama involves tension or suspense, and development of a theme to a resolution. The phenomena of *amok* and *latah*, with their suspense and development, may be termed drama without ritual, though the drama is of a relatively underdeveloped kind, and

elements of routine and convention are present. There can presumably be also some simple forms of ritual where the dramatic
elements are minimal, where the resolution of a situation is so
well-known or guessed in advance that suspense and development
are almost completely lacking. But drama also involves both a
formal or stylized character and some power of abstraction, so
that the situations to which it refers are not merely empirically
descriptive but have a more general quality and as such some
explanatory value. In these respects the spirit medium performances of Kelantan are rather deficient in dramatic character. The
language is stereotyped and follows conventional formulae; the
expository dialogue is also stiff and formal for the most part. But
it is relatively unstructured, of narrow range, concerned with
immediate circumstance rather than with more general problem.
The patient, the master of ceremonies, above all the medium,
each offers a special presentation of the self, a facet of his own
personality which is not shed completely when the show is over.
The audience, too, though spectators, are themselves for the most
part directly involved in the situation, as relatives, friends, neighbours, and may be personally concerned in the outcome. The
situation is not a constructed one, conceived with any representative character; it deals with real people here and now. The plot
is not worked out in advance but allowed to evolve as the action
proceeds. The end is not known at the time of the beginning.
Actors, spectators and patient all have a fairly clear idea of the
general plan of what is about to occur, but their speculations as
to the exact resolution of the situation may vary widely. It is like
a scene in a theatre workshop where the play is allowed to
develop freely out of the reactions between the actors. There is
lacking what Virginia Wolf has called the 'single vision' of an
author.

Now I revert to Jane Harrison. One of the points which I have
found of great interest in her analysis was the significance she
attached to the role of the *spectator* in this developmental theory
of the evolution of drama from ritual. She distinguished very
clearly between participants and worshippers acting and dancing
out the ritual, and spectators 'watching, feeling, thinking, not
doing'. She emphasized how it is in this new attitude of the
spectator that we touch on the difference between ritual and art.
'The dromenon, the thing actually done by yourself, has become
a drama, a thing also done but abstracted from your doing'

(1913: 127). Without necessarily subscribing to such a theory of development in Greek aesthetic history, I can note its relevance at the present time, in Kelantan. In the small household where a simple rite is performed over a sick person with a formula or two and some incense, perhaps also a mild act of spirit medium-ship without orchestra or controller, the spectator element is minimal. The people are assembled to do a certain job and few come to watch. The dramatic element is at a low level. But for the full village performance of the *main puteri* scores of spectators may assemble, attracted as much by the spectacle as by the interest in a cure. They assemble particularly of course also when the performance has a general exorcising effect for the village.

I want to elaborate a little this point of *spectator role*. In non-literate communities such as those of which I have spoken, art is used commonly to make statements about religious values – these religious values themselves being symbolic conceptualizations of human problems. This has significance in modern conditions. During much of this century the *main puteri* performances in Kelantan have been under some fire from the modernists on the one hand, especially the medical men, who think this a backward peasant custom, and from the Muslim orthodox on the other, who regard it as a challenge to the purity of Islam. The spirit medium experts themselves defend their position. They are good Muslims, performing all their religious duties at least as well as do their neighbours, and they regard themselves as invoking their spirit aids through the help of Allah for the repelling of evil spirits who otherwise would afflict true believers. But among Malays, followers of Islam, graphic religious art involving por-trayal of the human figure is forbidden – there are in a mosque no images or pictures of saints or angels, let alone of God, which would be a terrible offence. From the point of view of an ortho-dox Muslim dignitary, an Imam or other leader, the Kelantan spirit medium performance is suspect, I think, on two grounds. Firstly, it ascribes validity to jinn and other spirit beings who, while not figments of the imagination, are given a role far exceed-ing anything allowed them by the Koran which recognizes them but lays the direction of human affairs in the hands of Allah (Koran 1909, Sura lxxii, *Djinn*). The spirit medium then is traf-ficking with powers which he should leave alone or to which he should deny potency. Unless he is careful, he comes close to being accused of the prime heresy of 'giving God a partner' –

God who is One only, without associate. Secondly (though I do not remember to have heard this stated), he may be thought to be giving these powers a material form, a human figure, which is against the spirit of Islam.

Now for the spirit medium performance to be envisaged as drama rather than ritual, what is required is a detachment of the participant, or at least those who attend to watch, from a personal involvement in the issues portrayed. Drama has moral as well as aesthetic values. But such detachment allows the tension-pattern of what is being performed to be viewed as nonrepresentational, as a general statement about human values and actions and not a specific statement of the here-and-now kind. But for effective conversion of ritual presentation to drama another change may be necessary: a change in the validity ascription. Those who attend the spectacle in Kelantan village circles ordinarily believe in the overt truth of what they see and hear, in the sense that they credit the speech and action of the spirit medium and his companions as being correct portrayals of what they claim. But more sophisticated Malays, more highly educated, or more pious, or more committed to the Muslim theocratic system, either deny the reality of what is being claimed and done or admit its reality and deny its propriety.

This illustrates the two alternatives that commonly face a ritual performance which is in danger of becoming outmoded. If belief in its truth and validity remains, but its propriety is questioned, then in the long run it will tend to be abandoned. Two parallel ritual systems are in conflict and one must give way. Historically this has happened with many spirit medium cults when confronted by Christianity. In the Malay Muslim field it happened already to such spirit cults – at least those with orchestral accompaniment – in the highly pious Muslim state of Trengganu, adjacent to Kelantan. But a process of secularization, of 'de-mythologizing' of the spirit medium phenomena, may take place instead with the growth of education and general sophistication. If such a change of belief has taken place – if the performance be no longer regarded as a portrayal of actually existent spirits – then a way is open for the survival of it as drama rather than as ritual.

This is a hypothesis but not mere speculation since the present-day situation in Malaya offers a test case.

From time to time it has happened that a spirit medium performance, in common with shadow play and other entertainments, has been offered as part of the celebrations on some public occasion in Kelantan, such as the Sultan's birthday. Again, such a performance has sometimes been staged in order that visitors could make a film record. Here the *main puteri* is admitted as a cultural rather than a ritual spectacle. It entertains both those who believe in the reality of the spirits conjured up and those who do not.[8] This is the precedent for translating private into public spectacle. No sick person is needed as a subject; the performance can always be thought to have the effect of clearing away undesirable spiritual influences from the public place.

But the absence of a patient creates a problem: where is the drama without a central figure who can suffer and who can be cured? And what is to take the place of the unity of theme ordinarily enforced upon the action by the logic of the therapeutic diagnosis and treatment? And can such generalized recreational performances be thought really to command the attention of spirits?

Here two thoughts come to mind in a move from ritual to drama: one of content, the other of form. As regards content, it would be possible to create a purported performance, with a mock patient and a mock cure – perhaps even a mock trance, which is not unknown in the ordinary spirit medium display. It would be not just a bogus imitation, but a serious illustration of the village cult, an indication of how in less enlightened and less well-endowed times, the villagers met the problems of evil and human ills. As regards form, for dramatic effect the performance should obviously be enormously curtailed and the action tightened up. Moreover, the title might be taken out of Jeanne Cuisinier's book, and for aesthetic purposes these cult performances be regarded primarily as dances. One can envisage how they might be treated choreographically, with a good deal of miming, with development to climax and release, assisted by the orchestra in much the present style. What about the reluctance of ritual specialists to lend themselves to such public mime and to such modifications? Here is one great persuader – money. The sums which these spirit mediums get from their performances are not large, but they are keenly sought, in view of their low peasant incomes, and they are always eager to put on what is primarily a recreational show in a village when requested. Indeed, what I miss perhaps most in Jane Harrison's reconstruction of how ancient Greek ritual gave birth to drama is any reference to the place of economic factors in such a transition.

But there are several elements which may militate against the success of such a translation from spirit medium performance to secular drama in Malaya.

The first is the attitude of the Islamic authorities. If they continue to regard the *main puteri* as dealing or purporting to deal with real spirit presences, instead of merely being vaguely symbolic of human suffering and its folk treatment at the village level, then their opposition may well stifle its development as a dramatic form. The second element is competition from other forms of art and recreation, principally of course the cinema. In the village the *main puteri* still attracts an audience who look for thrills and amusement as well as for therapy. But what the Malays call the 'image play' (*wayang gambar*),[9] that is the cinema, and not the puppet play, is a terrific magnet, especially for the young, and for this they are willing to pay whereas the spirit medium performance is free for onlookers. Clearly, for a successful translation of spirit medium rite into drama the financial structure of the whole situation would have to be re-ordered, and also the career structure for the performers.

Finally, there is the question of belief and incentive. With detachment of performance from its basic objective, relief from affliction and suffering, the basis of credence is likely to alter. The performers may still believe in spirits but not in their presence on this occasion. If their belief in its extra-human validity disappears, then this may rob the presentation of much of its vivid quality.

But there is one possible stimulus to the creation of a new dramatic form, that is the influence of developing cultural nationalism. The new nations of today are keenly searching among their traditional practices for elements that can be adapted to modern needs. They want cultural background, historical respectability, unifying mechanisms that will help them to get more effective cooperation from their people, material to build up a more striking public image. Some of them have discovered in their rustic songs, dances and ceremonies, as also in some of their more abstract folk concepts, material for which they can claim the dignity of tradition, a cultural individuality and an aesthetic appeal. Re-worked to fit the requirements of the stage such material, some of it formerly of ritual character, has been presented by national theatrical and dance troupes all over the world during the last forty years. It is an ironic thought that the politician and his even more alert rival the public relations man are now discovering virtues in customs which previously only the anthropologist was prepared to defend!

The future of folk rituals is a question of much broader relevance than in the context of Malaysia. But it is a problem well worth investigation. It is too early yet to say what will be the future of the Kelantan spirit medium performance. It could be that the modern values of cultural nationalism will enter to replace those of traditional belief, that the state and not the local community will provide a career structure, and assist in the conversion of a ritual into a dramatical spectacle, with aesthetic and recreational interest, if not moral force. But one question will still remain: who in the village, when Western medicine has full sway, will give that psychological release and reassurance which the traditional therapy helped to provide?

Chapter 7

Faith and scepticism in Kelantan village magic

This chapter has several aims. Ethnographically, it gives data on Kelantan Malay magic in a coastal area, mainly from 1939–40, before modern education reached the people. It shows how folk beliefs and practices existed side by side with orthodox Islam. More theoretically, it explores the problem of local beliefs in magic and religion, and challenges common monolithic views of Malay magic as a unitary self-sufficient system of general credence. Even in recent publications one may read of 'the Malay world-view' or 'Malay magical thought' as if all Malays, even nowadays, shared the same ideas. My argument to the contrary is that certainly nowadays, and even a generation ago, in a part of Malaysia which has been recognized as a stronghold of magical practices, Malays have been more pragmatic, shown more variation in their beliefs, been more experimental in their attitudes, than could be inferred from the literature.

From material collected by my wife and me during two periods in Kelantan I examine some aspects of the magic of agriculture, of fishing, of personal protection and healing. Much of my argument revolves around the interpretation of specific incidents in which particular magicians and an audience took part, because so much discussion of Malay magic has been couched in general terms which obscure significant elements in the social setting. Certainly I agree that Malay folk beliefs used – and to some degree still use – a general conceptual framework expressed in such terms as *ilmu, tuntut, ubat, semangat, hantu, keramat*, which may be crudely translated as knowledge, revelation, medicine, soul, spirit, superhuman power. These and many other concepts can be integrated at an abstract level into a system, but it is a system with much variation in different sectors of Malay society and with different individuals; inferences from it alone may give a very false idea of what any actual person believes and does. Some people integrate such notions with their Muslim theological concepts, others reject a great part of them. The more magical aspect of them may not be denied, but depending upon the age, sex, occupation and education of a person they may be utilized more or less; their validity may be not so much questioned as ignored. On the other hand, obscure factors in a person's history, such as illness or other misfortune, may incline him more than others to belief in the greater immediacy and truth of such folk resources. So, in the same community, faith and scepticism in magical concepts and practices may appear side by side in different people, or even alternate in the same person at different periods.

By magic in this context I mean action, primarily ritual action, based on belief in superhuman power, directed to a specific aim, and regarded as efficacious in itself. (Anthropologists will recognize in this statement that I have taken position on some classical theoretical issues, but do not feel it necessary to defend this here.) The notion of faith has its own complexities. When it is said that a person believes in or has faith in a certain set of magical concepts and practices, there are several possibilities. He may think the concept is a true one, and be prepared to implement his belief by appropriate action. He may think the concept is true, but not think that it applies to his particular situation and therefore not be willing to do anything concrete about it. He may think that the concept is true in general, but that it is untrue as a description of the particular item before him. Or he may doubt the truth of the concept in general but think that in particular cases there may be 'something in it', so that he takes the precaution of acting as if it were true. From consideration of the Kelantan situations we observed, I would argue that instances of all this occurred, as well as more radical scepticism which would deny the validity of much that was put forward as magical knowledge and action. Insofar as faith is regarded as a confident expectation of a given result, it will be seen that this was often lacking among our Malay friends, whose attitude towards magical practices tended to be much more dubious, even experimental. And if, as sometimes is said, faith constitutes a defence against surprise, here too weaknesses in belief were revealed. On the other hand, magical practitioners often operated with assurance, displayed considerable authority, and were ingenious in reinterpreting untoward events in terms of their own system of extra-human concepts.

MAGIC OF THE 'RICE SOUL'

I begin with consideration of agricultural magic, especially in regard to the *semangat padi*, the so-called 'rice soul'. Consideration of the concept of *semangat padi* shows definite variation here from the conventional ideas of the homogeneity of the treatment of the 'rice soul' throughout Malaya (Skeat 1900: 250n; Shaw 1926: 20; Winstedt 1951: 39, 55; Endicott 1970; 23). In fields immediately inland from the Bachok coast, on the seaward side of the Kemasin river, a fair amount of rice was grown, by both 'dry' and 'wet' methods. The cultivators recognized the validity of the notion of *semangat padi* as the vital principle of rice, but tended to regard it as contextually determined for ritual purposes. Some did celebrate rites in connection with it, but to a limited degree; others did not celebrate it at all. The reasons given were pragmatic. It was said that more rites were performed elsewhere, in places nearer forest, as in Besut, where, it was said, offerings were formally set out. But locally, it was argued, offerings to the 'rice soul' were not generally made since the fields were 'in the middle of the land' with no 'ailments' such as pigs or other forest animals to destroy the rice (cf. Downs 1967: 171). Again, it was stated that only if a person cultivated a lot of padi (that is many hundred *gantang*, or gallons) did he *buat semangat padi*; and as I saw, many ordinary cultivators with small crops did not do so. Even if the cultivator was himself a magical practitioner in other matters he might not do so. One man, a line-fisherman who produced also 100–150 gantang of padi per season, practised as a *bomoh* with *siup* technique (see later); but though a ritual specialist for healing, using traditional concepts of soul and of magical protection, he saw no need to practise magic for his rice. And owners of fields which yielded large crops, but who had leased out these fields to other cultivators, took no pains to see that any *semangat padi* rites were carried out; they regarded this as entirely an affair of their tenants.

There were traditional ideas of a magical order about the local agriculture: a scheme of lucky and unlucky days; notions of a 'fruitful hand' akin to the 'green thumb' of English gardening. One man kept to hoeing and left all planting to his wife because the Lord didn't give him bounty, but what she planted grew. The concept of *semangat padi* was used at times in a concrete way, equivalent to the notion of quality of a rice, as having a 'harsh essence' (*semangat keras, padi dia keras nasi*) or a 'pleasant essence' (*bau bangin, bau sedap, semangat ini*). But there were also traditional ideas of the *semangat padi* as a being of a more personal order, highly sensitive to rough treatment, so that it would enter the dreams of a cultivator at night, weeping, to complain. Yet despite such ideas, I could not get any informant to admit the correctness of statements by Wilkinson and others (Wilkinson 1906: 50; 1932: 604; Skeat 1900: 227; Endicott 1970: 149) that the small harvest knife (*tuai*, in Kelantan *ketaman*) was used because otherwise the *semangat padi* would be angry. One man (a fisherman) said it might be true of the country of the person who alleged this, but it was not true of Kelantan. Another (a rice cultivator) denied that it made any difference to the *semangat padi* whether the knife or the sickle was used; he argued that the farmers of the west coast used the slashing sickle method, and their rice was better than that of Kelantan.

This last man did actually perform some rites over the *semangat padi*, though they were relatively simple. Awang-Meh Sari, though he used to go to sea before he had children, had spent most of his life as a cultivator. When I knew him in 1940 he had fifteen fields of rice, yielding between 400 and 700 gantang of padi a year. He grew vegetables extensively; he owned four cattle. Awang said that he himself did not actually *buat semangat* with full rites; he simply took a small sheaf (handful) of padi and put it away 'in the place' in the granary attached to his house. I asked if I might see the place and he became embarrassed; he said one could not go in at midday; that the old people said that if one goes in at midday the padi gets 'chilled' (*sejuk*, a common term in magical vocabulary to indicate lowered resistance). He added that in the early morning it would be all right, and when I asked again he invited me for the next day when the sun should be only a little above the horizon. At 7.30 a.m. I went to his house. He warned me not to speak when we entered the granary, and told me that children were not allowed there at all. I put out my cigarette as a sign of respect but noticed that Awang himself went in smoking. He took a lamp and held it down for me to see. In a large basket of the type used for storing rice or salt lay two sheaves of padi, together with a dry coconut, a working adze, and a small basket tray containing water in a shell, oil in the bottom of a china cup, bananas and sugar cane. There appeared also to be earth in the bottom of the basket, but Awang said this was not significant.

That there were two sheaves of padi was not particularly relevant; Awang said it didn't matter if there were one or two. But the dry coconut and the materials on the tray were significant, and were described in traditional classificatory rhythm: *nyior sa buteh; ayer (ai) sa chawan; minyak sa titek; pisang sa buteh; tebu sa ruah*: a coconut; a cup of water; a drop of oil; a banana bunch; a sugar cane node. All these were components of magical offerings. The working adze had caught my attention. I thought it might represent the sacralization of a working tool. No, said Awang, it was there only for security – he was afraid people might otherwise want to borrow it; it had no connection with the *semangat padi*. (This was a cautionary lesson to the anthropologist not to jump to conclusions!) The large basket was used as an ordinary rice store as well as a ritual repository, the tray of offerings and the sheaves of *semangat padi* being simply lifted up on top. The remainder of the rice crop was stored in a separate shed. At the end of each ritual season the old ritual sheaves were not thrown away but left at the bottom of the basket; only after ten years or so might the oldest ones be thrown out. There was thus a continuous succession in the *semangat padi*, since each heap had sheaves of successive years. (What I had taken to be earth at the bottom of the basket was probably the residue of former sheaves.)

Awang described his procedure in taking the ritual sheaves. He selected grain heads that 'look towards the house', that is, which curved that way. The idea of this was that the *semangat padi* should 'return to the house'. After these particular sheaves had been taken and deposited, the owner does not visit his fields for two days following; he may do so only on the third day. Why? 'The *semangat padi* doesn't like it.' the concept of the *semangat padi*, as described by Awang, was that it was like a child, easily disturbed, pleasured by simple things. He said that the sheaves of *semangat padi* were cut by himself alone, in the very early morning, when it was truly dark. He could speak to no-one, and he had to return at once. The *semangat padi* would become 'chilled' if these observances were not kept, and would 'flee to the west', which was its origin. And 'if the *semangat* is lacking, we will hunger, what will we do?' As for the offerings, the *semangat padi*, like a child, likes these things, but does not eat them.

According to local tradition it is good to complete all critical operations concerned with padi in the morning. With planting of either 'dry' or 'wet' rice it is good to finish and return in the morning, and it is good also to finish the padi harvest in the morning. The elders say it is not good to finish and bring back the last sheaves of padi in the afternoon – 'the *semangat padi* likes to return in the morning'. When the padi was harvested, said Awang, according to the elders, a little should be left standing for the birds, and the old people had an instruction (*pesan*) for this, in the form of a chant:

He! Semangat semangin	Hey! Spirit
Mu berusong berdola	You're carried in a litter
Beripung bertambun ka rumah aku	Heaped up to my house
Hampar-hampar	Spread out there
Tinggal ka burong berian	Leave a gift for the birds
Sedekah ka dia lah![1]	As charity for them!

So, said Awang, merit will go to a man who works padi.

But despite such views about the sensitivity of the rice soul and the possibility of loss if it were not ritualized, most rice cultivators to whom I spoke seemed tough-minded on the practical issue. So a woman rice cultivator confirmed the saying of the elders about bringing in the last of the padi at harvest in the morning; but she attributed it to prudence – otherwise it would be eaten by the chickens! When I asked about the custom of leaving a little for the wild birds she seemed indifferent – when they are hungry they come and eat anyway, she commented.

In general I had the impression that the attitude towards agricultural magic in this area, even among rice planters, was rather informal and casual. It was not so much sceptical as pragmatic: people who carried out the rites did so as precaution because of the scale of their operations, and from respect to tradition, not because they regarded these rites as obligatory in themselves. The rites were not of *pars pro toto* kind, done on behalf of the total harvest of the community. They were individual, often modified and curtailed, and small operators totally ignored them. There was some belief, some suspension of judgement, in their validity, and a general disinclination to implement ideology by ritual activity.

TRADITION AND NOVELTY IN FISHING MAGIC

The situation was very different with fishing. Earlier I have dealt very briefly (Raymond Firth 1966: 122–5) with the part played by magic in the Kelantan fishing industry, particularly in placating sea spirits and in enabling master fishermen to 'meet with fish'. Whereas rice cultivators who celebrated the 'rice soul' tended to rely on their own resources, and master fishermen might perform some magic rites, Kelantan fishing has often been supplemented by magical aids of other kinds. Apart from general belief in the over-riding concept of the bounty of Allah, which might be granted or withheld at the will of the All-Mighty, help was sought from men of learning or holiness in the Muslim religious field, and from professional magicians (*bomoh*),[2] some of whom had no direct knowledge of the sea and fishing.

To illustrate local beliefs in fishing magic, including beliefs in its relation to Islam, I describe here a particular type of rite performed by a Muslim religious man (*orang lebai*), and its effect upon the local circle of fishermen. To set this in perspective I outline the general course of events in the fishing season of 1940, especially as seen by several master fishermen closely connected with this ritual. (For convenience I indicate the magical practitioner as B, and the master fishermen as L, M and P – cf. Firth 1966: 109–11, 383, for some details of the fishing season and the receipts of L and M.)

I first consider the position of M. He was an intelligent man of long fishing experience who combined a rather self-consciously pious attitude towards Islam with a firm belief in spirits of the sea. With his dry, often subtle sense of humour and whimsical realism in discussing human relationships, his comments were among the most revealing offered to us. As the fishing season developed I noted several fairly distinct elements in his interpretation of success or failure. (The account is much compressed from my notebook.) Early in 1940 he like other fishermen was complaining about lack of success, and he had gone to a local holy man, To' Wali Awang of Bukit Merbau, to bless some rice he had taken, by stirring a finger in it. M spoke also of a net magician (*bomoh pukat*) living inland, whom local fishermen used. This man did not 'use *hantu*' but only the Koran; he too uttered formulae over rice. M said he had called in this man a year or so before but without 'agreement' – he got no good catches as a result.

When M began to get good catches his first statement was in orthodox Muslim terms, for the bounty of Allah, expressed particularly through prayer and the blessing of the holy man. Early in February M got his new net ready and on his first day out he brought in the best catch of his village. I chaffed him about this, because the day before he had been very vague about making the traditional net offerings, and I thought he had not done these magic rites. I said 'But you didn't make the offerings!' He answered with a twinkle 'Made them – last night!' He had nine 'pious men' to perform the 'prayers of hope' (Firth 1966, plate IIb) and one afterwards to make the offerings. For about a week he was very successful, and was elated, saying that other master fishermen would be very 'sick' at this outstanding performance; he likened their competition to cocks fighting and giving peck for peck. To draw him I said I supposed his success was due to his having had the fishing ground very much to himself, and to luck; he agreed, but added 'Tuhan Allah'. 'There it is – I think Tuhan Allah gives to me.' On another occasion he said 'Tomorrow, if Tuhan Allah grants, I shall get fish.' When he got a phenomenal catch, while many other nets got nothing, he said, obviously very pleased, that he was 'in agreement' – equivalent to being 'in luck'. He said that his success was due to To' Wali, the holy man, and hence to God. He added that six or seven fishing experts had gone to the holy man, but that he 'agreed' usually with only one or two. I asked why? He replied 'I don't know' but added with a laugh 'perhaps because if with all, they would all become rich, would all build tile houses, and the price of large boats would go up to $300!' But this idea that magical discrimination was necessary to avoid inflation was not meant very seriously. He said however that the arts of the holy man were often effective for only a week or so, instancing examples. (Note the pragmatic aspect of this: the chances are that one or two fishermen will have success, but that their success will not continue for very long unless they have exceptional skill. What success that occurs can then be attributed to the immediate selective virtue of the holy man's blessing.)

Traditional folk ideas also played a considerable part in M's thinking about fishing. Towards the end of February I met him one evening with a ritual smear of rice paste on his forehead –

he had just been dyeing his net according to his usual practice, weekly, with appropriate rites asking for blessing and the goodwill of sea spirits. As an instance of his magical belief, he said he had just met another expert who had just put ropes on his new net. 'I told him that he will probably get fish; a new net gets fish.' I asked if offerings would be made over it. He answered 'One must; if it is a new net, one must make offerings.' He went on to say that if it had been him he would not have put ropes on the net that day. Why, because it was Friday, the day one goes to mosque? No, because it was the 14th day of the 4th month (by local Malay reckoning) On the 4th, 14th, and 24th of the 4th month one should not do work on the net – nor also on the 3rd, 13th and 23rd of the 3rd month, and so on. The net would foul the lure, and break. 'But would you not go to sea?' I asked. 'Going to sea, that doesn't matter,' he replied. But he added that if it were for (ordinarily) the first time in a season, the opening day, he wouldn't. He quoted a colloquial saying which may be rendered as 'An ill-starred day, 'twill tear the net' – so old people said. Then he went on 'but if a *juru selam* has knowledge, a bit of revelation, it doesn't matter'. M was convinced that boat measurements could express relationships of good and bad fortune in fishing (Firth 1966: 145), and inclined to believe that there were ways of injuring another man's net so that it wouldn't get fish. He told me that an *ubat* could be prepared by mixing hair of pig or tiger (both animals unmentionable at sea) with an infusion of *lurak salah* (a medicinal plant, unidentified); if this were put in a kind of Siamese pot for keeping rice warm and secreted in the boat carrying the net, it would be prevented from getting fish. Such an *ubat* could cost $5 to $10 – a vast sum in 1940. He said that one fisherman alleged such magical interference with his net and so had not gone out to sea for a month; that a *bomoh* to whom he had gone for help refused to come, saying, 'That is a net to which people have done evil'. Yet M was doubtful about the efficacy of much-vaunted talismans such as ambergris (Raymond Firth 1966: 125). He distinguished between 'true' ambergris, which he described as the vomit of a large fish, and alleged ambergris from Mecca, which he had already used to no avail, and he held sceptically that while real ambergris was very dear that which people sold as such probably wasn't true anyway. Certain traditional taboos he categorically denied. I had been told that umbrellas should not be carried on a fishing boat. M argued that this was not correct. He said he took an umbrella himself in the rainy season, and suggested that I take one on my own boat; he said he had seen umbrellas occasionally on boats at Beserah in Pahang, and that when parties including women travelled to Semerak, Besut and other places they must have umbrellas against the midday sun. He added that people of the Perhentian islands, who were wise in all sea lore, brought umbrellas and even shoes with them when they came to the mainland. He certainly did not subscribe rigidly to a rule against mixing terrestrial with marine categories of objects. He was not without magical reservations. He said that one thing was prohibited on a boat, a certain kind of pandanus mat; if this was taken aboard a sailing boat there would be no wind. Yet even here he commented shrewdly, 'I think this is not true either – if it is taken in the season when there is plenty of wind, how will a mat stop it?'

With this critical intelligence and pious tendency, he might have been expected to reject the more purely magical rites connected with traditional *hantu*. Yet here he displayed an uncertainty, a swing in opinion, which showed his more orthodox and more sophisticated views to some extent at war with the strength of his involvement in his daily striving for fish and for reputation. He was no blind adherent of magic. Towards the end of the season, when fish were very scarce, P said 'There are no fish, so people are using *bomoh*.' Commented M caustically, 'When fish are plentiful *bomoh* don't matter; all men get fish'. But he also held that if fish were not in season then it was no good making offerings; the object of the offerings was to get men to 'meet with fish', not to conjure up fish out of nowhere. He said 'If I don't get fish for several days, and all other men are getting fish, *then* I make the offerings, so that the sea spirits will be pleased, and I will meet with fish.'

The critical elements in M's judgement of the validity of magical performance emerged especially in his attitudes towards the practices of B, who while generally a minor scholar and teacher of religion, also served on occasion as *bomoh*. At an early stage in the 1940 season M had employed B to make the offerings for his net, and continued to give him alms as a kind of retaining fee. But M was clearly ambivalent about B's powers. He said at the start 'B is only a little skilled; he's not a man of the sea', and attributed his own net's success as much to the blessing of the holy man (who, however, was not a 'man of the sea' either!). When M heard that another fisherman, L, whom he did not rate highly, was going to have B also make net offerings he was scornful – 'all the same, I think he won't get any fish; he is not skilled; if he makes the offerings today, tomorrow, he won't get above other people. You will be able to see; he's not skilled.' And he laughed and said 'We shall see'.

Now M's general estimate of L was about right, but in fact, whether through a spurt of enthusiasm generated by knowledge of the offerings or not, L's net did actually get a bumper catch the next day. This was generally attributed to the efforts of B. When next evening I asked M what he thought he replied 'I think B has magic power (*ada keramat*).' He said he thought that B was 'true' and skilled. Some day before, P, an old fishing expert and *bomoh*, had said to him that in making offerings to land spirits B was wrong; that one should invoke only sea spirits for fishing, and on the beach, not beside a house. Yet, M now thought, B was right: 'inland spirits can reach out to sea; sea spirits can reach inland.' However, M was much indebted to P, to whom he had been like an adopted son, and he added diplomatically 'when I am with P I follow him; when I am with B I follow him; I don't want to fight with them. But I think B is cleverer than P; I think B is *keramat*.'

Now this was a switch of opinion, as others too realized. Our servant Mamat, who had known B's father as a *bomoh besar*, and thought B himself was a clever *bomoh*, told me that four days previously M had said that he didn't trust B's performance. 'Now, he trusts!' (But P, with whom I discussed the matter, was still sceptical. His view was, let us wait and see; other nets for which B made offerings have got nothing as yet.)

A couple of days later M and I returned to the subject of fishing success. He held that only those master fishermen whose fathers had also been experts got fish. He quoted cases of men without ancestral heritage whose lack of success proved this. I asked why – do the dead watch over the sea? 'No, they don't come back,' he replied, but went on, 'I think they ask over there,' meaning that they intercede with Allah on behalf of their sons. He said that he himself went every Friday to the cemetery to ask his father, his mother and his dead child to make him rich and give him fish – he prayed to them. Their bones are in the grave, he said, but their spirits (he used the term *nyawa*) are yonder and have the shape of men. 'But do they hear?' I asked. 'People say they hear; if not, what is the good of going? It is simply work thrown away!' Then he came back to the subject of B. He said that about ten years before B had made offerings for one net, but no fish resulted, so he stopped. The net of M himself recently was the first net for which he had performed ritual since then. M then revealed that misleadingly he had told P – as indeed he had virtually told me too – that B had *not* made the offerings for him. He said he had told P, 'What is the good of getting him, a man of prayer, who doesn't go to sea . . .?' He said that he had talked in this vein, but then towards midnight, when all men were inside their houses, he had the rites performed. Afraid that if it were generally known that he had had the magic done, but got no fish, people would chaff him and he would be ashamed, he had given a false impression.

M continued to oscillate in his attitude towards the validity of B's magical technique. When other master fishermen were successful and he himself was not he said 'It is not that I am unskilled, no; I think that no fish have been given to me'. He had lost confidence in B. Retrospectively, he thought that on the days when L got large catches it was because Tuhan Allah had wished to give him fish; even if B had not acted as *bomoh*, L could easily have got the fish. M backed this up by pointing to two other expert fishermen for whom B had made offerings, and who had caught no fish. In order to draw him my wife commented 'It is as Tuhan Allah wills'. He replied rather sharply 'As Tuhan Allah wills – but the men of Perupok [his competitors] get the bulk of the cash'. He admitted that some people might have special powers: one fisherman, previously markedly successful, had lost his wife by death, and had had few good catches since. M commented 'I think his wife was *keramat*.' But thinking of the non-success of others beside himself he said in resignation 'Tuhan Allah gives to all the same.' He hoped that people would speak of himself as good-omened, of blessed mouth, and then he would continue to get fish. About *bomoh* he said that people went from one to another, seeking success, and if they couldn't go themselves they sent their womenfolk far afield, as far as Ketereh or Pasir Mas, to get rice or water that had been blessed. However, though M himself got no further large catches, when some fishermen for whom B had made the offerings did very well he reverted to his opinion that B was *keramat*. He also pointed out that P had

formerly acted as local *bomoh* for the nets, and was probably
ashamed to see that another had been successful where he had
not. He said 'perhaps the sea spirits like the offerings of B;
perhaps they don't like the offerings of P.' And he added rather
unfeelingly that P was an old man and perhaps he would die. M's
belief in B's powers was further demonstrated when his eyes
became very bloodshot from his work at sea. We put drops of
acriflavin in them but he also consulted B, who said that he had
been afflicted by sea spirits and recited a formula over them; he
then refused more medicine, saying that he would see the effects
of the formula first – though he consented to wear dark glasses
which we gave him, saying that B had also advised them.

So here was an expert fisherman who, having a great amount
of empirical knowledge of his craft, had also a set of beliefs of a
mystical order, mingling Islamic concepts of the bounty of Allah
with concepts of the power of sea spirits and the efficacy of
human ritual to placate them. But he did not have a simple blind
faith. He did not operate 'in obedience to the rules which the
superstitious people have followed for ages' (Clifford 1897: 148;
also Skeat 1900: 193). Doubt, suspension of judgement and even
scepticism were mingled with his belief. A constant theme in his
whole situation was his faith in the control exercised by the will
of Allah over the destinies of men – this he never questioned.
But a variable factor, in his judgement, was the degree to which
the bounty of Allah was being accorded to him personally. Yet
this was cross-cut by two other elements. One was the pragmatic
nature of the situation: if it was the season when fish were normally absent, or if fish were present but the interference of
another fisherman spoiled the shooting of his net, then he
attributed his poor catch to these empirical factors and not to
lack of Allah's favour. Nor were the rituals of magic, in his view,
designed for such situations; they were for situations where fish
were available but he was not getting them. The test in particular
was where other fishermen were getting catches but he was not.
This was where in his view offerings to spirits could be useful.
But offerings in themselves could not remedy lack of fishing skill
– hence his protests in the case of L. Yet if a *bomoh* were
powerful enough (*keramat*) then he might overcome even relative
lack of fishing skill, though only for a short time. Hence his
concession that, after all, the performances of B did seem to
give results. Note that his position was not quite that which

anthropologists have generally recognized – where the efficacy of the ritual in general is not questioned but only the proficiency of individual practitioners. The position of M was more complex. The efficacy of the will of Allah was not questioned, but the efficacy of the arts of *bomoh* was subject to continual scrutiny – not just individual *bomoh*, but all *bomoh*. Only when empirical evidence seemed to indicate that they had produced results was he willing to concede their validity. But his alternation of faith and scepticism about the performances of *bomoh* did not mean that he lacked a general belief in the significance of magical forces. Apart from his free use of the concepts of *hantu* and of *keramat*, for instance, he recognized various rules of a mystical order, especially when backed by the authority of the elders. What he questioned was not so much the operation of mystical forces as the abiity of men to cope with them. What did emerge very clearly with M was his tendency to retreat from faith in *bomoh* to faith in Allah – not at all the conventional picture of 'Malay first and Muhammedan afterwards' which is often offered in the older literature (e.g. Clifford 1897).

Another complicating element in M's attitudes was the problem of the extent to which modern changes had rendered old concepts and practices invalid. However, he did not seem as much bothered by this as did P, who as a *bomoh* of long standing had more of a vested interest in traditional matters. On one occasion P admitted with a laugh that while nets should be ritually sprinkled in order to get fish, as tradition dictated, nets which had not been sprinkled also took fish. He added, with a twist of his mouth, wryly, 'They don't understand, they haven't learnt, they don't know' – a kind of rather bitter 'ignorance is bliss' view.

The position of the *bomoh* B was also very interesting. He was a producer, not a consumer, of fishing magic; yet, a professedly religious man, he was operating with traditional local concepts of *hantu*. I was impressed by his apparent modesty and sincerity. He took the line that his role was to aid fishermen, not to substitute for them. 'Just to help', was his slogan. When L got his first phenomenal catch of fish B was sitting near by on the sand when the carrier boat came in. After the fish had been sold he asked me how much it fetched. When I told him he said 'Good!' So I asked him 'What if it had been a poor catch?' 'What about it, Tuan, I would help again.' His view was that his rites, if effective, helped to stop the fish from bolting the net, so that the fisherman had a fair chance to catch them.

B allowed me to be present when he performed his rites over the net of L; they began about 9 p.m. at the house where the net was kept, on the verandah. The master fisherman, who was also the major net owner, and four members of his crew constituted the group, apart from a few children on the outskirts. First the *bomoh* laid a cotton thread of three strands in the middle of some soft wax and moulded it to candle shape. A tray of conventional offerings had been prepared, and from it B took an egg, examined it close to his eye and then stuck the candle upright against it. He called for *beras kunyit* – rice with some shavings of turmeric root in it. Holding this in his hands and facing towards the sea (away from Mecca, in itself significant for a ritual address by a man of religious learning) he recited a long formula. From time to time he stirred the rice with his finger. (He was rocking slowly from side to side, a movement which I had noted he made also in ordinary conversation.) Most of the formula was inaudible, but occasionally he spoke more loudly, enabling me to hear what seemed to be characteristic phrases of the kind used by *bomoh*, addressed to jinn and *hantu* by name, and asserting that the reciter knew their origins. One of the principal spirits I heard addressed was Jinn Kuning, generally believed in Kelantan peasant circles to be very powerful. Then the *bomoh* passed the tray of offerings through incense smoke and recited another long formula.

The group then adjourned outside the house, on the earth below. A sail had been put up as a windbreak; the net remained on the verandah. I asked if I could see exactly what was to be done. B said 'Yes, but it is good if you keep ten feet away,' and I noted that part way through the rite he ordered one man who had inched forward to within about six feet to get back. At this stage the offerings were divided into three portions: (i) for consultation; (ii) for placing at the boats; (iii) for throwing into the sea.

(i) Consultation. The *bomoh* took a *parang* (short chopper) and with it dug a rectangular hole in the earth behind the sail screen. He stuck the parang in the soil at the side, then carefully slid the first portion of offerings on a banana leaf off the plate into the bottom of the hole. The top of the egg was broken with the parang and the egg added again to the offerings – having been opened for the spirits. The candle was lit from a lamp used hitherto to illuminate the scene, the lamp was extinguished, and the candle too was lowered into the hole. Then B, with knees apart, recited another formula, observing the flame the while. He sprinkled turmeric rice upon it, and also threw some of the rice up on to the net above, twice, part way through and at the end. Several times while the formula was being recited the flame died down, seeming as if it might go out, but then revived again.

(ii) Boat offering. Immediately afterwards, the rite over the boat took place. B sat in the boat, held rice paste in a brass bowl and recited a formula – a picturesque sight in the moonlight. The boat owner then sprinkled his boat with *ayer beluru* (medicated water, *beluru* being a large climbing plant, *Entada* sp., of which the bark has a pungent odour). B then sprinkled rice paste and burnt incense first under the bow and then under the stern of the boat. A similar rite was then performed for the carrier boat, used to bring catches of fish to shore. Each boat captain sprinkled his own boat with medicated water, one saying 'I just dare to do my own', as an indication of the awe with which the rite was viewed. The second portion of offerings was put by the sternpost of each boat.

(iii) Then the *bomoh* went down to the sea and stood in the water up to his shins; there he cast away the third set of offerings, and so completed the rite.

The formulae used, and most of the offerings, seemed to be part of the common stock of *bomoh*'s invocations and rites. But an idiosyncratic element, which was novel to the fishermen and which they did not pretend to understand, was the procedure with egg and candle, which seemed to involve very powerful spirits, needing special knowledge and confidence to control. Great interest was taken in the display and several fishermen came to discuss it with me. P emphasized that the results depended upon Allah and aid 'I have had no teacher for this; I don't understand the meaning of it. The people who use it know.' But he and the others thought that the candle flame gave sign of the advent of jinn of various kinds. He contrasted with this the procedures of *juru selam* who used only excerpts from the Koran as formulae, combined with smearing on rice paste. B himself took a very tentative attitude towards the efficacy of his rites. He was not sceptical about them, or cynical as M tended to be – it was rather that he seemed honestly to think that their outcome was uncertain. He said that he was the only man in the Perupok area to perform rites in this way – which was confirmed by the fishermen. He said also that he used the same technique in cases of sickness, but only a little – if a patient was crazy or had swollen limbs. His knowledge of what to do did not go far.

In accounting for the validity of his performance B explained that his grandfather and his father had been *bomoh*, but that while he had had a little instruction from his father his *guru* had been To' Mamat of Kota Bharu and Sungei Besar, who had been a pupil of his grandfather. B said that he used primarily Jinn Tanah, the Earth Spirit, in his rites (hence the adjournment to the ground outside the house, and the pit dug in the ground). As against the opinion of P he held that according to the teaching of his own guru, the spirits of the sea could ascend on to the shore, and spirits of the inland could be effective at sea. Hence he performed his rite inland, with the earth as location, instead of on the seashore – though he also invoked Anah, Manah, Ganah as spirits of the strand. He said that he had been told by his teacher not to invoke 'Sang Gano' (Sang Gana, cf. Cuisinier 1936: 163n), lest being always present but called upon only occasionally he be angry and make people ill. But he did use Semar (who, he said, originated in Mecca and was the first to become Haji – so in his view was obviously legitimate to invoke; this bears out Cuisinier (1936: 182n). Of the candle rite B said that he judged by the flame whether the jinn were 'in agreement', whether they desired the appeal. He obviously felt that in invoking these jinn he was dealing with dangerous forces. So he refused to recite his formula to me; he said that without the flame he was afraid – he couldn't tell what their attitude was. With the flame one could tell 'a little' about how the spirits would be likely to react: if the flame was small and red, it was Jinn Merah; if small and white, then Jinn Puteh; if clear, then Jinn Kuning. When the flame burned up brightly this was a good sign; if it died down, this was a bad sign. As for egg offerings (to Jinn Tanah) he used these according to the stage of the rite. On the first night he used only one egg, on the second night he used two; should his efforts still be unsuccessful he continued, adding an egg each night until he reached a total of seven. There he stopped – if no results had been obtained by then he would hand the case over to another *bomoh*, since it would be an indication that the jinn were not willing to cooperate with him. He explained the unique nature of his rites locally by pointing out that his teacher gave his *ilmu* to only one son, and to himself, B, who was like a son to him, and that he had no other pupil to whom he handed it on.

Though I did not challenge his religious orthodoxy directly I am sure that he regarded himself as doing a morally and theologically respectable job, controlling and directing the jinn in the interests of hungry and suffering humanity. I did question him on the general issue. He said quite definitely that an *orang lebai* might be a *bomoh*. Those with 'knowledge' might have it of two kinds – of the Koran and of the *bomoh* – and it was legitimate to use both if one had them. A religious man might 'blow' and make offerings. But he might not play the violin. Why not? Because the Prophet Muhammad didn't like it. Hence such a man couldn't conduct a *main puteri*. He himself could go into trance (*lupa*) but was embarrassed to do so. When I questioned whether the Imam and other dignitaries approved of religious men being *bomoh* he replied 'How can they be angry, when the Imam himself calls me in? When his son or his wife is sick, he calls me; he has been two or three times to do so.' He said also that To' Guru Bachok, a highly respected Muslim teacher, had the attitude, if a person is sick the thing is to clear it up – implying that the end justified the means. B said too that even *main puteri* was tolerated by Islamic dignitaries, provided it was held for one of their relatives in another house than their own. I emphasize that what I am giving here is essentially the viewpoint of a local man justifying himself, and a viewpoint in 1940; it is not necessarily a 'correct' view from the standpoint of the religious authorities, and it is not necessarily a modern view. But it was certainly widely held in the Bachok area fifty years ago, with sincerity and a sense of moral commitment.

The admitted uncertainty as to his results which B showed was the very antithesis of a common stereotype of a magician, often represented as boldly confident in the validity of his rites. Some Kelantan *bomoh*, such as my old teacher To' Mamat Mindok, were quietly and firmly convinced of their powers. This was perhaps partly temperamental, partly a matter of field – for, in the end, sick people probably get well more often than mediocre fishermen catch fish! But B behaved as a man who had in his possession a powerful but dangerous tool of the accuracy of which he was not certain, but with which he was willing to experiment, convinced of the propriety of his intentions. He might almost be described as a 'reluctant magician'. He certainly seemed very far from wanting to claim the quality of being possessed of supernatural power, as had sometimes been said of him. Gimlette, one of the most careful students of Kelantan magic, wrote of 'the self-reliance of the *bomoh* and his sublime belief in his calling' (1929: 52). As a general statement this can pass, but it must not be taken as applying to every instance, and it is important to realize this in order to understand the interplay between the producer and the consumer of magic, and the nature of interpretations given to it, including its relation to Islam.

THE CONCEPT OF KERAMAT

Though belief in Malay magic does not rest on the notion of *keramat* they are closely associated. The concept of *keramat* has often been discussed, and translations ranging from saint, shrine, venerable, sacred, miraculous, to prohibited, taboo, haunted have been suggested. It has been thought to apply basically to places and only secondarily to persons and things; it has been interpreted as representing a high concentration of *semangat*, of wonder-working power . . . and so on (Marsden 1812: 255; Favre 1875, I: 354; Skeat 1900: 673–4; Wilkinson 1903: 509; Cuisinier 1936: 31–3; Endicott 1970: 90–5). Many examples of the use of the term *keramat* were given to us in 1940. A *jitong (Gluta*-sp.), a large tree growing near the seashore, was pointed out as *keramat*. According to Gimlette and Thomson (1939, 97–8) such trees can yield an irritant juice used by 'vindictive natives of Kelantan' against their victims. We were not told this, but it was said that *hantu* liked such trees and were liable to strike people who passed beneath. A man of Kubang Golok who defecated beneath one could not rise from his crouching position until a *bomoh* was summoned, came and 'blew' upon him and hit him on the back. The *hantu* clawing at his posterior released their hold, and off he ran. When a *bomoh* neighbour of ours cut down a *jitong* tree he first made offerings near by; no one could take the wood for fires. An elephant by name Berma Sakti (the female principle of Brahma) was said by peasants to be *keramat*, and to be called every month to clear one of the Sultan's residences of evil. If a person was ill, and the elephant was called and given an offering of turmeric rice and bananas to eat, the evil was lifted. The animal was possessed by a *hantu* – 'If there's no *hantu*, there's no *keramat*; if there's a *hantu, keramat*' – but the name of the *hantu* was not known. The shadow play figures Pak Dogol and Wak Long were *keramat* as shown by the raw cotton threads round their necks. When a *dalang* presented me with a set of figures and asked me to choose which I would like he courteously refused to give me the current Pak Dogol, and gave me the current Wak Long with a request that I would let him take it away to his house for an hour or so (to be rendered innocuous). Other people told me that all Pak Dogol figures, even old disused ones, were *keramat*, and that if a woman were giving birth they should be kept under a platform or high on the wall where they could not be walked on, as they were dangerous. The *dalang* said that certain illnesses such as headache could be diagnosed as caused by Pak Dogol and consequently could be relieved only by his agency (cf. Cuisinier 1957: 83–90).

These examples are of objects regarded as possessing special powers which can be harmful to men but which may also be used to relieve illness. These powers are usually associated with *hantu*, and contact with them tends to be cautious, with elements of taboo. When the term *keramat* is applied to persons, especially to living persons, the associations are apt to be different. The taboo aspect tends to be subordinated to the creative power aspect; it is benefit rather than harm to people that tends to be emphasized. I think the best translation for *keramat* is usually extraordinary or superhuman power, with positive or negative aspects uppermost according to circumstances.[3] When the *bomoh* B was said by M to be *keramat*, elements of taboo were almost entirely lacking; it was the positive theme of recognition of his success that was expressed, success to an unexpected, seemingly superhuman degree. His success was thought to be due to his control of powerful *hantu*, but this putative control in itself implied that he had qualities lacking in ordinary people, and so worthy of respect. This positive aspect of the *keramat* quality that might attach to a living person came out very strongly in some of M's other remarks. When I asked him formally what the term meant he replied 'it's like the fever of a child – if To' Wali is *keramat*, he stops it' and he added significantly 'if the fever does not stop, perhaps he is not *keramat*.' This conditional attribution of *keramat* is a factor which I think should be strongly emphasized. It is essentially judgement by results. 'If a child loses a gold plaque, its parents may promise rice and bananas to To' Wali if they find it. If he is *keramat*, perhaps they will come across it.' The notion of *keramat* has a strong inferential aspect; it is an invisible power the presence of which is inferred from concrete events which are taken to be evidence. As an illustration of such power greater than normal M cited the behaviour of To' Wali Ismail, near Ketereh. To fishing experts with whom he was in good relations he gave blessed rice, passed his hands over their faces and said 'go to sea, tomorrow you will get fish'. But when M went to visit him he didn't appear – not that he was not present, but one could be quite close to him and not see him if he wished to be invisible, even if he was in the same room. On this occasion the Wali's son said he was in the room, but M could only hear his voice – the Wali announced that he was going to Mecca to pray, but would be back that afternoon!

Though to be *keramat* can connote sainthood, it was understood that a person who became *keramat* was not necessarily a man of great learning in religious matters. One of my friends said rather unkindly that the Wali of Bukit Merbau, who was *keramat*, would take thirty years of teaching before he could be the equal in learning of To' Guru Bachok, who was held in great esteem as a teacher. To be *keramat* could be the result of searching, a matter of obtaining special knowledge – *ilmu keramat*, it was stated, was different from other knowledge – and my informant said that he himself could ask for it. It was implied that in becoming *keramat* one came into the possession of a secret, and that one need not grow gradually into it. The Wali of Bukit Merbau was said, in 1940, to have been *keramat* for only a year, and he 'had become *keramat* at once' (I think, after the death of a predecessor). It was alleged that if To' Guru Bachok wished it, he could be ten times as *keramat* as the Wali of Bukit Merbau.[4] In all this, there was no suggestion of *keramat* being associated with any particular 'concentration of *semangat* (Endicott 1970: 93) which I think is a mistaken notion; *keramat* is an active, often offensive power, whereas *semangat* is a rather passive, sensitive, life principle.

In the local fishing magic, then, though there were recognized traditional procedures for seeking success, the attitude towards them tended to be exploratory, choosing between alternatives, testing by results, assigning or rejecting attributes of special powers to particular individuals. The fishermen by no means accepted and practised a completely unchallenged integral ritual system. The attitude to healing magic has much in common with this.

ROLE OF *BOMOH* IN PERSONAL PROTECTION

Concern for bodily health was a major field for exercise of a *bomoh*'s arts, since while agriculture or fishing were actually carried on by only a fraction of the coastal population, every member of it was liable to be afflicted by illness. While there was room for interpretation, illness commonly involved some concepts of spiritual attack and defence. Apart from any other specialism he might have, then, each *bomoh* usually had a set of magical (and putatively medical) procedures not only for healing, but also for protecting people against spirit harm. (For this reason some translations of *bomoh* have taken the medical/magical aspect of his work as primary.) Although there was considerable variation in individual procedures, the protective and healing techniques of *bomoh* in 1940 fell into several classes, involving formulae, 'blowing' and laying on of hands. (I have already dealt briefly with the more dramatic aspects of the procedures in chapter 6.)

LATER DEVELOPMENTS

In 1963, as in 1940, there was clear evidence of much firm belief in magical ideas and practices in fields where mental and physical elements of the personality were closely associated, and orthodox medicine was still far from secure in its therapy. On the other hand, much of the treatment of simple physical illnesses had passed, over the generation, from magical or spirit healer to modern medical dispensary. It was not so much that scepticism had replaced faith in magic in such spheres, but that the area of magical operations had become more circumscribed.

SUMMARY

In a way this analysis is a small contribution to the intellectual history of a part of Kelantan a generation ago, showing the kind of compound of mystical and pragmatic ideas then current about some important sectors of social affairs. If faith be the acceptance of the witness of things seen to things unseen, then there was much strong faith in magic. A strongly integrated framework of ideas expressed in terms such as *semangat, hantu, keramat*, and in actions such as use of *ubat, tiup, bageh*, etc., symbolized forces responsible for success and failure, health and sickness, ease or disturbance of mind. Yet this was not the only possible framework.

The quasi-scientific framework of empiricism was also important. However much inclined to respect traditional norms, Kelantan coastal Malays were apt to view their magic in a relatively sceptical, flexible way, which in its own particular setting at that period probably had distinct functional advantages for them. Advances in mechanization, medical care, education in the area over the last generation have tended to reduce belief if not in the validity at least in the necessity of magic. The broadening of interests since Independence may have drawn off some of the interest formerly focused upon magical practices. However much this may be seen as a gain in social and intellectual maturity, the traditional magical ideology should not be despised but regarded as worthy of understanding as part of the attempt to provide an intelligible framework for dealing with human problems.

Ostensibly, this chapter has dealt only marginally with religion. But it is intended to show how, at a level of folk behaviour and folk beliefs, the Malay ideas of Islam have been interwoven with elements of a magical order. For the peasantry, the relation of magic to religion has tended to be fairly equable. But there has been tension. This has often existed in the form of a vague disapproval of magical practices by many of the more literate or more pious members of the community. It has also emerged as a direct challenge to the magical practices by Muslim leaders. With the growth of Islamic fundamentalism in Kelantan in recent years it is likely that magical beliefs and practices may decline quite rapidly.

Chapter 8

Paradox in religious systems

Previous chapters have given much comparative ethnography of specific religious ideas and institutions, and shown their relevance to individual and social life. The aim of the present chapter is to sharpen the argument. It generalizes the material from a different angle in order to bring out more clearly the essentially human character of religious phenomena. To do this I focus on the diversity of religious systems, including the concepts of supernatural beings. I indicate their incompatibilities and their paradoxes as well as their positive achievements. And I demonstrate how such incompatibilities and paradoxes are either ignored or explained away in terms of reaction to human problems. All this requires no over-arching assumptions about divine revelation, involving God or other transcendental extra-human beings, minds or forces.

DIVERSITY OF RELIGIOUS SYSTEMS

The diversity of religious systems is due in part to the different environmental and economic settings in which the people who have formed them have lived. Concepts of spirit entities controlling the destiny of rural or forest-dwelling peoples vary greatly from those of industrial urban dwellers. But diversity *within* religious systems has arisen very strongly through differences in interpretation of doctrine or ritual, often associated with struggle for control of the religious organization itself.

Granted that all religious systems share some common features such as some belief in spiritual beings of mystical powers, and some general patterns of formalized behaviour in ritual, their diversity is remarkable. In scope, in patterns of ritual and of belief, in institutional structure, they show much individuality. They also vary greatly in relation to the society in which they operate. In most of the small-scale, technologically simple communities studied by many anthropologists the congruence between religious belief and ritual, and the forms of political and social structure has been close. But even in such a small, compact community such as that of the traditional Tikopia there was room for divergence between institutional arrangement and personal charisma. Alongside the highly formal worship of gods and ancestors through the agency of lineage heads as hereditary priests, was the operation of a spirit medium cult, with practitioners primarily self-selected for their capacity to enter into trance and serve as mouthpieces of gods or spirits of the dead.

In most small-scale religious systems, 'particularistic' in that their beliefs and ritual have been unique, limited to each specific society, there has been little overt concern for individual *belief.* All the emphasis has been on *practice.* Proper performance of ritual and fulfillment of economic and social obligations associated with the religious system have been paramount. Some common set of beliefs by members of the religious body has been in operation, else the rituals would not be carried out. But no clearly formulated body of doctrine is asserted, to which everyone is expected to conform. Just *what* any single person believes has not been a matter of moment to his fellows or to the ritual leaders. There has been no concept of heresy. Such absence of concern for definition of belief has been associated with the absence of any competing religious system. Proselytizing moves by religious leaders have been unnecessary. The complex issues of faith characteristic, say, of many Christian believers, have not arisen. Changes in the system have no doubt occurred, from personal pressures, external forces, or demographic movement, which have involved the creation of new gods and the demise of old gods. But sceptics have been rare and confined to doubt about the efficacy of specific rites or priests or the power of particular supernatural beings.

In marked contrast has been the history of major 'universalistic' religious systems. Religious belief has been a very powerful, often critical, force in holding large groups of people together and marking their difference from other groups. But running counter to the unifying force of the religious system, its promotion of fellowship, its collective ideational commitment, have arisen variant beliefs, even fission. Strongly marked, even violent separation of bodies of the faithful have occurred (see Factionalism, p. 188). An ostensible reason for separation has often been difference of interpretation of religious concepts. But associated with this have often been divergent group interests of an economic or political kind, or personal conflicts of ambition and struggle for power in the corporate religious body.

The diversity of religious systems is shown by their varied claims to general validity. Christians and Muslims are used to the assertion that their faiths are of universal application, for all mankind. Small scale particularistic religious systems make no claim to universality. In their view each local religion is valid only for its own society; the gods and ancestors whom they worship are theirs alone and cannot apply to folk of different culture. But the major religious systems have no such modesty. Each claims universal truth. Each holds its conception of the divine and its interpretation of the state of the world and the nature and future of mankind as uniquely correct. Each claims to have the sole clue to an understanding of the role of transcendent beings in relation to humanity. Yet the greater the claim to universal validity, the more is the potential for variation. So one characteristic of all the major religions is their marked history of diversity.

CONCEPTS OF TRANSCENDENT BEINGS AND POWERS

In defining a religion one of the most convenient criteria for use is the recognition of beliefs in a transcendent element. This involves a concept of dualism – an order of human beings and an order of spiritual beings or mystical powers. E. B. Tylor, one of the great synthesizers in nineteenth-century anthropological study, gave as the 'minimum definition' of religion the belief in spiritual beings. But this was speedily enlarged to include belief in non-human forces or powers of a less clearly personalized form. It is this transcendent element which distinguishes a religious from a political faith, often held with great intensity, but in this-worldly, not other-worldly style. Marxism has sometimes popularly been described as a religion. But while crowds may have queued in the Kremlin to visit the tomb of Lenin and pay respect to this most powerful symbol of a communist regime there is no record of their having prayed to Lenin's spirit to intercede for them with the spirit of Karl Marx, as multitudes of Christians appeal to saints or to Mary the Mother of Jesus to intercede for them with Almighty God.

The concept of transcendence has a long history and various meanings in western philosophic and religious thought. It refers ostensibly to beings or powers of another order than that of mankind. But the nature attributed to the transcendent in religion does involve human as well as extra-human characteristics. It displays an amazing fertility of imagery.

Most religious systems endow man with a spiritual nature, and hold that this spiritual aspect of the personality, the soul, endures after the death of the body. Such souls may then help to populate a vast transcendent afterworld. Belief in the fate of such spirits is however very varied. In some religious beliefs the spirits of the dead just fade away; in others they hold active communication with the living. In some the spirits of those who were leaders in life are worshipped with offerings after death; in others, though worship of dead saints may be forbidden, reverence for them and invocation of them may be permitted (see saints, pp. 183–5).

The extent to which human and transcendental or divine natures can be intermingled or merged is a matter of extreme interest to the three major 'religious of the book' – Judaism, Christianity and Islam. Since every religion is oriented towards human ends, there is a constant problem of how to bring the transcendent within human grasp. Christianity solved this by a radical affirmation that Jesus, the Jewish prophet, was the Son of God, the Almighty God incarnate, born of a human mother. This paradoxical concept of Jesus as both divine and human has furnished a cardinal bridge between the transcendent and the world of man. It has presumably helped many of the faithful to feel their religion as close to their personal needs. But this concept posed a theological dilemma: how can Jesus have been at one and the same time both God and man? Many solutions have been offered to this problem. One of the most ingenious, though one of the least acceptable to most early Christians, was that of the docetists. They understood Jesus's historical existence to have been appearance, not reality. He was a divine being dressed as a man in order to communicate revelation, and withdrew his spiritual presence from his body before the crucifixion. Other views, identifying Jesus with the Logos, the Word of God, seemed to make Jesus secondary, God's messenger, inferior to God. The

Arian doctrine that the Logos represented the principle of change in the divine, while God himself remained unchanged, also gave Jesus a subordinate position. This hierarchical concept of the Trinity was branded as heretical by fourth-century church councils. They insisted on the commonality of essence in the Holy Trinity, giving God, Jesus and the Holy Spirit equal status. Such elaborate theological arguments have been quite alien to Judaism and to Islam, each sternly monotheistic. Like Buddhism, Islam has regarded its putative founder as a human teacher, of sacred character certainly, but not divine. Indeed, for Islam, the assignment of divinity to Jesus Christ, who is regarded as a veritable prophet, is an example of the heresy known as *shirk*, giving God a partner.

It is a problem in many religions to envisage how far the transcendent can or will manifest itself in immanent form, that is, participate in events within the world. Traditional African religions offer many variants of view on this. Among the Lugbara, Adro (which may be translated as God) is believed to be the ultimate source of all power and of the moral order. Unlike the conventional God of Western religions Adro has no distinction of gender, and is not necessarily regarded as a person. In an immanent form Adro is credited with will and understanding, and seems to be conceived in basically anthropomorphic terms. In the transcendent aspect Adro is an ultimate creator, remote, living in the sky, beyond human control and knowledge. But in his/her/its immanent aspect Adro is close to human being, living with offspring on earth, especially in rivers, responsible for changes in human affairs, including the structure of Lugbara society. In particular, Adro is responsible for all deaths. No moral relation is ascribed to Adro in contacts with men. But since he/she/it is responsible for misfortune, including that of man's dissolution, Adro is feared and vaguely regarded as 'bad'. In their traditional moral concepts, then, the Lugbara faced a basic problem inherent in most religions – is the origin of evil in some extra-human, spiritual source? Unlike a religion with a personal God, such as Christianity, however, the Lugbara have not been troubled by the paradox of theodicy – how can an almighty God who is a God of love also suffer evil against his creatures?[1]

Another variant of the transcendent has been described for the Dinka of the Sudan in chapter 4. The Dinka divinity is largely withdrawn from men, and the moral order he sponsors often eludes them. He is also represented in the nonrational forces of nature, the unpredictable, chance and uncertainty in life. His existence is given as the ultimate answer to the question as to why things happen to men, an answer beyond further question. The ambiguities and contrariness of human experience are attributed to him. Lesser transcendent beings or powers, called by Lienhardt 'free-divinities' and 'clan-divinities', named though formless, have been believed to be responsible for illness and trance states, and may have been associated with various material emblems in natural species. But essentially the Dinka notion of divinity is both single and manifold, corresponding to a common experience of complexity in human affairs. The paradox that this concept of divinity is both a principle of certainty and a principle of uncertainty is seen by Lienhardt to be a reflection – 'image' in his terms – of the human condition (Lienhardt 1961: chs 1, 2, 4).

To believers in what a Muslim regards as the 'religions of the Book', that is Judaism, Christianity, Islam, the apex of the transcendence concept is God (Yahweh, Allah). In all these religions he is believed to be creator of heaven and earth, of all things visible and invisible, endowed with infinite power, wisdom and goodness. He is believed to have existed from all eternity, the giver of life and death, the arbiter of good and evil, equipped with all knowledge. As a humanist, I do not share such belief in the existence of such a being, either external to or immanent in the human world, representing the ultimate reality. But it is not enough simply to deny his existence; for neither affirmation nor denial of the existence of God can any ultimate proof be given. An anthropological humanism offers an alternative position. Considering the diversity of religious phenomena worldwide, in all their human contexts, the existence of an omniscient, omnipotent, all-pervasive spiritual entity becomes a question of probability. To a humanist, the explanation of religious phenomena in human terms seems adequate, the probability of the existence of a God with the qualities described seems so low as to be discarded, and the postulate of his existence seems unnecessary, redundant. God then is a purely human construct, a concept shaped in many forms to meet the great variety of human interests and human problems (see chapter 4).

THE NATURE OF GOD

However this be, to Western religions God is a central feature, and it is appropriate then to examine their interpretation of his nature and attributes. There are deep semantic and philosophical problems involved in any enquiry into the nature of God. But even a brief survey of the theological positions adopted in various phases of the issue reveals their essential preoccupation with human interests.

One type of approach, especially characteristic of Eastern Christian thought, is that of apophatic theology. This assumes the existence of God, but denies that his nature can ever be fully known to human beings. Much more than a thousand years ago the Neoplatonist doctrine of the One stressed how the divine unity and simplicity was incapable of being grasped by human thought or expressed in language. In the history of Christian thought the theme of God as 'incomprehensible being' runs through much exposition, even to the point of assertion of his total unknowability. Fairly recently, there has been the forceful argument of Karl Barth, that *religion*, in the sense of doctrine and ritual, is essentially a human construct, but that this is radically different from the *revelation* of God in Jesus Christ. God, as wholly Other than man, reveals himself to man independently of any human effort. This and allied ways of talking about God as unknowable, beyond all categories of thought and sensation, even beyond conceptualization, can be appealing to those of mystical temperament, with their suggestion of the hidden, the unknown, the unattainable. But logically they mean that communication with God is held to be impossible. The soul, it is argued, can only come closer to God in a kind of mystical darkness, stripped of all vestiges of the senses. So it is contended. But dispassionately viewed, such assertions are pure speculation. Acceptance of such a view would inhibit – perhaps is meant to inhibit – any effective discussion of the issues of divinity. As human utterance, such expressions can be seen as defence mechanism against enquiry, attempts to make propositions about the transcendent self-validating.

Such an apophatic position, however, has been generally held to be unsatisfactory, since it limits the freedom of the worshipper to communicate with the Almighty. Theological argument about the nature of God in relation to human affairs has stressed

a variety of themes. The cosmological argument stresses the role
of God as non-contingent 'prime mover' of the universe; the
universe must have been divinely created or it would be inexplic-
able. (The position of God as creator of the universe has tended
to shift in accord with current cosmological scientific theory.) The
teleological argument is parallel: it rests on the improbability of
the universe having come about by chance; a divine designer
must have been at work to provide for the infinite complexity of
the world and its creatures. An ethical argument appeals to the
source of morality. No human origin, it is held, is enough to
account for the moral rules by which human beings try to order
their existence; some external, superhuman origin is a necessary
postulate. The ethical argument is perhaps the most powerful in
its human appeal. But it has posed serious dilemmas, for the
faithful as well as for theologians. How is the existence of a God
of infinite power, knowledge and love to be squared with the
widespread existence of evil, the sufferings of the innocent, or
the idea of 'a curse of supernatural dimensions' in the notion of
punishment of the damned? Questions of ultimate origins may
remain for ever a mystery, but they are not solved by simple
assertions of divine intervention.

Classical ontological argument for the existence of God makes
some delicate distinctions. In the eleventh century Anselm's
famous argument for Divine Being was based upon the proposition that if we are able to conceive of an absolutely perfect
being then such a being, namely God, must exist in reality outside
our minds, as something greater than our conception. But this
argument has been challenged on various grounds. It has been
held in particular that the concept 'existence' as such is unprov-
able/unknowable without observation of the qualities of instances
pertaining to it. Another critique has been that we can know
things only as they appear to us in our minds, not how they
really are in themselves. But a nineteenth-century variant of the
ontological argument has claimed that the human mind has innate
direct knowledge of being as such, which is identical with God,
but that this knowledge does not come with clarity but confusedly.
On this view the ontological argument is not a logical proof of
the existence of God but rather a description of the nature of our
knowledge of his existence.

All such subtle intellectual argument can be very satisfying to
Christian theologians. In the event that God should exist, it is

illuminating, but in itself does not compel truth. As a distinguished theologian has said, with caution 'If, as seems to be the
case, God's existence cannot be philosophically proved, it does
not necessarily follow that there is no God'.[2]

But to an observer outside the religious sphere then such a
postulated existence of God is a reality in merely a linguistic
and conceptual sense, a reality of idea in human minds, but not
necessarily anything more.

The exclusivity of God is a question that has concerned many
religious systems. Judaism and Islam are uncompromising, claims
to the power of other gods are false. More rigorous views even
deny the existence of any other gods. But less exclusive views
have been common. Many religious systems are polytheistic, such
as that of Hindus. And even 'pure' monotheism has had its
qualifications. In early Israelite days it seems to have been
thought that other gods (such as Baal) existed, though the authority and power claimed by their practitioners was believed to
be a pretence. The role of angels and archangels as messengers
of God, endowed with some measure of the divine, has at times
seemed ambiguous, in both Judaism and Christianity. Concepts
of evil and sin have sometimes been given concrete form in the
notion of a Devil, Satan. Often regarded as a mere creature of
God, Satan has sometimes been treated as an independent entity,
God's antagonist. And as already mentioned, the Christian idea
of Jesus the prophet as Christ the Son of God has posed serious
problems of identity of the divine exclusiveness. (This was
exemplified by the early Arian doctrine of the sovereignty of
God by declaring the Son to be a secondary, created being.)

A problem of another order about the exclusivity of God arises
in the ethnicity of Jesus (Firth 1973: 406–11). Since in Christian
doctrine Jesus was born of a human mother and assumed human
form, the question is what ethnic shape he presented. The problem reveals itself clearly in the paintings and sculptures of Jesus
which Christianity encourages. For many centuries, before proselytization had reached far into Africa or Asia, portraits of Jesus
showed him as pale faced, rosy cheeked, with fair or reddish hair,
conformable with a general Western or Mediterranean physical
type. But in recent times, images have appeared of an Asian
Christ, a black Christ, as local artists have wished to portray a
figure with more immediate meaning for their own people. Here
is a paradox. For if Jesus has any historicity it must be as a

Middle Eastern personality, and so any literal reader of the Bible should depict him. But if he is to be regarded as a divine personality of universal relevance, then symbolically it is intelligible that he should be rendered in multiple local types of man, who can be recognized by the local congregation as one of themselves. Yet the acceptance of a Chinese Christ or a black Christ may be hard for a Western congregation.

Problems about the exercise of God's will have occupied many religious thinkers. Islam tends to be the most uncompromising of the monotheist religions by insisting that all events that occur are the outcome of God's will, and in a sense are pre-determined. In Christianity the problem of the freewill of the believer is a perennial paradox. Whether man has the capacity to choose between good and evil has been a worrying issue, in the light of God's omniscience and omnipotence. On the whole in modern times it seems that a libertarian position is most favoured, with an idea of God as self-limiting in this respect, allowing an area of human choice.

CONCEPTS OF SACREDNESS

A marked feature of most religious belief is that the transcendent beings who constitute the core of belief are endowed with a special quality, called ordinarily in English 'sacredness'. Derived from the Latin *sacer*, which had a general meaning of 'holy', this word implies respect, care in approach, a mystical aura of positive grace and power of a different order than those of ordinary human virtue. But a paradox appears here. The Latin *sacer* also had a more specific negative meaning, a sinister dedication to one of the infernal deities of the nether world, hence 'accursed', 'devoted to destruction'. The concept of sacredness in English refers primarily to the most positive, intangible, power-endowed aspect of the quality. It is a diffuse abstract concept, but is given specific concrete form in ritual injunctions about behaviour on religious occasions when transcendent beings are believed to be involved. The most negative aspect of *sacer* is paralleled by prohibitions regarding the sacred, including notions of untouchability and pollution.

The quality of sacredness attributed to gods and other spiritual beings has tended to be applied also to things associated with them, such as temples, altars, ritual vessels, sacrificial offerings.

These material things serve as media for promotion of worship and use of symbols of the faith. But they can also be objects of power manipulation and struggle for control – as exemplified in medieval competition for Christian relics of saints and martyrs or modern contests for administration of sacred places, as in Jerusalem. As anthropologists have often pointed out this notion of a special quality of sacredness that ritual things acquire, implies both grave respect and prohibition from contamination, and it acts as a marker for behaviour of believers towards them. For example, in religions with a basis of literacy, the texts in which their doctrines are enshrined are commonly treated as having a special sanctity. Though Christian scriptures are often handled as everyday objects, they are described as the Holy Bible, venerated and frequently treated with great care. The Muslim Koran (Kuran) is treated as sanctified in itself, and used with great respect. Guru Granth Sahib, the scripture of the Sikhs, is a focal point of worship in a Sikh temple; upon entering the building with covered head and bare feet a worshipper's first act of supplication is to the holy book located at the back of the temple. Scriptures of this kind tend to acquire an absolute value, as divinely inspired, inerrant, containing all the truth necessary for salvation. As such they are a witness to the faith. But they may also serve as a basis for controversy. They can be used as instruments of aggression, as Luther used the inspiration and inerrancy of the Bible against the Catholic church.

Modern historical scholarship has posed serious problems for scriptural interpretation, and hence for the attribution of sacredness to the texts. It has become clear to all but the most fundamentalist believers that most of these 'holy' scriptures cannot be taken literally. Historical scrutiny of the texts has shown that their authorship is often not as claimed, by named scribes, apostles or prophets as messengers of God, but anonymous, perhaps the work of several hands, even at different periods of time. So, one of the most important canonical books of Mahayana Buddhism, the Lotus Sutra, reputed to embody the very words of the Buddha in his final teaching in Nepal, has been shown to be the product of an unknown author of a much later period (Soothill 1930: 3–13). In its turn, historical scrutiny has provoked defence by supporters of the traditional religion. Apart from producing disagreement about texts, accusations of blasphemy may be levelled against textual critics of 'sacred' works.

A dignified if tendentious retort to the iconoclastic critics has sometimes been that the rules of critical judgement of ordinary literature cannot be applied to divinely inspired scriptures!

The sacredness attributed to material religious objects has historically given rise to popular misconceptions. To an anthropologist a literal naïve Western idea of pagan people in a religious rite 'bowing down to wood and stone' is absurd. The people are worshipping not these material objects as such but symbols of their gods and spirits. There is always some concept of a spiritual presence associated with the tree or stone slab in question, in quite a complex of ideas. The stone or tree is used as a resting place, or temporary habitation or as a mnemonic sign. As Robertson Smith pointed out a century ago a deity might inhabit or manifest himself in a sacred stone without being necessarily identified with it (1907 [1889]: 188).

But the issue is by no means always simple. An analogous problem of relation of representation to spirit arose in the early history of the Christian church over the veneration of images (icons). The iconoclasts of the eighth century argued, rather as Muslims do today, that the Godhead cannot be depicted, and that images of Christ as a man are therefore highly improper if not blasphemous. The iconodules, the supporters of the cult of images, held that the creation of such images was an act of loving devotion which expressed the true nature of divine activity. The controversy was about much more than the propriety of sacred art. It involved a difference of understanding about the incarnation of Jesus and the general Christian attitude to the material world. So, in the Eastern Orthodox Church, victorious in its contention since the Ecumenical Council of Nicaea in ad 787, the holy icons by which the worshipper is surrounded express in visual form the central doctrines of the faith. They provide a 'window upon the divine'.

But one of the more bizarre features of the veneration accorded to material religious objects deemed sacred has been the cult of relics. All the major religious systems have had cults of relics – remnants of bodies of saints, great teachers or ritual leaders, such as their alleged teeth, nails, ashes, hair; or things said to have been used by them and passed on to their followers – such as a cup, a ring or a garment. Such relics have tended to become objects of adoration to the cult believers, and have often had miraculous powers attributed to them. In medieval

Christendom the possession of sacred relics gave prestige to a religious foundation, and the scramble for these sometimes became unseemly. Constantinople was reputed to have the greatest store of ancient Christian relics. An account of the looting of the city in ad 1204 reports an abbot of an Alsatian monastery as having made off with a trace of Christ's blood, a piece of the Cross, a 'not inconsiderable piece' of St. John the Baptist, the arm of St. James and other important relics of saints (Haskins 1957: 234). Sacred relics are often accommodated in shrines, which themselves tend to acquire a special sanctity, with alleged power of response to requests in prayer to the saint concerned.

Theologians of religious systems have from time been uneasy about these cults of relics and shrines. Popular behaviour has implied very strongly that miraculous powers can be attributed to the objects and places *per se*, giving them a kind of magical value. So interpreters of a more abstract turn of mind have been careful to point out that the honour given to relics and allied objects is only relative, and that the only true object of worship is God. He may use the relics of saints as channels of grace and instruments of healing. But as with iconic images, a clear distinction must be drawn between *latrei*, worship, which is paid to God alone, and *doulia*, reverence or veneration which is the proper attitude to assume towards such memorials of saints and other holy personages. (St. John of Damascus, who drew these distinctions in the eighth century, spoke of *hyperdoulia*, a special kind of veneration, for Mary the Mother of God.)

An external observer, however, may note that this abstract distinction, while satisfying to a theologian, is perhaps not so easy to recognize for an Italian or Spanish peasant! Such a one, eager to get relief from some form of suffering, focuses on the immediacy of the situation and welcomes any suggestion of power that may be thought to come from touching or praying to the sacred object.

COMMUNICATION TO THE TRANSCENDENT

Religion is not just a matter of belief, of internal commitment to the notion of existence of some transcendent power. It also involves ideas that this power is related to human interests. And almost everywhere it is thought that a believer can take the initiative in communicating with this power. This communication normally takes two forms, verbal and nonverbal. But the initiative of the individual is rarely taken completely personally and randomly. It follows models; it is patterned upon religious forms, governed by rule in shape and timing, a part of ritual. Such ritual behaviour is often traditional and symbolic, its meaning legitimized by past practice and interpretation.

Verbal communication with the transcendent may take the form of a simple announcement of offering (see chapter 5) but commonly takes the form of address known as prayer. Usually uttered aloud, but sometimes silently articulated, prayer is ostensibly a manifestation of a personal tie with the transcendent. Prayer may have great variety according to occasion. It may repeat a formal model, as in the Christian 'Lord's Prayer' or be spontaneous and informal. It may be mandatory, to be uttered in prescribed times in regular worship, such as the orthodox Muslim recital of prayer at five periods of the day. It may be recited by a priest on behalf of a congregation, or uttered in unison by the whole religious assembly.

Prayer represents an initiative, an outward-looking approach to a listener who is unseen; it therefore constitutes an act of faith or hope that it will reach its mark. Some prayer in moments of stress may be little more than a pure ejaculation – 'Oh, God help me!' But most prayer envisages a recipient, though whether the recipient hears, and if hearing, will answer, is quite unknown. Much prayer is routinized, so the degree of alertness and emotional and intellectual commitment of the worshipper who is praying is often problematical. But broadly it may be assumed that prayer expresses one or more of the following attitudes. It may give praise to the divine being, and emphasize the asymmetrical position of the worshipper, his inferiority. Much prayer embodies request, but modern Christian prayer tends to avoid requests for God to intervene with natural process – though prayers for rain still are made. It focuses on hope for betterment of oneself or others in less material ways. The Christian plea of 'Give us this day our daily bread' is a formal request of a traditional kind, significant if at all, of only a general recognition of divine control of human welfare.

In the Islamic tradition, prescribed daily prayer is not an occasion for a worshipper to put forward requests to Allah, whose will is already determined. In the Judaeo-Christian tradition, however, a worshipper may pray freely, with requests which God may 'answer' in his wisdom. But there is a distinct air of uncertainty about this situation. Theological subtleties apart, an anthropological impression is strong that the chief function of prayer in such a system is twofold: to reassure the worshipper that he/she continues in a proper relation with the divine; and to provide an outlet for the compulsion of people to express in words their preoccupations and problems, talking to somebody, even an unseen person. Prayer is then part of a personal release mechanism. In systems where morality and religion are closely connected as in Christianity, prayer may be treated as means of expressing personal defect or breach of the moral code, and seeking forgiveness. Prayer can then be cathartic, purgative in a psychological sense, a contribution to the internal stability of the personality.

Even for members of a major religious system, belief in the external efficacy of prayer can vary widely. The cult of saints, from the time of the early Christian church, has involved prayer at their places of burial or other associated places, requesting them to continue to pray for their fellows still on earth. This type of surrogate intercession has analogy in cases where agents – priests, for example – are paid to pronounce prayers on behalf of the people who pay, or of others whom they nominate. This indicates belief in a kind of autonomous validity of prayer. Such prayer is transferable, detachable, has power in itself, independent of the original author. This is an aspect of the power of 'the word', a feature found commonly in religious systems. One of the most marked examples of transferable invocation rather than of prayer of a more personal type, is the mechanical repetition of Buddhist texts of *sutras* on rotary drums, the so-called 'prayer wheels'. By their constant movement these drums convey virtue or merit to the people associated with them. In some religious systems an obligatory quality is introduced into a prayer by the citation of sacred, often secret, names which are believed to have the power – in effect magical – of inducing the spirit addressed to listen to the worshipper and to do what he requests.

But prayer may express a diversity of attitudes. With mandatory phrases adjuring the deity to listen and perform some service may be mingled expressions of praise of the deity and abasement on the part of the worshipper. So, a traditional Tikopia pagan prayer began by naming the deity and commanding him to pay attention to the rite being carried out. But then the address continued with a kind of 'dust under your feet' metaphor. 'I speak simply to the sole of your foot; you are sacred; I address the dirty sole of your foot' meaning 'I am not worthy to confront you face to face'. Another description given by a priest was of himself as 'an orphan fingernail'. This was a double metaphor. It meant that he was in a very inferior position, and without protection – 'parentless' unless aided by the deity. In a further phrase a priest described himself as a 'thieving person', implying that he was so poverty-stricken and devoid of food that he was driven to steal. All these were set phrases of a routine order, intended to convey to the spirits that their worshipper was in dire need of help. But they were figurative expressions, pathetic stimuli to arouse the sympathy of the deity, but not factual indices of the actual economic position of the worshipper. Some of the phraseology needed a special gloss. A common Tikopia phrase of depreciation addressed to a deity in prayer was 'I eat your excrement'. Clearly, this indicated an attitude of great humility, a condition of miserable inferiority. It was not a statement of personal moral defect, or even failure to fulfill a ritual obligation. The verbal assertion of eating another person's ordure was a statement of degradation. Yet the assertion was double-edged. For in Tikopia metaphor the gods were conceived to create food crops in the land and fish in the sea by symbolic acts of excretion. To speak of their eliminations was a figurative way of speaking of man's food. Hence under the form of extreme, disgusting humility the Tikopia priest was also saying in effect 'I eat of your bounty in food', so virtually thanking the deity (Firth 1970: 256–8; 1973: ch. 7.).

A comparative analysis of the phenomena of prayer shows then several features of human significance. Many if not most religious systems have forms of prayer in which man expresses his dependence upon transcendent beings. This often manifests a desire for a personal relation between a human being and a transcendent one. But it may show a wish to avoid responsibility, to have the prayer so routinized that it is performed by a representative of the religious body, not by individual worshippers. (And many people professing adherence to a religious system do not in fact ever pray at all.) A Christian theological interpretation of prayer is that it is man's personal approach to God. But this may be paradoxical, ambiguous. If, as in the Christian system, God is conceived as all-knowing, all-powerful, all-wise, all-loving and omnipresent, he should have no need of man's communications.

He is already aware of the plight of his worshippers and of their attitudes. And if, as some theologians argue, prayer is permissible only in the name of Jesus Christ, who 'at the right hand of God' makes intercession for the person who prays, this is surely superfluous.

An anthropologist therefore seeks the functions of prayer elsewhere. If indeed there is no God, then the worshipper is uttering into the void. But an important function of prayer, individual or collective, or through an agency, is in providing a means of common ritual action. It is an affirmation of common belief, a restatement of sacred values of a community. In many religious systems, prayer, as formal or informal spoken word, is an explanatory mechanism accompanying a material nonverbal act such as offering or sacrifice (see chapter 5). Prayer is thus a means binding people of a congregation together. Individually, prayer can be a cathartic mechanism, an act of articulation helping to clarify issues of significance to the person who is praying. It often seems to give emotional release thereby. Whether there be any listening transcendent being or not, then, prayer is significant as a form of human action, an attempt to enlarge the domain of the self by seeking assistance, even if illusory.

COMMUNICATION FROM THE TRANSCENDENT

Prayer is conceived essentially as an outgoing from a worshipper to a transcendent being, with response left open. But in many religious systems it is believed that transcendent beings such as gods or spirits themselves are active in communication with their worshippers. They are alleged to do this by signs such as oracles, or by spoken words, issued through mystics, prophets or spirit mediums, often in trance.

There is a basic polarization in all religious systems. This is associated with the contrast, even opposition, between individual and society. On the one hand there is the notion that the religious system is best served by emphasizing its corporate aspects, and using selected persons, especially trained or privileged, to mediate between congregation and transcendent being. Hence the importance of priests (see pp. 178–80). But in contrast to this stress on officialdom is the notion of individual religious freedom, allowing members of a congregation direct access to the divine, with communication on a purely personal basis. In a broad Christian field the contrast is illustrated by the difference between Roman Catholic and Nonconformist traditions. The one makes much use of official intermediaries between worshipper and God, the other minimizes the intermediary in favour of a personal approach. Methodist theology, for example, emphasizes the importance of individual conversion, of the saving power of grace through faith in ensuring personal salvation, and the value of individual spontaneous prayer as a mode of communion with God the Father of Jesus Christ. Lacking is the traditional concept of the Catholic priest as one with power to offer sacrifice and offer forgiveness of sin.

Mysticism, occurring in many religions, is one form of an alleged personal relation with a divine power (Firth 1964: ch. xii for an anthropological view). The phenomena show great variation. But the essence of a mystical experience, as often described by mystics themselves, is the search for or attainment of a sense of nearness to or unity with a transcendent power, usually God. This means an enhancement of the self, a heightened state of awareness which seems to the mystic to throw a new light upon the nature of reality. Interpretation of their experience by religious mystics has produced much imaginative, penetrating, stimulating reflection upon the nature of man and his relation to what is conceived as the unseen world (cf. the admirable study of Jewish mysticism by Gershom Scholem 1955, and of Muslim mysticism by Nicholson 1914). But mystics at times have been a disturbing element in the religious systems to which they have been attached. In Islam and Christianity their claims to a highly personal unique relationship with divinity have challenged the more orthodox interpretations of the faithful. An assertion sometimes made by a mystic of unity with God has been seen as plainly heretical. In the 'religions of the book' therefore, mysticism has tended to be treated with caution, sometimes with hostility. The claim of the mystic to have direct experience of God is usually admitted, but the implications of such a claim have often been unacceptable to established authority. Linked with mystical claims have often been antinomianism, a rejection of the law, both religious and moral, in the name of the mystic's own access to divine authority. One of the most remarkable instances of this was the emergence in the Jewish field in the seventeenth century of Sabbatai Zevi, a manic-depressive Kabbalist, who was convinced by his prophetic follower Nathan of Gaza that he had messianic interpretation. Fired by this he became a 'holy sinner' – an attractive anti-establishment concept – and centrepiece of a strong heretical movement. (That Sabbatai himself later became an apostate adherent to Islam complicated but did not destroy his movement, which had some importance in leading to later reforms in Judaism (Scholem 1955: 287–324).)

To an anthropoligist, these accounts of mystical experience seem to fall within the human range of imaginative perception and sensation, without any necessary assumption of an extra-human entity responsible for them.

Another mode of purporting to display a direct personal relationship with transcendent powers has been that of ecstasy. Ecstasy, a sense of being taken out of oneself, covers a very wide field. In a religious context, as a 'transport of delight' it may be linked with mysticism. It may involve the notion of deliverance from the body in a kind of divine inspiration. One type of ecstasy can be manifest in a trance, in which the human being may assume an alternative personality, and speak or otherwise behave with what is regarded as spirit action. There are many varieties of such spirit medium cults, in which the words of an alleged spirit are taken as diagnostic and as guides to action for purposes of healing the sick or dealing with other pressing problems.[3]

From the point of view of the person primarily concerned, who is deemed to be a medium for communication with spirits, this offers a field for the exercise of individual fantasy. The religious system still provides controls, and for the most part mediums seem to remain within the bounds of the theological and ritual conventions of their faith. But the belief, by themselves and their audience, that they are in direct linkage with spirits gives them a freedom of thought and expression which an ordinary worshipper does not enjoy. Hence many mediums claim that they are guided and protected by a 'familiar', seen from an external observer's point of view as a claim to an alternative personality, who makes independent statements not necessarily in line with orthodox religious opinion. In some religious systems spirit mediums pur-port to engage in adventures in the spirit world, talking with the dead or with other spirit beings, clearly indulging in inventive fantasy encounters.

In this way it would seem that members of a religious system use this method of fantasy elaboration as to some degree an escape from the rigours of the system. They present no overt challenge to belief or dogma; the conventions of the mediumship cult protect them from accusations of unorthodoxy or even heresy. But through the cult practices persons of an imaginative, perhaps unstable type can find a freedom of mental activity and verbal utterance otherwise denied to them.

Such spirit medium behaviour is commonly institutionalized, and incorporated into a cult. The personal experience of an individual with special quality of trance entry is turned into a social phenomenon of functional significance and practical usefulness. Terms commonly used in this connection are 'spirit possession' for the attribution of trance state to control by extra-human agency; 'spirit medium' for the individual who in such state purports to serve as a vehicle for spirit communication; and 'shaman' (ultimately a Siberian term) for the human controller who as principal director of ceremonies is regarded as master of the spirits concerned. (See chapter 6 for Malaysian example.)

In the modern Christian church, a movement of charismatic renewal sometimes takes in part the character of ecstasy. It insists on the element of grace in the church, and guidance by the Holy Spirit as conferred by adult baptism. It is manifest in concrete evidence, such as speaking in tongues (glossolalia), prophecy and healing through spiritual agency. It is revivalist, evangelist, evoking legitimacy by reference to the first Christian Pentecost when the Holy Spirit is believed to have inspired the apostles to ardent proselytization. Sprung mainly from Methodist and Baptist congregations these ecstatic movements, the Pentecostal bodies of the twentieth century, with their ultra-fundamentalist bent, have worked independently of, often in opposition to the established hierarchical main-line churches. Description of worshippers 'drunk in the Spirit' or 'slain by the Spirit' in fainting and hysterical laughter at Holy Trinity Brompton church, Knightsbridge, London have been given by The Times religious correspondent (18.6.94, 2.7.94). The phenomenon is said to have originated in a small church in Toronto, Canada; hence it is sometimes referred to as the 'Toronto Blessing'.

The charismatic practice of 'speaking in tongues' offers an interesting example of theological subtlety. Its essential feature is not just that it is believed to represent human speech inspired by divine spirit, but that it is unintelligible in the context in which it is uttered. This presents a problem in interpretation. If, as is claimed, such speaking of alien sounds is evidence of the baptism of Spirit, then it would be impertinent to call it meaningless babble, as an external observer might think it be. So various ingenious explanations of it have been put forward. Occasionally the 'speaking with tongues' has been identified as an actual foreign language spoken by people who have never learned it but who have been endowed with mysterious knowledge of it in the ecstatic state. But investigation of this view has shown it not to be convincing. Some commentators have argued that some cases cited evade all rational explanation. Tendentiously, it has been held that any attempt to experiment and collect more data on the issue may inhibit the phenomena and 'upset the delicate conditions in which they occur'. Theologians are unwilling to dismiss as irrelevant or absurd a phenomenon which purports to have spiritual origins and which is intricately bound up with the practices of some Christian groups. So they have tended to take the line that any verbal expression, however unintelligible to ordinary hearers, is a means of communication, and creates a bond between members of the congregation. It is a reminder of 'that important and deep dimension of language which we tend to suppress in our discussion on language' (Walter J. Hollenweger, in Richardson and Bowden 1983, 'Glossolalia'). This is close to an anthropological theory of the magical use of language, where it is not the actual form of the words spoken that is socially significant but the act of speaking as a means of social communication. The difference is that, unlike a theologian, an anthropologist is very familiar with cases of personal excitation in which individuals show unusual, bizarre behaviour, without need for any postulate of spirit agency.

RELIGIOUS LEADERS

Some religions imply or insist upon a direct relation of believer to the transcendent being believed in. But in most religious systems the relation of worshipper to transcendent is often indirect; an established intermediary plays the role of communicator and interpreter with the divine. Yet the recognition of an agent in spiritual affairs is apt to bring problems of a mundane as well as spiritual kind. The existence of a religious agent can be in conflict with a thirst for self-expression on the part of a worshipper. The performance of leadership in spiritual affairs easily moves over into an assumption of control over the secular affairs of the faithful. There are also practical problems of selection and training of leaders, allocation of them to spheres of duty, and provision for their economic support.

Different religious systems have adopted widely varied solutions to these problems of organization of their leadership. A simple type of religious leadership structure, paralleled in many other small rural communities, has operated in a traditional Polynesian society such as that of Tikopia. What may be called the priests, who uttered prayers to gods and ancestors on behalf of their people, and made material offerings of food and vestments to these spirits, were In fact lineage or clan heads by virtue of seniority. These leaders were all men. They had important economic and social roles in the community, and though they received substantial gifts as part of a complex system of exchange, they were responsible for their own subsistence. The leadership was hierarchical, and the religious functions of the leaders were a reinforcement of their secular political roles (see Firth 1970: ch. 2).

By contrast, a leadership structure of more complex kind has existed in the Malay state of Kelantan, Malaysia. Though not theocratic, as Muslim states have often historically been, it acknowledges the strong influence of the Sunni version of Islam as the state religion.[4] In conformity with general Muslim views about the equality of man before Allah, the main type of leader for major religious purposes is the Imam, whose basic defined function is to serve as a leader of prayer. He is not a priest, by any special ordination. However, he is an important religious official, basic to the state administrative structure of religion. Imams not only lead Friday prayers but also supervise mosque affairs, solemnize marriages, oversee the burial of the dead, and collect religious taxes. Historically, many rural Imams, often hereditary, have been attached to prayer houses built by themselves or their families, and occupy themselves with local pastoral duties. Formerly, Imams have had no fixed salaries, but have relied upon a share of religious taxes upon persons and crops for a living. This has given rise to friction between them and the state religious board (*majlis ugama*), which has tended to claim an increasing amount of such receipts. While the Imams represent the everyday aspect of religious leadership other types of religious leaders cater for more technical religious matters. Administration of the *shari'a*, the Islamic law, has resulted in the creation of powerful functionaries concerned primarily with the application of Muslim personal law, for example, relating to divorce, inheritance, religious bequests and offences against religion. The *mufti*, a major Islamic judiciary official, also has the function of issuing authoritative opinions (*fatwa*) on questions of public interest from a religious point of view. Kelantan has also been noted among Malay states for its religious teaching. Traditional religious schools (*pondok*) are headed by leaders known as To' Guru (ultimately a Sanskrit term), whose reputation as spiritual guides is often widespread. Religious leadership in Kelantan is thus threefold: at a local pastoral level; at the level of more abstract legal interpretation; and at an exalted spiritual level. Analogous structures exist in most Muslim communities.

In general terms the secular obligations of religious leadership may be quite heavy. Many religious groups are property owners, if only of the temples in which their worship is commonly conducted. But the long-established religious organizations may be holders of immense property and other wealth. The Church Commissioners of the Church of England control a great deal of land and house property throughout the country, giving them immense economic power. For the Roman Catholic church, world-wide, it was stated twenty years ago that about five million people – priests, nuns, lay doctors *et al.* – worked for the Christian community, twenty million boys and girls were being educated in Catholic schools and universities, and thirteen million adults and children received assistance from Catholic charitable institutions. To maintain this vast organization involved huge financial operations based upon enormous wealth in cash and investments. Regular gifts from the faithful (Peter's Pence) provided many million of dollars annually to this end. Problems of administration of such vast resources impose an enormous secular load upon the religious institution and necessitate intricate relationships between spiritual considerations and lay demands.

The relation of secular to spiritual functions of religious leaders is highlighted by the great array of diverse practices in Christian sects and denominations. Issues of the degree of authority that should be exercised by leaders, and of the extent to which they should really represent the views of their followers are well illustrated by usage of the terms bishop, priest, minister, presbyter for different types of religious leaders. In the early Christian church *bishop* came to be the title of the chief leader of the local community, chosen by the community itself. But as the Bishop of Rome assumed pre-eminence as Pope, papal appointment of bishops became the rule. In the Roman Catholic and Orthodox churches a bishop has been regarded as the supreme governing and liturgical authority in a diocese. Collectively, bishops are believed to be direct successors to the original apostles and therefore capable of stating Christian doctrine with authority. *Priest*, a term of wider application, refers primarily to a role in worship, originally in sacrifice. But in the Christian church it applies to the operation of the eucharist, as consecrator and transformer of the holy elements. A priest then speaks to God on behalf of the congregation. But historically this focus on the authoritative nature of the bishopric and the sacramental nature of the priesthood ran counter to more egalitarian views of the religious process and the spiritual life. Moreover, it was seen to lead to arrogance and corruption among its practitioners in the mediaeval church. So, many churches arising from the Reformation of the sixteenth century discarded bishops and priests. Retaining the administrative and pastoral activities of their leaders, the churches have left them with greatly reduced liturgical roles. Hence the prevalence of the term *minister* for leaders in many Protestant churches. A minister may be ordained for his special religious duties by some such rite as a laying on of hands. While this may be symbolic of conferment of the Holy Spirit, the emphasis is upon dedication to community service rather than upon the possession of any special spiritual attributes given from the divine power. The term *presbyter* is in similar secular vein. Originally from the Greek, meaning elder, it referred to the system of government of the ancient Christian church. But since the sixteenth century, under the inspiration of John Calvin, presbyterianism has characterized the government of many reformed churches. Calvin's theology, emphasizing the supreme dominance of God, was harsh in many respects. But his insistence on the uniqueness of the biblical scriptures as a source of knowledge, and upon the sovereignty of the individual conscience in interpretation of the will and word of God meant a rejection of any other authority such as that of bishop or priest. Hence a presbyterian form of leadership and church government came into existence. This was believed to be laid down in scripture, involving both laymen and ministers in constant secular as well as theological discussion.

Throughout the whole field of religious leadership runs the constant problem of the spiritual nature and bounds of authority of the leaders. Are leaders to be recognized as divinely appointed or inspired, or are they simple human beings with special functions? And how far does their authority require obedience, in thought as well as act? A priesthood of hierarchical order, claiming divine sanction, is a strong defence mechanism for a religious system. As the sole legitimate interpreter of doctrine a priest helps to safeguard the purity of religious belief and ritual among the faithful and maintain the integrity of the congregation.

My analysis of religious leadership so far has tended to focus on the strength of the individualistic, egalitarian elements in it. But it is clear that for many religious people there are great attractions in the idea of submission to authority, of being supplied with dogma, of being assured that the conduct recommended to them has divine sanction. In some religious systems with vast numbers of adherents, there have emerged prime leaders of such power that they have claimed absolute authority, both spiritual and temporal, over their congregations. Best known is the Roman Catholic Pope, whose traditional status has grown over the centuries to the assertion in 1870 of the doctrine of papal infallibility, a claim that the Pope is preserved from error when speaking *ex cathedra* on matters of faith and morals.[5] So, it is held to be unquestionably true, as pronounced as an article of faith by Pope Pius XII in 1950, that the Blessed Virgin Mary after her death was bodily assumed up into heaven. Though the writings upon which this early tradition is based are apocryphal, and as a physical fact the notion is absurd, the strength of religious commitment is such that millions of people give credence to this papal statement (see Palmer 1953: 101–14).

In the Church of Jesus Christ of Latterday Saints (Mormons) their president is the 'mouthpiece of God' able to enunciate laws of the church by divine revelation. In 1976 Spencer Kimball, president of the Mormon church, in a timely statement announced that a divine revelation had commanded him to order the cessation of the practice which had formerly been stringently followed, of denying black people any membership of the priesthood. In the traditional Tibetan Buddhist system the supreme ruler, the Dalai Lama, has been regarded as not only the representative or interpreter of the divine; he is treated as being himself a god, the embodiment of Chen-re-zi, the Tibetan name for the Buddhisatva Avalokita, the deity of mercy. He has thus been properly described as a god-king (Bell 1931: 130, 141, 186). But even the most elevated and authoritarian religious rulers have not been immune to challenge. In the nineteenth century the Old Catholic churches in Europe broke with the Pope over the doctrines of infallibility and the Immaculate Conception. So too the Reorganized Church of Jesus Christ of Latterday Saints was constituted in mid-nineteenth century as a result of the rejection of Brigham Young's claims to a revelation on polygamy for church members. Again, some edicts of the present Dalai Lama have given rise to much controversy among his followers, some of whom do not accept all his statements as divinely inspired. No claim to absolute religious supremacy can be completely self-validating!

Much religious leadership has been what is called charismatic, a product of special qualities in the person rather than the prestige of office. Basically associated with the idea of grace, a spiritual endowment, the term charisma has been popularized in sociology by Max Weber. He saw charisma as giving rise to a type of authority specifically in conflict with the 'routine' structure of power having legitimacy in an established institutional order. In the religious field, the operations of charisma are not perhaps as opposed to those of the established leadership as Weber postulated. But two types of authority of a charismatic order, that of prophets and that of saints, have often displayed a separation from the 'official' institutionalized system (Firth 1970: 31–2).

A prophet is someone who has a personalized vision of the significance of the transcendent and who proclaims this vision, often in a call to a new way of life. Thus Jesus may be seen as a Jewish ethical prophet with a new message for salvation of souls. Though his prophetic role has been accepted by Christians, it has been obscured by claims that he himself was the Messiah, the Christ, the 'anointed one', the Saviour, and that he was divine, the Son of God. His importance as a prophet has been recognized by Islam, which, however, denies his divinity. Muhammed was a prophet in a stricter sense, being the interpreter of the word of God in a new form, but having his character as a human messenger preserved. The claim that he was the 'seal of the prophets', the last with special divine authority, has however given him an outstanding sacredness in the prophetic hierarchy, and led to the Muslim categorization of all later prophets as impostors. In religious history generally, prophets have tended to arise in times of social stress as corrections to or in opposition to established religious orthodoxies. This is recognized theologically – and sociologically – as a necessary dialectical development. But in time what Weber called the routinization of charisma has often given established form to what was originally a breakaway movement founded upon an intense personal vision.

The term prophet is not of very precise usage. In popular understanding it often has some connotation of prediction of the future. In Bengt Sundkler's notable study (1948) of Zulu cult leaders in South Africa the term 'prophet' is used in a conventional local sense of a religious leader with unusual personal qualities. These are often deemed to be supernatural in nature. Such a prophet, outside the hierarchy of the regular churches of long establishment, is believed to have powers of divination and of healing, in addition to an original interpretation of the Bible. Commonly, such powers are said to have been received by the prophet in a dream or other special bodily and mental experience such as trance, his 'call'. Some of these prophets, such as Isaiah Shembe, who founded the Nazarene (Nazarite) sect of Bantu Christians, have been men of impressive, magnetic personality, though illiterate. Others, such as Shembe's son and successor, though literate (he held a college degree) have been credited rather than endowed with special qualities, owing their position to a process of 'routinization'.

A marked feature of prophetic and associated cults, such as those of a messianic order, has been their political significance. Their leaders, stimulated by mystical visions, have often been reacting not only against the established religious organization, but also against more secular pressures. In many parts of the world during the last century or so, these have included the Western drive for land and industrial development, which have deprived local people of basic resources and led to a break-up of their traditional way of life. Many politico-religious movements arising from the tensions and conflicts due to the impact of Western culture upon the indigenous cultures of Africa, the Pacific and elsewhere have been described by anthropologists and historians. These movements have combined revival of past glories – imaginary as well as actual – with attempts at transformation of contemporary conditions. Here the inspiration of charismatic individuals has been often spurred on by what they believed to be traumatic encounters with a transcendental spirit world. Notable has been the strength of the engagement with the cult, the intensity of the religious conviction backing up the sometimes imprudent political protest.[6]

If prophets have been conspicuous by their utterances, saints have tended to operate in less articulate ways. Saints are people of special charisma, recognized as holy in the quality of their lives, and commonly venerated as having a special relation with the divine. In the Christian field the cult of saints has a long history. In the Roman Catholic church the holiness of saints represents the image of God, so that after death they are in heaven and can continue in communion with men, being appealed to by prayer. This church has elaborate procedures to establish saints, including examination of the virtues of a saint, and 'proofs' of miracles performed during life or after his or her death in response to prayer. But the process of sanctification (canonization), depending on the decision of the Pope upon the advice of the Congregation for the Causes of Saints, does not always pass nowadays without challenge. The normal Catholic process of sanctification involves a progress through the stages of being declared Venerable, and then Blessed. The first demands a recognition that the person has lived a life of heroic virtue, the second requires proof of a physical miracle such as the overnight cure of someone with a disease designated by experts as incurable. The recent beatification of Josemaria Escrivà, founder of the Catholic action group Opus Dei, raised considerable opposition within the church. Only seventeen years after his death, this declaration was seen as a step on the way to declaring him a saint, a position to which the objectors thought he was not entitled, either by his life history or in view of claims of others such as Cardinal John Henry Newman, who had been waiting much longer for elevation (*The Times* 16–18.5.92).

In Islam the saintly attribution is much less centralized and much more flexible. In sophisticated Muslim theology saints (walī) are persons who are 'close to God' and strictly speaking are known only to him. They have no function as mediators between God and man, as saints do in Catholic belief. But in more popular Muslim conceptions the notion of sainthood is linked with that of the possession of *baraka*, supernatural blessing resulting in health, prosperity, the fertility of crops and other human benefits. As such it is embodied in living men of distinction, such as the

Moroccan Arab *marabout* and the hereditary Berber *igurramen*. Such men are thought to have a special relation with God, and able to exercise their powers on behalf of their followers or clients (Gellner 1969; Eickelman 1976; Nicholson 1914: ch. v).

Historically, cults of saints have been associated with belief in miracles. In ordinary physical terms, a miracle may be regarded as an event contrary to the laws of nature. In religious terms, such an event is due ultimately to divine intervention, perhaps actuated by prayers offered to a saint. Belief in miracles is still strong among some congregations of, say, peasant Roman Catholics or urban Pentecostals. But sophisticated religious thought has tended more and more to interpret the classical field of claims to miraculous happenings such as recovery from what has been diagnosed as a terminal illness, to obscure psychosomatic process. More sociologically, claims to miracles can be regarded as attempts to bolster up the religious or social status of individuals or groups.

COMMITMENT AND CLAIMS TO UNIQUE AUTHORITY

Especially remarkable about many religions is the strength of commitment of their followers and their claims to unique authority. Basically the transcendent elements in religious belief are non-rational figurations. Yahweh, God, Allah, the Boddhisattvas, Shinto gods and spirits, the Nilotic Jok or Polynesian nature deities, though defined intellectually by their 'otherness', have been essentially creations of human thought, often of long tradition and often changing in description. Yet belief in these and in a multitude of other transcendent entites throughout the cultures of the world has stimulated momentous forces for social action. Since it is believed that these imagined entities have power, limited or unlimited, and greater than human power, the implication is that this power and its associated authority can be transmitted to and used by their followers. The result can be a terrific focusing of human energy in ways which radically affect conduct.

The variety of modes of engagement of people with their religion is very great. There is a meditative tradition, in which the individual adherent is preoccupied with his or her personal understanding and perhaps personal salvation from sin and evil.

This can take such forms as strict observance of rules, mystical introspection or ascetic renunciation. Then there is a more outward-looking tradition, in which a religious individual is concerned to demonstrate the truth of the faith to others. This may be expressed in justificatory argument such as preaching or theological writing directed primarily to the needs of the faithful. Or it may take a more active evangelical form, endeavouring to disseminate the faith by making converts to it. Historically, in the West, as a religion of a 'Chosen People' Judaism has shown little enthusiasm for making converts – though much seepage into as well as out from that religious and cultural body seems to have occurred. But of the 'religions of the book' both Christianity and Islam have shown great zeal in proselytization. Technically, evangelism is proclamation of the gospel, the good news; but accompanying this is the very strong implication that hearing of the good news should lead to acceptance of it as true. Conversion has therefore formed part of the programme of the main religious faiths, including Buddhism and Hinduism. Unfortunately, in many cases the proselytizers have not been content to rely on the cogency of their arguments alone. Directly or indirectly, consciously or unconsciously, they have often employed more material, even violent pressure, including war. Undoubtedly economic considerations were important in the conversion of many Pacific island peoples to Christianity, while Islam in Africa has made use of oppressive military means.

Religious commitment can be seen at its most powerful when it is engaged to protect the religious body. Aggressive religious alignment can take the form of massive even violent physical action, where the positive values of religious solidarity assume a negative, destructive shape.

Hinduism is a very complex religion, with much stress on tolerance and many moral treatises. Some schools, like that of Saiva, give great emphasis to the concept of love, 'the only quality of God which we can comprehend', and which we should extend to all our fellow beings (Shivapadasundaram 1934). Yet at a popular level Hinduism has shown most violent antagonism towards fellow Indians of Muslim faith.

This has been recently evidenced by the Hindu destruction of the Babri mosque at Ayodhya, Uttar Pradesh, alleged to have been built on the site of the birthplace of the Hindu god Ram. Representatives of the World Hindu Council led the attack upon the mosque, and the nationalist Bharatiya Janata Party supported the building of a Hindu temple on the contested site. In the resulting riots hundreds of people died, across India (*The Times* 8.1.93 *et seq.*). Observers have seen the danger of a transition of India from a secular state into 'an abyss of sectarianism'. There can hardly be a more powerful demonstration of the disruptive force inherent in religious commitment of a fanatical order.

Where a religious ideology does seem peculiarly powerful and often paradoxical is where it is associated with ethnic or nationalistic issues. This has been so throughout history and persists into modern times, as recent events in Yugoslavia have shown. Ethnic individuation may take various religious forms. As with the 'black theology' mentioned earlier, it may involve only a reinterpretation of doctrinal issues within the religious system. It may however lead to the creation of separate corporate bodies, as the many Black Baptist churches in the United States have developed in parallel fashion to their white counterparts. Again, completely new religious organizations may be formed, as the 'Black Muslims' of the United States were organized under the leadership of Elijah Muhammed. These congregations regard themselves as very different from ordinary Muslims, particularly in their rejection of equality of skin colour in adherents. They regard whites as alien, evil and incapable of inclusion in the same religious system. Their stigmatization of white people initially struck a sympathetic chord in many black people who did not wish to join the cult but resented the social discrimination against blacks by whites.

The identification of religious ideology and practice with specifically nationalistic alignment and aspirations has been very marked in recent years. The case of Iran is outstanding. The religious enthusiasm of the Shi'a masses was used by their leaders to overthrow an autocratic, corrupt Westernizing government and install a strongly nationalistic fanatical theocracy. In Iran, veneration for symbols of the Muslim religion, including the person of the leader Ayatollah Khomeini has verged at times upon mass hysteria. The case of Poland is also very marked, though of different content. For many years of this century the Catholic church remained the only overtly organized critic – sometimes opponent – of the communist Polish government. It had a large body of faithful church adherents, but it also gained support from a lot of intellectuals of no very firm religious persuasion because it stood for a nationalistic anti-Russian attitude against the compliant pro-Russian government. In a neighbouring region in earlier times the religious division between Russian Orthodox church and Polish Catholic church played an important part in the formation of national stereotypes. That religious allegiance, used as a banner for ethnic or communal divisions, is capable of generating fierce emotions, often expressed in violence, has been amply demonstrated historically by clashes between Hindus and Muslims or Sikhs in India, Christian Armenians and Muslim Azeris in the former Soviet Union, or Protestants and Catholics in Northern Ireland.

Fundamentalism in a particularly aggressive form may operate where a religious body tries to enforce its religious norms and values on people of the community who are moderate by ordinary practice or whose normal way of life is secular, following no religious patterns at all. So in India of recent years the hardline political party, Bharatiya Janata, aims to turn the country into a Hindu state, with appropriate conformity by every citizen. It was reported early in 1992 that the state of Kelantan, Malaysia, planned to implement the *shari'a*, the Islamic law, including penalties of stoning, whipping, and amputation of hand or foot of severe offenders. The chief minister who stated this was leader of the Parti Islam Se-Malaysia, the Muslim Party of Malaysia, a fundamentalist organization (*Independent* 3.4.92). In Algeria, fundamentalists of the Islamic Salvation Front attempted in 1988 and 1991 to demand reforms which would end in the setting up of an Islamic state; their demonstration led to riots and much loss of life. Early in 1992 their success at the ballot box led to a military coup to restrain them. Even in Jordan, a secular Arab state, the advance of Muslim extremists in the government has resulted in the application of religious rules of sexual segregation in schools and government offices, to the indignation of many ordinary citizens who resent this interference with their usual way of life (*The Times* 30.5.91; 6.6.91).

There is a real dilemma here for public policy over a wide range. Fundamentalists in Christianity, for instance, are mostly content to seek the original purity of the doctrine and practice of their religion, without attempting to force their practices upon their co-religionists and others, except by persuasion. But in Islam the prescriptions of the Koran are so mandatory upon believers, holding that all social, economic and political affairs come under the domain of Allah, that logically a good Muslim may feel bound to adopt extreme measures to secure the desired state.[7]

FACTIONALISM

The strength of an engagement with the nonrational is demonstrated by the unity of a religious group, which may even lead it to violent confrontation with another religious group. But it has also been responsible for much division among religious bodies when sections of them develop different interpretations of basic religious concepts or practices – or their leaders engage in power struggles. The significance attached to antagonism between different Christian doctrinal views is indicated by the theological precision given to terms such as creed, confession, schism, heresy, apostasy (Richardson and Bowden 1983: *passim*).

Any student of the history of Christianity must be struck by the extreme factionalism it has displayed. Basic to this has been the very human effort at distinctiveness, the assertion of individual rights to interpretation of the faith and exercise of authority over the faithful. In doctrine, this has been illustrated by the profusion of creeds and confessions, and by the care shown in defining divergence from them. A creed is essentially a statement of the rules of faith, and has been intended to be ecumenical, rooted in the common life of the church. A confession – a term used for credal statement by Reformation churches – is not so much an alternative to older creeds as an interpretation of what is meant by them, according to some particular understanding. Both creeds and confessions have been important for preaching and teaching. But significant too has been their oppositional character. It has been said that the task of a creed has been to defend the church against heresies. So, the notable Nicene Creed (of ad 325) rejected Arianism, the doctrine that Jesus Christ was not divine, of equality with God, but a subordinate creature. A basic job of a confession was to distinguish one church from another, as the Westminster Confession of 1643 became the formulary of the Church of Scotland in 1689.

Schism is now generally applied within the Christian church to the division of the church into separate and mutually hostile organizations. But though in the early centuries schism was regarded as blasphemous and sinful, marked by only one body possessing the truth, later views have held that a body could be termed schismatic and still retain the faith and the sacraments which it had acquired within the original church. The modern view, with its ecumenical trend, is that despite schism between the Eastern and Western Christian churches, and between Roman Catholicism and Protestantism, these are internal divisions. Their schism is not outside the church, though in itself it is still a sin from the original Catholic view. Schism is marked off from heresy, which is also a sin, but consists in specific denial of defined doctrine after instruction in what is alleged to be the truth. Historically, heresy has been very severely punished by the Catholic church, as by burning a heretic at the stake. But with the growing flexibility of modern theology, the identification of formal heresy has now become more questionable. Apostasy is a deliberate denial of belief, not just of an item of doctrine, but of the whole body of doctrine and practice, made by one who formerly was a believer. But despite the apparent precision in definition of all these terms, there is still room for ambiguity, since classification of persons or religious bodies in their terms is a matter of opinion. For instance, though both Christian Scientists and Mormons claim belief in Christ as a central part of their doctrine, more orthodox opinion is apt to regard them both as apostate rather than as schismatic Christians.

In Christianity, the Roman Catholic church claims primacy in deriving authority from the apostle Peter, chief of the apostles to whom the keys of earth and heaven are alleged to have been entrusted by his Lord. By the fourth century ad this figurative authority, regarded as crystallized in the bishop of Rome, was admitted as extending over the whole Western church, and by the fourteenth century the Pope had claimed that all temporal and spiritual powers belonged to the Roman church. Even now the papacy maintains its claim to universal spiritual jurisdiction and authority. But the Roman church has succeeded in retaining its structure of unified authority only at the cost of some losses. The Great Schism from the tenth century onwards separated the Eastern Orthodox church from the Western church on grounds both of dogma and of authority. The Eastern church became episcopal and collegial, governed by an ecumenical council, not a Pope. Later dissidents like Martin Luther broke away, partly in protest against the church corruption suffered by the papal structure, while others of the faithful such as Henry VIII of England were primarily reacting against ecclesiastical demands for sovereignty and political control. In the last century challenges to Roman Catholicism have arisen in the refusal of some Catholics to accept the doctrine of papal infallibility in official pronouncements on faith and morals, while the revolutionary interpretations of Marxist theology and 'liberation theology' have shown marked divergence from the central tradition. These views may not have given rise to any marked factional re-alignment of a separatist kind, but they indicate the strong differences that can arise within a dogmatic system claiming absolute authority.

By comparison with the still relatively unified Roman Catholic church, Protestantism has produced a spectacular crop of separate sectarian organizations. Over two hundred have been described for the United States alone in mid-twentieth century (Mead 1956). Characteristic of such organizations on the whole have been their exclusiveness, their intolerance of beliefs and practices of other, often allied or parent sects, their conviction of rightness in their scriptural interpretations, their use of sect allegiance as a primary factor in a member's social identity. Often sects have been generated by or associated with some forms of charismatic leadership. Expressed faith in the tenets of the sect is often a cardinal attribute of membership (cf. Bryan R. Wilson 1961).

Superficially, the patterns of division in Buddhism and Islam are very different from those in Christianity, but actually there are strong parallels among them. Both Buddhism and Islam suffered major cleavages at an early stage of their history, though from different causes. Nominally at least, Buddhism divided over an extent to which an individual, through the aid of Buddha, could personally obtain his release from the world of suffering. The older teaching of Theravada (Hinayana) – the Doctrine of the Elders (Small Vehicle) – linked salvation with the acquisition of merit by self-effort. The Buddha provided a model but was thought not to intervene actively in the fate of the worshipper. The Mahayana – Great Vehicle – a later development, held that vicarious salvation is possible through faith in the Buddha alone. (This is reminiscent of the bitter controversy in Christianity about justification by good works as contrasted with that by faith.) But though separation of doctrine was a prime issue in the split in Buddhism, more mundane considerations also operated. A strong regional alignment with political implications came into being, with Theravada being characteristic of Burma, Sri Lanka and Thailand, and Mahayana of China and Japan. Factionalism of various kinds has been rife throughout Buddhist religious history. Burmese Buddhism, of the Theravada school, has been noted for the way in which the Sangha (order of monks) has formed segments or sects on complex grounds such as degree of orthodoxy in following the rules of discipline, or differences of interpretation of the sacred texts by charismatic teachers. One of the most curious controversies, with strong political overtones in its factionalism, was the eighteenth-century argument over whether monks should wear their robes over one shoulder only, or over both shoulders, when seeking their daily food in the villages (Mendelson 1975: 58–62 *passim*). Japanese Buddhism, of Mahayana type, has seen the development of at least a dozen major sects, all tracing their origin to China, but differing in their canonical texts and their mystical interpretations. Perhaps best known in the West, if often in garbled form, is Zen Buddhism. An appealing legend is that Zen was generated by a smile of the Buddha – though it owed its origin to a succession of idiosyncratic human teachers. Zen is noted for its doctrine of detachment – 'the doctrine of Thought transmitted by Thought', its individuality of behaviour, and its pretension of placing no special virtue in canonical texts.

The term Zen is derived through Chinese from the Sanskrit *dhyana* meaning meditation. Unlike other Buddhist sects, Zen holds that enlightenment can come only by direct intuitive perception, relying neither upon sacred formulae nor upon the power of a merciful saviour. Zen is said to have contributed much to intellectual and aesthetic development in Japan. But it has had its enemies. In its early years Zen was bitterly opposed by older sects such as Tendai and Shingon in 'a fight for privilege rather than a battle for truth'. On occasion hostile parties attacked and burned down Zen monasteries (Sansom 1932, 320–32; Steinilber-Oberlin, 1938: 126–84).

Factionalism in Islam seems first to have arisen not primarily from divergence of religious belief but from disagreement over the form of succession to the authority of the Prophet after his death. The traditions are complex and at times contradictory. But a major division occurred at the outset of the succession between those who favoured as leader one of the elder Companions of the Prophet and those who wanted a man of closer relationship,

Ali bin Abu Talib, a cousin and son-in-law of the Prophet, married to his daughter Fatima. In the event Abu Bakr, a senior Companion, and allegedly the one whom the Prophet regarded as second to him in leading prayers, was chosen as Caliph (*khalifa*, deputy, delegate). He was succeeded in turn by two other Companions, and Ali became only the fourth Caliph. But it was a period of great civil strife, provoked in part by the personal ambitions of leaders, and in part by deep underlying tribal and urban rivalries. In this situation the partisans of Ali and of his sons Hasan and Husain, grandsons of the Prophet, suffered severely. Hasan, as Caliph, was poisoned and Husain was killed in the battle of Kerbala, which has become a traumatic symbol of suffering, with its site a pilgrim shrine, for Shi'ite Muslims.

In the centuries after Muhammed's death, the major sectarian divisions between Muslims crystallized into Sunni, the orthodox majority, followers of the Sunna, the path or custom; and Shi'a, the then unorthodox minority, named after *shi'a*, a party or sect. But the history of changing religious and political authority in Islam is exceedingly complex, with Sunnite and Shi'ite ruling dynasties tending to alternate. As time went on a regional alignment developed, with a major Sunni population in the western territories and a corresponding Shi'a population to the east, notably in Iran (Persia).

Both Sunni and Shi'a accept the sources of the law of Islam expressed in the Koran as the direct Word of God, and the traditions (*hadith*) regarding the sayings and doings of the Prophet. But the Shi'ites have many variant traditions of their own, more favourable to the cause of Ali than those of the main Sunni canon. The Shi'ites regard the first three Caliphs, the Companions, as usurpers of the authority of Ali. In the course of time Muslims recognized a divorce of the Caliphate, with leadership in political authority over the Muslim empire, from the Imamate, with leadership in religious authority over the Faithful. The role of Imam came to assume a mystical significance for the Shi'ites. Most recognize twelve Imams after Muhammed, in hereditary succession. These came to be regarded as infallible and sinless. But the twelfth Imam, a young boy, disappeared in mysterious circumstances in his own house, in Samarra (if historical, probably a victim of foul play). This was about the middle of the third century ah of the Muslim reckoning, or towards the end of the ninth century of the Christian era. The disappearance of the twelfth Imam was treated not simply as a physical, possibly criminal matter, but of critical mystical significance. He has since been known for the last thousand years by the Shi'ites as the Hidden Imam. He is believed to be alive, staying in concealment, expected in due course to return and assume leadership of the Faithful. (Analogy with the Jewish Messiah, and the Second Coming of Christ are obvious.) For the first seventy years or so the Hidden Imam was in the 'Lesser Concealment' and represented by agents, but the fourth and last of these refused to appoint a successor. So from ad 940 the Hidden Imam has had no visible representative on earth (Donaldson 1933: *passim*).

This brief outline of the major division of Islam has ignored the bewildering diversity of doctrinal views from the early centuries of the religion. The influence of Hellenistic Christian thought affected Muslim theology in Syria, as did Gnosticism in Iraq and Manichaean dualism in Iran. The result was sectarian movements such as the puritan, rationalistic Mu'tazilite and the fanatical Khawārij who pursued the Muslim obligation to do good to such extremes that they made war on the orthodox, more tolerant community. Even the Shi'ites showed fissiparous tendencies, the Imāmi sect of Iran recognizing twelve Imams, the Ismāili holding that the last proper visible Imam was the seventh, Ismail. (One of the offshoots of this sectarian movement was the notorious so-called 'Assassins' of the Middle Ages and later.) From time to time attempts were made by the jurists to incorporate the Imāmi sect of Shi'a into the orthodox framework of Islam as just another 'school' but so far without success (Gibb 1949: 107–36).

While both Sunni and Shi'a share belief in the major elements of Islam, Shi'ites reject the prescription of *ijmā'*, the obligation to abide by the 'consensus of the community', which in practice means the dictates of the scholars of the majority. They also differ in views about the Mahdi. The Hidden Imam, the Master of the Age, is identified by Shi'ites with the Mahdi – 'one who is absolutely guided by God', an eschatological figure of messianic type who will come at the End of Time. From the ambiguity of traditions and Koranic reference, Sunni theologians have not required belief in the coming of the Mahdi as part of their creeds. For Shi'ite theologians, on the other hand, belief in the expected coming of the Mahdi is essential.

Each of the great Western religions has at times had a belief in the coming or return of a mystical leader who will rectify the state of the world and sit in judgement on believers and infidels. But belief in a hope deferred can impose a great strain on organizational solidarity. Within the Shi'ite community itself impatience sometimes developed about the Great Concealment. Some visible representative of the hidden principle was sometimes sought. During times of great suffering, in the period of the crusades and of the later invasion of the Mongols, the Hidden Imam did not appear. Towards the end of the eighteenth century a heretical sect of Shaikhis sought for guidance in the revelation of a new leader. Later, about mid-nineteenth century, Mirza 'Ali Muhammed came to be recognized by some Shaikhis and other Shi'ites as the Bab or Gate of communication with the Hidden Imam. He himself believed this claim, and maintained it before orthodox Shi'ite theologians. He also interpreted the Koran in a largely allegorical sense, and gave little value to the laws on ritual purity. Since by this period Iran (Persia) had embraced Shi'ite doctrine as its state religion, it is hardly surprising that Mirza was imprisoned and executed. But the faith he had enunciated was promulgated and extended by his follower Baha'ullah, who claimed to be an emanation of Allah. He led his supporters into what became a religion entirely separate from Islam, with world pretensions, emerging ultimately as the synthetic faith of Baha'i. This has now a large international membership, devoted to spreading ideas of universal brotherhood of man, the unity of all religions and general peace (Donaldson 1933: 362–9; Gobineau 1933: 131–319).

Islam, a strongly monotheistic religion, attaches great importance to the rule of law, which is essentially believed to be the law of God. The term Islam means 'complete surrender', that is to the will of God, and the *shari'a*, the law of Islam, deals primarily with the relation of God to the human soul. Theoretically, nothing in the human world is free from the rules of the *shari'a*. Sovereignty belongs to God alone and the prime duty of a ruler is to enforce the divine law and protect the rights of Muslims.[8]

But the divine law needs human interpreters. Early in the history of Islam there arose learned jurists who gave their own opinion on the meaning of the various phases of the law – from marriage, inheritance, administration of estates, charitable gifts to identification and punishment of criminals. In the Sunni division of Islam four main jurists have been recognized, each offering some variation on the canon derived from the Koran and the traditions. Within some 350 years of Muhammed's time, the readings of these four jurists – Shafi'i, Hanafi, Hanbali, Maliki – had crystallized into a received set of interpretations or schools, mutually acceptable in wisdom, with fairly definite regional distribution. Being a sacred canon, the Word of God, it became hard to allow new streams of legal thought, so the idea of the closure of the Gate of Interpretation came to be accepted. By this in theory no change in the *shari'a* was possible, though in practice some modifications or alleviations have crept in over the centuries. Also, descendants of converts to Islam, for example, from Hinduism have in some cases retained elements of their traditional customs in their local interpretation of the law. But in general the scholars of each generation, the *ulamā*, as legal interpreters of the sacred writings, have become the source of authority, often treated as almost infallible, through the principle of *ijmā'*, community consensus.

But such formal authoritarianism provoked reaction. Parallel, in some cases antagonistic, to the juristic scholarship of the *ulamā* have been the *sūfi*, who have displayed more emotional as well as intellectual individuality. In theory by prayer and meditation, the *sūfi* endeavours to gain insight into, even reproduce the mystical experiences of the Prophet, as related in the Koran. But in the history of Islam, the influence of Christian asceticism and Hellenistic philosophy have also been discerned in *sūfi* thought. Islam has had many notable *sūfi*, renowned for their poetical imagery and their philosophical and mystical insight. Some among them, inspired by the doctrine of mystical union imparted by divine grace, even asserted an intense personal relation with God of an unorthodox kind, which brought them close to heresy. The distinction between *ma'arifa*, knowledge given in ecstasy, and *'ilm*, intellectual and traditional knowledge, tended to separate *sūfi* from the ordinary body of the Faithful. The symbolic developments of their esoteric knowledge often gave *sūfi* leaders an elite position among scholars. Yet despite its vagaries, sūfism was able to remain within orthodox Islam, and was responsible for much conversion to the faith.

The spread of sūfism was facilitated by the development of *tariqa*, orders or 'ways' by which followers clustered round a pious man credited with miraculous powers and formed a kind of brotherhood. Such orders developed from the twelfth and thirteenth centuries onwards, in large numbers. They have differed from one another in ritual and litany, and in the degree of their tolerance of the rules of the orthodox religion. Their leaders became shaikhs or saints according to the emphasis on their social or mystical role; some saints were hereditary. Members of some orders sought ecstasy by swaying in convulsions to accompaniment of music and chanting of religious formulae. In other orders such external stimuli were forbidden, and identification with the Prophet rather than with God was sought by contemplation of the essence of the Prophet and imitation of his conduct. An order tended to provide a way of life, and many of the activities of its members were highly pragmatic, often of political significance, as with the well-known Wahhabi of Saudi Arabia or the Sanusi of Libya. The relation of sūfism to such orders has been complex, sometimes tenuous, but historically of great importance. Essentially, sūfism became a spearhead for a popular movement of religious thought and practice, getting away from the rigid dogmatism of the orthodox scholars and helping to supply a more personal aspect to what appears in some respects as a very formal religion. The *sūfi* orders often provided a bridge between elite and folk cultures.[9]

Diversification if not factionalism has also been characteristic of Hinduism, as reference to any general work on this religion will show (for example, H. H. Wilson 1958) who lists over sixty divisions in what he has called 'sects' of this faith.

In this examination of factionalism I have indicated a kind of dialectical process in the development of religion. Formalization of belief and conduct is a necessary step in the institutionalization of a religion. But this is continually being challenged by assertion of more individual relation to the transcendent, and in turn the results of individual innovation become routinized into more regular patterns. Ideas attract followers, and dissident ideas serve to crystallize the views of many individuals. So factions arise. All this takes place in a social environment, by which thought and conduct are radically affected, and ambitions of individuals seeking power complicate the situation. Any dispassionate analysis of factionalism in the great religions makes clear the essentially human character of the forces in operation.

RELIGIONS IN CHANGE

Historically, religious belief has supplied people with major patterns for apprehending the world, and religious ritual has supplied them with periodic patterns for conduct, in daily life and in crises of existence. Established forms of belief and ritual, seen as traditional and given legitimacy thereby, have been very important in maintaining the stability of society. But such stability has been in part an illusion. Religion, like other social institutions, is continually in process of change, due partly to external pressures of an economic or political kind, or to internal pressures of doctrinal debate or personal ambition.

Even the small-scale particularistic 'primitive' religions would appear to have suffered change, if only because of population changes. But our information about this is very limited. By contrast every major religion has given clear evidence of change. From the early days of the Christian faith it is clear that the influence of other faiths, such as Gnosticism, influenced the formation of Christian doctrine. Roman Catholicism, which claims nearly two thousand years of traditional patterning in the apostolic succession, has undergone various doctrinal modifications, for example, concerning the dogmatic position of Mary the mother of Jesus. Historically, the church suffered defections, notably that at the Reformation. And recently, in response to modern demands the Vatican Council II approved substantial changes to its ritual, including the substitution of a vernacular mass for the tridentine Latin mass – to the indignation of many of the more conventional faithful.

At an intellectual level, throughout the Christian world, theologians have been wrestling in a sophisticated way with some of the fundamental problems of their belief, such as the conception of the Trinity or the meaning of the Eucharist. Once prominent concepts of strong emotional value such as Heaven and Hell have now been given a marginal value only, and demoted from spatial to spiritual states. Orthodox and liberal theologians disagree on interpretations, but the more radical thinkers 'may assume that theology is the self-description of the Christian community, and doing it is far more like a cultural anthropolgist giving a "thick description" of a culture than like a philosopher identifying the structure of either reality or consciousness' (Kelsey, 'Method, Theological' in Richardson and Bowden 1983: 367).

A significant modern development at an international level is the growth of the notion of theocentricity – that the great world faiths are just different perceptions and responses to the one divine reality which Christians call God. For some Christians, then, instead of belief in the uniqueness of their own religion for salvation, there is a recognition of Jews, Hindus, Muslims, Buddhists as 'anonymous Christians' who in default of knowledge of the gospel, are saved by grace and sacrificial power of Christ. Patronizing as this notion may seem to those of other faiths, its eclecticism is one manifestion of the response of the Christian church to the pressures of world ethical opinion (see Hick, 'Theocentricity', in Richardson and Bowden 1983: 563).

But this eclecticism and toleration at an intellectual level has not inhibited the advance of proselytizing agencies, 'missions', notably from Christianity and Islam, to proclaim their faith and seek to convert people of other belief. Historically, the moves to proselytization have often been accompanied by or followed economic and political pressures, or military adventure, against the objects of religious assault. What the process of conversion then often seems to have been is not a religious awakening 'from darkness to light' but a concession to expediency. Intellectually, as I myself have observed it in the Solomon islands, it has commonly taken the form of a shift in the framework of ideas about the world. It is believed that the spiritual forces controlling events have God as their apex, rather than residing exclusively in God; the traditional spirits are inferior or quiescent, not non-existent. The truth of the new faith is relative, not absolute.

Religions, especially those of a universalistic order, are dynamic thought systems. They manifest a ferment of idea, defended by their protagonists with vigour and at times with rancour. A most marked change in Christian religious thinking has come with the development of scrutiny and interpretation of the Bible. Since the early centuries of the faith, the basic approach of most Christians to the Bible has been that it is a holy book, inspired by God, of unrivalled spiritual and moral impact. But many differences have arisen, as to the value to be attributed to the text itself, and to the meaning to be attached to it. At a very early period there was argument as to which books of Judaic and Christian origination were to be included in the sacred canon. The result was an apocrypha of Judaic books recognized by Jews as outside their canonical set, and a parallel series of gospels and sectarian writings excluded from the Christian Bible. But opinions as to their authenticity varied. The Council of Trent specifically admitted Tobit, Judith, Wisdom and some others to the Roman Catholic holy scriptures, whereas on the whole Protestant scriptures have tended to omit such works or to relegate them to a special section. Modern scholars view all such apocryphal material as historically inferior but not necessarily of less authority than the canonical books. They treat the non-canonical texts as certainly very informative about religious thought and conditions at the time in which they were written. The case for the Bible as the Word of God has come to be seen then as a product of some very human decisions as to what should be represented in it.

A basic question about the Bible has been the status of its message. A fundamentalist belief, still current, but which has early roots, is that the scriptures are divinely inspired, must be literally interpreted and are inerrant, incapable of wrong statement. Such a view insists for example, on the historicity of Adam and Eve in a material Garden of Eden. But Origen's view at an early period was that scripture had three modes of interpretation: literal, moral and allegorical. This gave a great deal of room for variation in understanding and in judgement of its truth. A modern historical and critical approach to biblical studies, by theologians themselves, and in other intellectual Christian circles, sees the Bible as a set of literary documents offering wisdom and moral teaching of high order, with views about a transcendental sphere and suggestions about conduct with reference to a present and a future life. Though they are credited with a diffuse authority emanating from a divine interest, the books of the Bible are now seen as messages prepared by human hands, not assuming any divine form.

Religious change has often been a result of social pressures upon guardians of the doctrine and ritual. This comes out clearly in what may be called a 'dark' side of a cult, where scriptural authority and tradition are invoked, even as the 'word of God' to justify a range of opinions based ultimately upon male chauvinism, class privilege or other very human interests. An example is the asymmetry historically apparent in the main three monotheistic religions, in regard to the position of women. In Islam females are almost totally excluded from official religious leadership in public worship, though they may be active in leadership in private worship. In Judaism women are barred from leadership in the orthodox synagogues, though in modern times a more liberal group has had a woman as rabbi. Opinions in Christianity are diverse. In the Roman Catholic and Orthodox churches, admission of women to the priesthood is still ruled out, on traditional grounds, ostensibly with reference to some divine sanction. With Nonconformists, in general the issue does not seem to have taken doctrinal form, though the number of women ministers is probably not large.

In the Anglican community, there has been great agitation in recent years over the issue of female ordination to the priesthood. Female deacons have existed for many years. But in the English church at least, no woman could enter the priestly order, exemplified by the ability to conduct the Eucharist, seen by traditionalists as an essentially male office since the days of Christ's apostles. In an attempt to soften the pressures from those who wished and those who opposed the ordination of women, the church once officially sought spiritual guidance, but this was ineffective. The liberal wing was moved by what is regarded as modern ethical and pragmatic considerations, though serious differences existed within it about timing and conditions of entry of women to the order. The traditionalists were aghast at the proposed change, which they saw as having mystical as well as ritual implications. They accused their opponents of 'situationist ethics' in yielding to the assumed morality of current fashions of thought. In particular, they quoted scripture in defence of the established practice of the church. Threats of splitting the Anglican church on the issue were made. When the issue finally came to the vote in the general synod in 1991 there was a very narrow majority for the consecration of women as priests. This has not ended the controversy. Ways are therefore being sought of avoiding fission within the church by making special arrangements to accomodate the traditionalists, as by special dioceses in which bishops would ordain male priests only.

All the major religions in this century have seen challenges to their doctrines and to the established position of those in authority. The most powerful challenges have had political roots, as reactions of the apparent lack of effectiveness of the religion to cope with modern social and economic conditions. To take only Christianity, movements of particular importance have been those of Marxist theology, liberation theology, feminist theology and black theology. These have all been concerned with themes of social justice, of discrimination and exploitation. They have all demanded a reinterpretation of Christian doctrine and practice. In its traditional form such doctrine and practice have seemed to be a reflection of much Western political and social ideology, legitimizing an unjust world order. Such movements have led to a reappraisal of the scriptures, with emphasis upon freedom from domination, care for the oppressed, even revolutionary protest. It is difficult to estimate, even for an expert, the effect of such theological revisions and associated behaviour upon the mainline churches, but in some areas it would seem to have been considerable.

THE EXALTED AND THE BIZARRE

Religions present many paradoxes. Inconsistencies and contradictions can be found in the ideas promulgated, and in interpretations of the beliefs or precepts enjoined upon their followers. And it is a matter of common knowledge how often their followers do not demonstrate in conduct the behaviour laid down by the rules of the religious belief.

Belief is a very general term of complex meaning, often implying an emotional as well as an intellectual commitment to a conviction that any given statement or appreciation of a situation is true. Doctrine, basically meaning 'teaching', in its narrower sense is a formulation of belief in some specific field, such as in Christianity the doctrine of salvation, or of resurrection as a divine act of new creation. In the major religions it is expected that the members of the religious body will recognize and accept its doctrines, though usually there is no absolute requirement for this. (Note the perturbation in 1994 in some Anglican communities in Britain when some priests declared that they did not believe in doctrines which their church expected them to believe – *The Times* 1.8.94.)

Dogma, originally meaning merely 'opinion' is an intensification of doctrine, placing more weight on the notion of authority. Members of the religious body are formally required to have adherence to the doctrinal formulation on pain of exclusion from some aspects of the work of the religious community. In Christianity a liberal interpretation of dogma views it as divinely revealed truth proclaimed as such by the church and binding on the faithful, but to be regarded in its historical context and not to be seen as ultimate norm. In Roman Catholicism, however, the interpretation is more stringent. *The magisterium* of papal authority, treated as infallible since 1870, lays a burden of absolute belief upon the faithful – a burden which some renowned Catholic theologians such as Küng have refused to share. Anthropologically, it is clear that the exercise of this papal authority, if prescribing what adherents should believe, is a powerful instrument in assisting conformity to church discipline.

Whatever the diversity of religious systems, from the more simply organized to the most complex, one is struck by a paradoxical contrast between what may be termed their 'exalted' and their 'bizarre' aspects. They explore some of the most abstract and profound human problems, of existence, life, death, love, achievement, suffering. They set out propositions purporting to explain the human dilemmas arising in critical situations, to provide rules for conduct in coping with them and salvation from their deleterious effects. They often cloak such teaching in impressive literary form, and in moving aesthetic presentations of music and drama. They use the narrative resources of myth and legend, and philosophical and theological skills to embroider their argument. Yet on the other hand they also at times employ some quite bizarre ideas about the events and personalities involved in the religious cult. Some religions even flaunt these ideas by requiring them to be held by their followers as items of belief, as dogma.

The church music of the Western world has given evidence of the most exalted ideas and experiences, to mention only Tallis, Byrd, Schütz, Monteverdi, Johann Sebastian Bach. Their contributions stand at the apex of aesthetic sensibility, combined with deep emotional thoughts on the nature of human life. Yet even in this musical sphere paradoxical elements can enter.

A charming if minor example of the mingling of the exalted and the bizarre is given in the history of the Song of Songs (Song of Solomon) in the Old Testament. Already in the third century ad the scholarly Origen had observed that on the face of it the poem held no profit to the reader, and that therefore it should all be given a spiritual meaning (Raymond F. Collins, 'Exegesis' in Richardson and Bowden 1983: 198). In the early fifteenth century, in the development of Marian piety, much church music was devoted to Mary. John Dunstable, the greatest English composer of the time, composed some of the most beautiful Marian antiphons, including *Regina celi letare* (Be glad, Queen of Heaven), and *Speciosa facta es* (Lovely to Look at are You). In praise of the Virgin Mother of God he also composed the motet *Quam pulchra es* (How Beautiful You are) as antiphon for Sundays from Trinity to Advent. The text of this motet was based upon chapter seven of the Song of Songs, presumably from the Latin Vulgate. In the context of performance of the hymn, the attributes of the lover and the loved are clearly attributable to Mary, in a delightfully solemn rendering. But in the Authorised Version of the Bible (1611) nearly two centuries later, and of Protestant not Catholic origin, the interpretation had changed. Now the song was regarded as conveying the mutual love of Christ and his Church, in glosses which have strained the credulity of many of the faithful. In the Revised Version (1885) and the Old Testament text of the New English Bible (1970) no theological or ecclesiastical glosses to the song appear. The New English Bible indeed treats the text with its highly emotionally charged, personally directed, physical expressions of passion, as a secular love song – which seems most probable. It indicates bride, bridegroom and companions as separate speakers, as some original Hebrew texts imply. It is ironic that over about two thousand years a magnificent love song should have been treated unconsciously as part of a sacred canon, expressing solemn religious values of the highest order! Such a sacralization of erotic poetic expression is touching, if unintended!

To label a belief or an action 'bizarre' means that it seems unusual, odd, out of keeping with the ordinary rules of behaviour in man or nature. Hence it is productive of astonishment, even regarded as incredible. Yet most religions show examples of what to an external observer would be classified as bizarre events or conditions, but treated by the faithful as true. A good field of instances may be taken from ideas about the human body. It may be regarded as behaving in an unusual physical manner, as when the Prophet Muhammed is believed to have made a bodily journey by night to Heaven. Under the guidance of the archangel Gabriel he made a journey from Mecca to Jerusalem, thence ascending by stages through the heavens into Paradise and the presence of God himself. In most versions of the story he rode the winged beast Burāq. Some Muslim commentators have treated this incident as only a dream or a vision. But a common interpretation, portrayed by Muslim painters, treats the journey as an actual occurrence, elevating the Prophet far above the rank of ordinary men (Arnold 1928: 117–22). In the Christian field a dogma which flouts any ordinary conception of natural process is that of the bodily assumption of the Blessed Virgin Mary to heaven. Stories of the miraculous preservation of Mary the mother of Jesus from bodily death and corruption began early in the Christian church, linked with ideas that the corruptibility of the body was a consequence of sin. These notions of Mary's purity culminated, after pressure from Marian pietists, in a declaration by Pope Pius XII in 1950 that the Bodily Assumption of the Blessed Virgin Mary was henceforward to be an article of faith of the church. What has never been satisfactorily explained is the exact situation of that physical body now, if the declaration is to be taken in any but a figurative sense!

Another idea about the human body which is bizarre to ordinary apprehension is that of bodily resurrection after death. This notion has been central to Christianity from its beginnings, since salvation of believers depends upon their trust in the idea of the resurrection of Jesus after his crucifixion, his death and deposit in the tomb. Ideas of bodily resurrection have not been unique to Christianity, but the Christian doctrine has given them a unique value. Literally interpreted, the resurrection of Jesus was a divine act which resolved an earthly contradiction. Regarded anthropologically, it is an assertion which demands from the faithful a suspension of judgement in natural process, a claim to the extra-human, divine nature of Jesus, and hence part of the defence mechanism for the cult. But the historical evidence for this alleged reversal of a natural process is understandably much open to question. Hence it is little wonder that the more sophisticated Christians tend to regard the story as essentially symbolical, a kind of parable to illustrate an aspect of God's love for mankind.

The complexity of the human body, its role as a vehicle of expression of a personality, offers a rich area for religious conceptualization. On the one hand the body is given a kind of earthy, mundane position, the seat of primal urging and desires; on the other hand it is seen as linked intimately with more elevated mental activities, figuratively given spiritual status. In many religions too there is an idea that the human body of officiant or worshipper can become the abiding places of a separate spirit form. As an anthropologist taking part in a traditional Polynesian religious service of offering to ancestral gods, I have been well aware of the deep conviction of people present, that the spirits of their ancestors were among us, registering and approving what was taking place. To a Western observer this would be a bizarre notion, but intelligible in the light of local attitudes about the dependence of economic prosperity and human welfare on such spiritual beings. Even more bizarre was the belief that at a certain moment of a critical rite of communion, the body of the presiding priest, the leading chief of the community, was actually possessed by the spirit of the founding ancestor of his clan. 'The god has come to sit in me' the chief declared to me. The idea of this supernatural presence was but one instance of a common religious phenomenon, that of spirit possession, in which the speech and actions of a human being are interpreted as those of a spirit being, and given due respect as such. The ritual over which this chief-god presided was a kind of communion feast, in which the participants were believed to partake of the flesh of the god himself by the act of eating a vegetable (a yam) which had been consecrated to the deity (Firth 1967b: 156–9).

Now such beliefs in spiritual presence in bodily shape and material form may seem odd to a Western reader. But of course they have their analogies in Western Christian religion. A most marked parallel is the Eucharist of the Christian church, when bread and wine are offered in commemoration of what is held to be the 'Last Supper' in which Jesus participated with his disciples. Theologians have given many interpretations of the Eucharist. But a common traditional view is that the bread and wine of the sacrament are changed into the body and blood of Jesus Christ by a process of 'transubstantiation'. The Polynesians with whom I took part in the ceremony of eating the vegetable flesh of the god did not seem to have any theory about the relation between material and spiritual substance. But Christian theologians have distinguished very carefully in Aristotelian fashion between the 'substances' of the bread and wine which were transformed into Christ's body and blood and the 'appearances' or 'accidents' of the bread and wine which kept their outward form unaltered. Hence it can be asserted that what the believer feels on his palate is still the taste of the ordinary materials, while receiving the essence of the divine Christ spiritually. Such an interpretation may be regarded as bizarre. And indeed some theologians have rejected it, holding that the ritual is essentially commemorative and symbolic, but not involving the presence of the bodily elements of the Christ. It is a 'thanksgiving' in the Greek sense of the term 'Eucharist', a sacramental ceremony emphasizing the cardinal concepts of the Christian faith (cf. Firth 1973: 414–26). Such views recognize the sociological significance of solemn ceremony without relying on an essentially esoteric interpretation.

One can see from these examples, and others such as the belief in the conception of Jesus by a virgin, that in many religious contexts the notion of the body is used as a field for embroidery, figurative to an outsider, but literal to a believer. Notions of bodily assumption into heaven, of resurrection of the body, of inhabitation of the body by spiritual powers, of transformation of bread and wine into body and blood invisibly are all contradictory of what we know about natural processes. Their function is essentially as declarations of the truth of the religion, in that it can overbear the natural in favour of the supernatural.

Striking examples of the bizarre in religion occur in tales of miracles. A miracle, in a conventional sense, is an unexpected performance resulting from supernatural power, exercised by direct divine intervention or through the agency of a divinely inspired person, such as a saint. Many modern theologians regard claims to miracles as simply testimony to the impact of a religious personality upon his followers, or an attempt at power manipulation. They abandon or leave open any question of divine intervention in human affairs. Most anthropologists would adopt a similar position, stressing the significance of claims to a miracle as propaganda devices, reinforcing the pretensions of a religion to credibility.

But in the major religions there is still much belief in miracles, visions of holy personages, messages from the spirit world, or even physical manifestations in the human body of what is regarded as spirit influence or possession. To a Buddhist, according to Conze (1951: 84), however refined and intellectual he may be, a belief in miracles is indispensable to the survival of any spiritual life. The folk religion of Roman Catholicism has provided many examples of miracles. Indeed a properly attested miracle is a criterion for elevation of a Catholic to sanctification. Especially popular has been the apparition of holy personages, including Christ and the Virgin Mary, to children and impressionable young women. Perhaps the most famous has been the apparition of the Virgin in 1858 to Bernadette Soubirous at Lourdes.

This image declared 'I am the Immaculate Conception', four years after the dogmatic definition of the feast of the Immaculate Conception in 1854 by Pope Pius IX put this notion among the revealed truths of the church. But also very celebrated have been the apparitions of Mary seen by three peasant children in Portugal, near the village of Fatima, over a period of years beginning in 1916. To one child in particular the Mother of God spoke many messages, saying that men must ask pardon for their sins and amend their lives, and insisting on the necessity of devotion to her 'immaculate heart'. She also pleaded for the consecration of Russia to her Immaculate Heart. The Sacred Heart of Jesus had already been enthusiastically described after a vision by Marie Alacoque at Paray-le-Monial in the seventeenth century, and the cult had blossomed with vigorous promotion by the Jesuit order. Here was an object of parallel devotion in the heart of Mary (Kearney 1950).

One of the oddest developments in the apparitional field of Catholic propaganda was the institution of the cult of the Miraculous Medal. In 1830 the Blessed Virgin was alleged to manifest herself to Sister Catherine Labouré, a young novice in the chapel of the mother house of the Sisters of Charity of St. Vincent de Paul in Paris. The Virgin revealed to the novice the design of a medal to be struck in her honour, and embodying the message of her conception without sin. Mary complained in the vision of delay in putting her mission into execution, but in due course the church, after careful enquiry, declared in favour of the supernatural origin of the medal. In a few years many millions of the medal were struck and distributed among the faithful throughout the world. Towards the end of the nineteenth century a special ritual for blessing and investing with the medal was inserted in the Roman Rite, and many indulgences were granted to those who wore it. To the medal, animated by prayer to the Immaculate Mother, were ascribed miraculous powers – diseases such as leprosy, dropsy, epilepsy disappeared with the application of the medal, and through supernatural intervention unbelievers and apostates were converted and hardened sinners abandoned their evil ways. The medal was also recorded as having proved a safeguard in shipwreck and accidents. As a result of this 'ineffable mystery' Sister Catherine, after beatification, was solemnly declared a saint in 1947.[10]

Looking back over its history, one can see the cult of the

Miraculous Medal as a feature of the pressure of Marian piety to establish dogmatically the doctrine of the Immaculate Conception of Mary, free from the taint of original sin. The ingenious nature of this development was that Mary herself was depicted as appearing in visible form to insist on the importance of the doctrine. The accounts of such apparitions are obviously firmly believed in by large numbers of the Catholic faithful. But despite arguments about 'mystery' a commonsense interpretation of them, in accord with much psychological and anthropological knowledge, would focus upon the suggestible character of the young women and children to whom they occurred, and the exhibitionism, bias and ambition of those in the religious orders who took such pains to promote the cults.

The existence of so much paradox in the belief and action system of even the most sophisticated religions calls for some explanation. One element is that the paradoxes often fit the beliefs of the ordinary folk; they correspond to the wants and anxieties of members of the congregation. They wish for healing to be done when medical science is ineffective; prayers are answered and miracles occur because science cannot cope with the randomness of individual activity. Another element is the stark contrast of the paradoxical item with the occurrence of ordinary events. The Mother of God who ascended bodily to heaven, the Shi'ite Imam who has remained alive in seclusion for a thousand years and who will reappear in the fullness of time, the Buddha who sends forth from his forehead a ray of light which lights up 18,000 worlds – to believe such things marks off the sacred character of the Beings involved and can be taken as proof of the cult. The mundanely impossible, absurd, is embraced as counter to a pragmatic, materialist world. Another defence of religious paradox is sometimes given by the more sophisticated members of the faith who themselves do not believe in the more extreme improbable events. They argue that these serve the less enlightened, and help to lead the mass of the faithful to adhere to the religion as a whole.[11]

Modern religious developments in belief may tend to increase rather than reduce the elements of paradox. Traditional Christianity has long embraced a paradox – the Eastern Church calls it a 'mystery' – in the concept of the Trinity, in which three persons, God the Father, Jesus Christ the Son, and the Holy Spirit, are united in one divine person. The paradox is heightened by some recent pronouncements which appear to accept the notion of addressing God as 'Mother' as well as 'Father' (see chapter 4).

All such examples indicate how often religious assertions, so satisfying to believers, can correspond to secular concerns, and can suggest alternative interpretations to a sceptical mind.

RELIGION AND MORALITY

In the 'great' or 'universalistic' religions another set of paradoxes lies in the field of morality.

Many small-scale, 'primitive' religious systems have not been much concerned with moral issues. The society has relied upon social sanctions to control moral behaviour among its members. But all the major religious systems treat moral problems as an essential feature of their theory and practice. They may vary in the degree to which they extend their moral precepts beyond the bounds of their own membership. But by and large, each of the major religions enunciates a set of moral principles which should regulate the conduct of its followers, towards equable relations towards other people, with truth, honesty, charity, loyalty among their prime tenets. In all the great religions, and also in others of lesser note, eminent men and women have led lives of virtue according to such precepts, serving as notable exemplars to many people. Yet it is clear that to profess a religion is no guarantee of a moral life. All the moral injunctions of Judaism, Christianity, Islam and the rest have not saved their followers from actions of self-assertion, greed, pride, cupidity and aggression. The results are deplored by leaders of the faith, but it is recognized that religious sanctions are not strong enough to control human impulses. Hence an elaborate vocabulary of concepts such as sin, confession, punishment, repentance, redemption has arisen to try and fill the gap between moral precept and failure to conform. Religion may promise salvation for the soul, but the road thereto may be rough!

A notable paradox is in the attitude of some religions towards the theory of peace and the practice of war. The ambiguity of Christianity here is marked. The religion of Christ is explicitly a religion of peace and love. From time to time, attempts are made to validate the concept of a 'just war', though apologetically. And through the course of Christian history adherents of the faith have killed one another, for sectarian or broader nationalistic reasons, in pursuit of power or territory, with little ideological check. The Napoleonic wars illustrated this. The comment of Tolstoy in *War and Peace* was very apt. Of about twenty years of war in Europe at the beginning of the nineteenth century he wrote 'millions of Christian men professing the law of love of their fellows slew one another'.

Islam has taken a different line. The Koran is full of moral injunctions towards good conduct. But these are directed primarily towards behaviour to fellow Muslims. Islam explicitly allows a morality of violence. The Muslim doctrine of *jihād*, the Path of God, can be interpreted as a call to a holy war, in which Muslims who are slain do not die but are translated living into the presence of their Lord. Such a holy war is justified as a revolt against the tyranny of an infidel government, or against alien non-Muslim forces. Some modern fundamentalist revolutionaries would like to invoke it against a secularist state. But the calling for a *jihād* is looked upon with caution by the learned men of Islam. Some schools of law hold that a *jihād* should be begun only with reasonable prospect of success (Gibb 1949: 66–7; Jansen 1979: 28); some, that a *jihād* should be undertaken only after an opponent has begun warlike action. Basically, *jihād* means 'effort', religiously sanctioned, and hence obligatory upon every believer once it has been declared. In Islamic history *jihād* has supplied the ideological strength for war of Muslims against infidels – from Saladin's medieval battles against the crusaders to the proselytizing campaigns of Uthman dan Fodio against pagan Hausa in West Africa in the eighteenth century.

But the moral impact of the religious sanction has been variously interpreted, according to more material considerations. In the Sudan about the end of the eighteenth century theocratic states became dominant, with an *imam* as the head of the community, his authority being regarded as resting upon the rule of God. Anyone who revolted against his (often severe) authority was treated as an enemy of God. So those fellow Muslims who did not accept his authority were persecuted in what was declared to be a *jihād*, a holy war. Here religious fanaticism gave an interpretation to political ambitions which led to very questionable moral judgements (cf. Gibb 1962: 102; Trimingham 1959: 152; Hurgronje 1906, II: 347–51).

For modern militant Islam the temptation to declare *jihād*

against alien forces has been great, though on the whole more moderate Muslim groups have not recognized the obligation called for. So the struggle of Muslim against Hindu in the Indo-Pakistan war of 1965 was labelled a holy war by some leaders. And after a Western air strike against Iraq in reprisal for Saddam Hussein's infringement of United Nations resolutions, he informed his people that 'another battle of *jihād* has begun which God wants to be a certain victory for you' (*The Times* 14 and 15.1.93). It is clear that the moral imperative of the religious appeal is differently interpreted by different Muslim groups.

In Islam, then, as with other religions, the actual behaviour of adherents does not correspond to the ideal as expressed in doctrine. This is recognized as a problem in all the major religions. It is commonly expressed as a contrast or incompatibility between human failings and frailities on the one hand and the purity of divinely inspired values on the other. But the contrast is unreal. Believers compromise with the world and with their own desires, and betray their religion, precisely because their religion, like their desires and the false values of the world, is essentially a human creation, a part of the whole intellectual and emotional make-up of human beings.

But despite these paradoxes, it appears that the major established religions do still provide codes of conduct and backing for moral action for many of their followers in many aspects of their lives. Morality can rest upon social foundations, without a concept of divine validation. But the creation of a moral system, which many individuals have managed for themselves, is nevertheless not an easy matter.

Chapter 9

The truth of religion?

So what is one to make of this immensely diverse, often paradoxical set of phenomena known as religion?

All religions probably would claim that they represent the truth, though some are much more articulate about it than others. It is said that Mahatma Gandhi tried to give a definition of Hinduism in the words 'Hinduism is a relentless pursuit after truth. It is the religion of truth' (Bouquet 1948: 12). But similar claims are stoutly made by many other religions, usually on an exclusive basis. Yet in this plethora of propositions about the transcendent and truth, it is logically not possible for every one to be true. Indeed, it is possible that no one set of propositions can be exclusively true against all the others. To save the notion of a universal truth, and an ultimate transcendent reality of a broad kind, concepts of pantheism, universal mind or spirit, theocentricity have been invented. But they have had to ignore so many differences that their effort has not been convincing, even to most religious believers.

Among Western scholars concern for the 'truth' of a religious position has perhaps tended to recede in urgency during the present century. This may be because philosophically the notion of 'truth' has become more ambiguous. Indeed it has been argued that an affirmation of the truth of a proposition can be no more than a re-statement in other words of the original proposition.[1] So to say that the proposition 'God is love' is true is no more than affirming 'God is love'. It may be that doubts of the uniqueness of the truth of a religion have also crept into the theological field. Be that as it may, modern Christian theologians seem to be more preoccupied with questions of consistency and intelligibility in argument, and with the context of statements made, than with the issue of 'truth' alone. There is still a division however, between thinkers who believe in the truth of a supersensible, transcendent reality, made known by revelation, and those who hold that all truth is confined to human experience, without recognition of any extra-human entity.

A question has been asked: is theology rational? One may divide the answer according to whether one is thinking of assumptions or argument. In general terms, much theological argument is quite rational. If the premises be granted, the discourse is logical, conforming to the ordinary principles of reason. Theological argument may be irrational only if it exhibits contradiction, an obvious gap between premises and conclusions. But while most theological argument is rational, the problem lies with the premises. Theologians assume the existence of God, and of an array of qualities pertaining to him/her such as omnipotence, omniscience and source of all moral values. But to an external observer assertions such as these about God's existence and qualities are nonrational. They are untestable and belong to another order than that of reason. They are justified by believers in terms of special knowledge, revelation not dependent upon reason. Yet such claims to special knowledge are not self-validating. Experience has shown how often what is claimed as knowledge is no more than strong conviction, and knowledge by revelation would seem to fall into that category.

In this regard, my own position is clear. From a comparative analytical point of view religion represents a vast series of rescue operations and fields for exercise of the human imagination. Everywhere belief in religion arises from attempts to save man or console him from the consequences of his own and other peoples' impulses, desires, fears and actions. The simpler religious systems are concerned in effect to help their people to cope with the stresses of their individual living and provide a setting in which these individuals can cooperate with their fellows in formal relationships. They also often offer some assurance of continuity of the human personality after death. In the more sophisticated religious systems, theology or its analogues of spiritual analysis, discuss the nature of God, Allah, Brahma, Buddha, combine with much examination of the concept of the human soul and its relation to the transcendent, with notions of redemption by suffering, salvation from sin. Such discourse attempts to cope at an intellectual level with the problems and paradoxes which a religious system presents to its devotees, in their efforts to match human frailty to the absolutes of the other-worldly. These other-worldly absolutes – whether universal love, eternal justice, the abolition of desire, according to the religious system – are postulates, hallowed by tradition, to offset the inadequacies and imperfections of the ordinary material world and provide ideals for human conduct. But they are essentially of human creation.

But these concepts of ultimate reality and absolute qualities easily become confused. They become identified with a range of very human interests, personal ambitions and status involvement as well as struggles for power at every level. They can become closely linked with ideas of control of material property. Hence what might seem a foundation for a general faith of a cult can be broken up into a bewildering mass of paradoxes, factions and struggles, sometimes of a violent kind.

Reviewing this vast array of divergent religious ritual and belief, my conclusion is then, like that of many thinkers before me, that we are faced by a massive output of human enterprise. It is a question of probabilities and necessary assumptions. An alternative interpretation to that of a conventional religious outlook is that an assumption such as the existence of a God has a very low probability. Such a concept is not a necessary assumption in the interpretation of human affairs, and can be explained in human terms. In the sophisticated major religions, for example, concepts of the divine, of 'ultimate reality', and of the extremes of knowledge, wisdom, morality and power associated with the divine, are just a summation of the absolutes of human imagination. Each religion has its ambiguities in regard to responsibility for human conduct. All this is elaborated in a huge intellectual appraisal of theological contributions, often of great beauty. It may seem harsh to say that God is an example of the fallacy of misplaced concreteness. But while at an abstract, figurative level the ideas of God, Yahweh, Allah, Brahma can provide spectacular symbolic expressions and penetrating thoughts upon the human condition, at bottom they are just essentially human constructs.

Religious people will probably find such statements unacceptable. They are apt to take on a patronizing attitude. They see the position of a humanist in such metaphors as that of a tone-deaf person attempting to write about music, or a colour-blind person attempting to judge a colour-print. But such assumption of superiority equates an intellectual refusal to share their appreciation of religion with a physical defect, and for this there is no evidence at all. What they are doing is putting up a defence mechanism, a re-assertion that their position is correct.

To a humanist such as myself, religion is not a set of truths about the divine or transcendent. The idea of revelation from on high is an illusion – every religion has its own different revelation. But to me as an anthropologist, each religion, even that which may appear to be intellectually not very sophisticated, contains some explanatory ideas about the world, some rituals as guides to conduct, serving as patterns for human relationships. Therefore I would argue that there is a truth in every religion. But it is a human, not a divine truth. In every society the beliefs and practices of religion are modelled on secular beliefs, desires, interests, fears and actions. These are raised by religion to a higher power, given an alleged external authority and legitimacy, because in their abstract, figurative, often symbolic form they are ultimately an outcome of the human condition and an attempt to remedy its difficulties. This is not a relativist position. I believe that there are values, truth among them. But they lie in the facts of human cooperation, in development of the human personality, not in any scheme of divine revelation.

The pity of it is that the followers of all these various religions so often betray their truth by failing to carry out the rules for conduct which so many religions lay down. From a realistic point of view, world society is in a parlous state. Most obvious are the violent conflicts that have erupted in so many parts of the globe, setting state against state and party against party within states. Less obvious but much more threatening, is the overhanging burden of possible nuclear warfare, with the prospect of new political units developing nuclear explosive potentiality. So far from followers of major world religious taking action to implement the peaceful dictates of their religions, Christian, Muslim, Buddhist, Confucianist adherents are busily engaged in internal slaughter of one another. Their religious leaders, if not actively engaged in partisan conflict, are impotent to control their followers and lead them to more peaceful forms of social living.

Many of the values of these religious faiths are true values, in the sense that if honestly adopted, they make for more viable social life – self-sacrifice, thought for others, avoidance of deceit, care for more vulnerable members of society, integrative meaning of rituals, strength in cooperation. Recognition of them is fortified by a belief in their transcendent nature, in their absoluteness independent of human initiative. Yet because they are *not* transcendental, *not* of divine origin, they can be easily set aside by the pressure of individual or group human interests. As many wise men have seen, the real battle of religion is not that of conflict with other religions, but of a religious follower within himself, in order to try to preserve the true values of his faith.

Notes

2 RELIGIOUS BELIEF AND PERSONAL ADJUSTMENT

1 The Koran, Sura iv, *Women*, verses 94–7.
2 The Koran, Sura xxxiii, *Confederates*, verse 49.
3 Cf. the view of a Chinese scholar on this point. 'Since men have knowledge, many religions regard God as having knowledge, though there is this difference, that he is omniscient. Since men have power, many religions regard God as having power, though with this difference, that he is omnipotent. Since men have a will, many religions regard God as having a will, though with this difference, that his will is perfectly good' Fung Yu-Lan 1947: 126.
4 From an article 'God's Trust in Man', *The Times*, 13.11.43.
5 'The Will of God – Man's Response', a correspondent in *The Times*, 10.1.48.
6 Ibid.
7 See, for example, Randolph 1923: 10.
8 Hughes 1942: 100, 321–5; Fung Yu-Lan 1947; Soothill 1929: 205.
9 The Lotus Sutra, the great canonical book of Mahayana Buddhism, expresses the teaching thus:

> The cause of all suffering
> Is rooted in desire.
> If desire be extinguished,
> Suffering has no foothold.

In this form of the religion, salvation, freedom from suffering, pain and evil is attained by faith in the Buddha and Boddhisattvas, and in the Sutra which proclaims the Way of the Law (Soothill 1930: 97–8 *et passim*). The inclusive pantheistic doctrines of the Tendai sect lay stress on the absolute nature of the Buddha, in which animate and inanimate are of the same essence; in the last resort, therefore, evil is also comprised therein. 'Since we are all of the same nature, some good can be found in the lowest of us, and reciprocally there is also some evil, in Buddha.' The idea is also held that the world is compounded of three thousand *dharmas*, of fundamental elements. 'The spiritual, and that which appears to us as material, good and evil, all our sentient universe and our illusions, are the different aspects under which the play of these three thousand *dharmas* reveal themselves to our senses and to our mind . . . This universe is so constructed that although it is constituted in its infinity by these three thousand *dharmas*, a single thought, mean as it may be, contains them all . . . The *dharmas* form the world and are all in our thought' (Steinilber-Oberlin 1938: 77–8).

10 Soothill 1929: 222–4.

11 The Koran, Sura xci, *The Sun*, verses 7–10; Sura iv, *Women*, verse 81.

12 Hasting's *Encyclopaedia*, article s.v. 'Theodicy'.

13 Cf. Zimmer 1946: 136. 'Hindu wisdom, Hindu religion, accepts the doom and forms of death as the dark-tones of a cosmic symphony . . .'

14 Muslim theology has its parallels in this field. For example, take the arguments of Ibn Maskawaih, a medieval historian who died in the early years of the eleventh century, nearly 150 years before St Thomas. In his 'Proof of the Maker', the first chapter of his book entitled *The Smaller Work on Salvation*, he puts forward a case very similar to that of Aquinas, and probably derived from the same Aristotelian sources, for the existence of God in terms of a need for a Prime Mover, who is the cause of all effects but not himself the effect of any cause. The proposition that God exists, he holds, is obvious as, if not more so than, the proposition that the sun exists. The difference is that the latter is clear to the senses whereas the former is clear to the reason. To free reason from its veils and reach the knowledge of God and the real, that is, spiritual world, requires discipline. And that is, who lacks reason is debarred from apprehension of God's existence, as a bat from the lack of the appropriate sensory faculties is debarred from an apprehension of the sun's existence (see Hamid 1946). Here we meet the thesis familiar in other contexts, that failure of an opponent to agree on the nature of the phenomena under discussion must be attributed to a gap in his perception, and not to error in the original identification.

15 Cock 1918: 20.

16 Webb 1929: 36–40. He proceeds to draw a comparison between the recalcitrance of such a hearer and resistance to poetry or music in a soul incapable of aesthetic emotions. But this is an imperfect analogy since only in a figurative way is it ever suggested that aesthetic expression carries within it any qualities of a personal supra-human kind akin to those claimed for religion.

17 Stocks 1934: 19–20.

18 Ritchie 1945: 73–4.

19 Thornton 1930: 27.

20 William James (1929: 27) has argued that this is only one of many sentiments which can be put as the basis of religion.

21 Webb 1929: 8; Temple 1924.

22 This idea is dramatically and movingly expressed in Marc Connelly's play *Green Pastures*, which symbolizes God learning from experience – specifically, the experience of suffering. See also the preface to the play by Vincent Long.

23 The metaphorical nature of beliefs formerly held as literal, for example the spatial notions of heaven and hell expressed in the Apostles' Creed, is examined by Ritchie 1945: 75–6.
24 Rev. J. G. Laughton, as reported in the *Auckland Weekly News*, 18.11.42.
25 Soothill 1930; introduction and chapter ii.
26 Gobineau 1933: 284. See also Huart s.v., 1941.
27 The value of the conception of progressive revelation from this point of view has been understood by Ritchie 1945: 75–6, who states, 'Unless God is now in process of being revealed to us, whatever revelation there may have been in the past, we must inevitably be atheists. The atheists are those to whom God does not reveal Himself or who reject His revelation.'
28 This point of view is epitomized by St. Paul: 'Now we see through a glass darkly; but then face to face: now I know in part; but then shall I know even as I am known.' The Buddhist *Avatamsakasutra*, a canonical text of the Hosso and Kegon sects, puts it thus:

> How exquisite is our physical eye,
> It has not the power to see our condition,
> The affirmation of its power betrays an illusion,
> And it is inapt to understand the incomparable Law . . .
> The Perfect law of all the Buddhas is incomprehensible.
> For it surpasses the power of our comprehension . . .
> Believe in Buddha with the simplicity of thy heart,
> Be unshakable in thy faith . . .
> Enter in the torrent of Buddhism,
> To reach the beauty and the calm of Wisdom.
>   (Steinilber-Oberlin 1938: 285–6)

Cf. also the view that in the present period, which is one of degeneracy, 'we are now too corrupt to understand alone the whole light of the Buddha. An act of faith in the sacred text which is suitable for the men of our time is necessary' (ibid: 241).
29 In the social sciences the existence of observer-effect, the participation of the observer as an element in many situations being studied, complicates the problems of determinate measurement. There are phenomena which defy logical and empirical reconstruction – the intuitive process for instance, as in that ability to perceive hitherto unnoticed relations and integrate them into a general principle which is the mark of the true scientist.
30 Qureshi 1945: 4. It will be observed that it is not argued that the Koran's ideas of today may become the mythology of tomorrow.
31 One gathers that by this the more accurate the determination of the position of an electron, the greater is the uncertainty as to its momentum; conversely, the more accurately its momentum is determined, the greater the uncertainty in its position. The degree of uncertainty, which is due to the nature of measurement itself, is laid down by Heisenberg's principle, by which it is assigned a value never less than a specified constant.

32 The new physics has 'renewed and stimulated a sense of the ontological mystery of the world of matter', Maritain 1940a: 65.
33 Stebbing 1937: 7, *et passim*.
34 See e.g. Brown 1946: 35–7, 39, etc.; Wach 1947: 4–5, 14; Sorokin 1941: 296.
35 See Fisher 1933: 62–72, 76 *et passim*; Shivapadasundaram 1934: 14.
36 Thornton 1930: 17–18, 23.
37 e.g. Bishop Walter Carey, in an article entitled 'Can We Ever Think Clearly?' *Sunday Dispatch*, 1.9.46.
38 'The terrible voices which rise up in man crying out Enough of lying optimism and illusory moralities . . . of liberty . . . of idealism; take us back to the great spiritual fruitfulness of the abyss, of the absurd, and of the ethics of despair' (Maritain 1940b: 5).
39 Maritain 1940b: 9.
40 See e.g. Mazenod 1943.
41 'So far as this Civitas Dei enters into the time-dimension at all . . . it is as a spiritual reality interpenetrating the present' (Toynbee 1946: 527–9).
42 See for example the illuminating essay by Webb 1929.
43 See the illuminating article of Talcott Parsons 1944: 176–90.
44 Expressed even by Malinowski (1925: 57, 64), who is usually so insistent on the importance of individual variation.
45 Allier (1925, I: 525) argues that conversion does not consist in intellectual conviction – but that such conviction must necessary follow if the conversion is not to be sooner or later only a memory of violent though fleeting emotions.
46 Hirn 1912.

3 SPIRITUAL AROMA? RELIGION AND POLITICS

1 The 'canopy syndrome' metaphor for such national statements of a religious kind was in my mind before I was aware of *The Sacred Canopy* as the American title of Peter Berger's book *The Social Reality of Religion* (1969). While I find his very scholarly approach most congenial, his use of the term 'canopy' is much broader than mine.
2 I have drawn illustrations from so wide a field that I can give references only for the more critical points, or those of particular anthropological interest. From the ample anthropological literature on divine kings and allied statuses it is enough to cite Frazer (1890, i: 107–20; 1909: 4–16); Seligman (1911); Fortes (1945: 182–4); Evans-Pritchard (1962: 66–86); Firth (1964: 71–80); Richards (1969); and Schapera (1955: 70–1).
3 As an example of a specific Christian formulation, the Calvinistic Scottish Independents, founded in 1797, 'insist, that the Scriptures contain a full and complete model and system of doctrine, government, discipline and worship; and that in them we may find an universal rule for the directions of Christians in their associated state. . . . They require Scripture for everything and reject the author-

ity of the civil magistrate in matters of religion' (Nightingale 1821: 242). These Independents argued that the kingdom of Jesus was spiritual, neither interfering with human governments not allowing interference by them. A critical issue of course was the boundary between religious and nonreligious affairs.

4 This highly compressed statement on Islam has drawn upon many standard sources impossible to list here, as also to some extent upon my own contacts with Islam in Malaysia, and the work of colleagues in various Muslim regions. Anthropological studies illustrating *inter alia* the diverse relation of Islam to local custom include, e.g., those for Java by Clifford Geertz (1960) and Robert Jay (1963); for Atjeh by Siegel (1969); for Malaysia by Swift (1966), Firth (1966, 1967b, chapter 7 of this book), Peter Wilson (1967), Winzeler (1974), Kessler (1974, 1978); for Morocco, Geertz (1968), Gellner (1963, 1969), Eickelman (1976); for tropical Africa by I. M. Lewis (1955–6, 1966). Two thoughtful general studies of Islam, fairly sharply contrasted, are by Clifford Geertz (1968) and Gellner (1981).

5 The history of Muslim reformism and its connections with nationalism over the last century has been complex, with differential emphasis on tradition, consensus, and individual interpretation. In addition to sources in note 4, see, e.g., von Grunebaum (1955: 185–236). For some anthropological contrasts see Badur (1964), Peacock (1978a, b), and for a more committed, more popular account, Jansen (1979). The influence of conservative evangelistic pressures, as that of *Da'wa*, the 'call' or 'message', upon Malay university students has been very perceptible in recent years. According to report (*The Times* (London) 2.10.80: 6) a recent political example of reformist influence occurred in Iran – the Minister of National Guidance (Information) closed his ministry after only a short period in office, telling employees that it was 'unIslamic'. In an analogous field, that of Burmese Buddhism, Mendelson (1975: 26) has noted the powerful effect of the 'rhetoric of purification'.

6 Political expediency may be further justified in a Shi'ite context by the doctrine of *takiya* (caution, dissimulation), a technical term for dispensation from the requirements of religion under compulsion or threat of injury. This allows conformity in speech and act even though the mind and heart do not acknowledge the legitimacy of the demand. See Donaldson (1933: 195, 253–4, 291), Madelung (1980: 27), and Strothmann (1934). Cf. Gobineau (1933: 25 *et seq.*) on *ketman* (disguise); and Minorsky (1955: 200) who explains the Iranian penchant for 'secrecy' and 'duplicity' in terms of their long subjection to foreign rule, and the Shi'ite 'aroma' of opposition, martyrdom and revolt.

7 For evidence of Marx's readings in religion, see Index of Authorities Quoted in *Capital* (Marx 1976: 1095–119), and Krader (1972). (The only considerable notes made by Marx from anthropological materials on religion were four pages on Lubbock's three chapters on stages of religion). For a succinct account of some modern Marxist anthropological views on religion, see Basilov (1980).

8 Cf. an analogous expression by Eickelman – 'Patterns of social structure and the prevailing systems of meaning through which religious
  beliefs are expressed are not always isomorphic' (1976: 233). Such
  views are generally in line with the intellectual tradition from Max
  Weber. (For more general critique of Marx, see Firth 1974, 1979b).

9 Anthropologists are fairly well familiar with literature dealing with
  millenarian movements and connections between religion and
  nationalism. Malaysia offers some interesting data in the latter field.
  The historian William R. Roff has shown (1967: 56–90) how reformist
  Islam in Malaya never succeeded in colonial times in elaborating a
  political nationalism capable of attracting mass support. On the other
  hand Margaret Roff, a political scientist, and Clive Kessler, an anthropologist, have indicated in quite separate cases how after independence, when 'democratic' political institutions are developing rapidly,
  religion may provide an instrument for political party organization
  and aggrandizement (Margaret Roff 1974: 111; Kessler 1978).

10 Cf. Macintyre (1969); Van Leeuwen (1972, 1974). Cf. also my own
  statement (a lecture given in 1948) that in the Western world religion,
  by its compromises, has allowed some of the most important symbols
  of distributive justice to pass to its opponents (Firth 1964: 189). For
  a Marxist Islam, see Lewis 1979: 15.

11 Analysis of the state of religion in Eastern Europe and the Soviet
  Union has been given by Beeson (1974) as a result of a British
  Council of Churches of Working Party initiative. My comments on
  the situation in China are based partly on an interview by E. E.
  Whyte with Bishop Ting Kwang-Hsun (reported in the BBC *Listener*
  3.4.80) and partly on a few informal inquiries of my own. (The
  original essay for this chapter was written before the dismantling of
  the Soviet Union.)

**5 OFFERING AND SACRIFICE: PROBLEMS OF
ORGANIZATION**

1 This chapter is an expanded version of a lecture delivered first in the
  Department of Anthropology, University of Chicago, in April 1955,
  and in a revised form before the Royal Anthropological Institute in
  October 1961. I am indebted to Dr Alice Dewey for helpful comment.

2 In R. H. Lowie's work on primitive religion, for long a standard text,
  all that can be found in the index is the one reference, 'Sacrifice,
  bloody, in America'. On following this up one reads that most
  noteworthy is the excessive development of bloody sacrifices in the
  Amerindian region, human sacrifices being especially common among
  the Aztecs, though in North America bloody sacrifices, even of animals are definitely rare, the Pawnee (Nebraska) offering of a maiden
  and that of a white dog by the Iroquois being notable exceptions
  (1936: 173).

3 Robertson Smith 1907: 466. The sacrifice of an animal originally wild,
  but caught and kept in custody or as a pet falls broadly within the
  domestic category, since the capture and keeping of the animal has

converted it into an item of personal property, e.g. the bear sacrifices of the Ainu.
4 Hubert and Mauss 1899: 63, 104; Kuper 1947: 192; Krige and Krige 1943: 278. Even the Dinka have to recognize limitations to their cattle sacrifices, and sometimes substitute sheep, goats or even chickens (Lienhardt 1961: 25).

6 RITUAL AND DRAMA IN MALAY SPIRIT MEDIUMSHIP

1 See the perceptive analysis by Kessler 1978.
2 For a general account of Malay spirit mediumship see Winstedt 1951. For a valuable account of the phenomenon in Kelantan see Cuisinier 1936
3 Gimlette 1929; Gimlette and Thomson 1939. Few of these folk remedies seem to be used in modern times.
4 See Yap 1952.
5 *Gong* in Kelantan means: a musical instrument of the percussive type; a rising ground or hillock; crazy or 'touched'. See Wilkinson 1932. I have been informed by Mr Ronald Ng that in Cantonese *gong* means hillock and by Professor Maurice Freedman that in Hokkien it means foolish, silly.
6 *Puteri* traditionally means princess, and the spirit medium's performance is sometimes translated as 'play of the princess', with a traditional but probably apocryphal attribution to a royal lady (see Gimlette 1929: 8; Cuisinier 1936: 94–5).
7 cf. Rentse 1936.
8 I remember seeing at least one example of performance of *main puteri* as part of the Ruler's Birthday celebration at Pasir Puteh in 1940, and saw the preparations for filming one at Bachok in 1963.
9 *Wayang* seems to have originally meant 'shadow' and later from the 'shadow play' to have been applied to all forms of theatre.

7 FAITH AND SCEPTICISM IN KELANTAN VILLAGE MAGIC

1 Difficulties in rendering spoken Kelantan Malay into writing have been indicated by C. C. Brown in his classic study (1927), and are appreciated by Malay linguists to whose competence I cannot lay claim. But I would note here that the richness of Kelantan dialect offers a problem in the theory of communication which is not solved in written Malay by simply converting it into standard romanized form (cf. Raymond Firth 1966: 388–91) even though Malays in Kelantan write in this form.
2 Variance in spelling and in meaning have been given to this term in the literature. Howison (1801: 100) has *boomo* (as doctor); Wilkinson (1903: 134) has *bomor* and *bomo*; and *bomoh* (1932: 150); Swettenham, (1905: 30) has *bomo*. Favre (1875, II 226) gives only *bumu*, as elephant-hunter. Pak Che Mat once gave me *bo'omor* in what he seemed to think was high-class pronunciation. Like Gimlette (1913:

29; 1929: 18 *et seq.*; and Cuisinier (1936: 31 *et seq.*; 1957: 89) I have tended to favour *bomor* (1966: 122–4), which has also had official authority in the State of Kelantan Estimates, 1938: 23 – 'Bomor for H. H.' (cf. Gimlette 1913: 31). I here follow the recent *Kamus Dewan* (1970).

3 The concept of *keramat* seems to me to be very similar to that of *mana* in Oceania, as I noted in 1940 (Firth 1967a: 192n). Nicholson, (1914: 122) terms a miracle performed by a Muslim saint *karāmāt*, that is, a 'favour' bestowed upon him by God, and links it with the Greek *charismata*.

4 To' Guru seems to have had a contempt for the local Wali. He was alleged to have said that to claim to be a saint while sitting in a kampong (and eating in luxury) was no good – it was known from the Koran that saints sat on hills and ate green shoots!

8 PARADOX IN RELIGIOUS SYSTEMS

1 Middleton 1960: 252–8. For an enlightening comparative study see Parkin 1985; compare also chapter 5 of this book.

2 John Hick, 'Argument for the Existence of God', in Richardson and Bowden 1983. See also T. Patrick Burke, 'Ontology', op. cit.

3 See I. M. Lewis 1991; Firth 1967a: ch. 14; 1970: ch. 9; and chapter 6 above.

4 Raymond Firth 1966: 12–14, and chapters 6 and 7 in this book; also the admirable study by Clive S. Kessler on the relation of religion to politics in Kelantan, 1978; also essays in William R. Roff (ed.) (1974) *Kelantan*.

5 Modern Catholic challenge to this dogma of papal infallibility has arisen among theologians. Cf. also the powerful argument of Hans Küng 1995: 318, 463, 514.

6 For important general works see Worsley 1957; Lanternari 1963. For particular studies of Melanesian 'cargo cults' see Burridge 1969; Lawrence 1964; Cochrane 1970.

7 Particularly distressing in any modern, ostensibly democratic state has been a claim by some Muslim extremists that any Muslim critic of the Koran should be put to death. The case of Salman Rushdie, condemned by a *fatwa* of an Iranian Islamic leader for his satirical treatment of the 'Satanic Verses' of the Koran, is well-known. More recently, the feminist Bangladeshi author Taslima Nasreen has been accused of saying that the Koran is the work only of the prophet Muhammed, not of Allah. In consequence it has been claimed by some fundamentalists of her faith that she should be hanged. Such reactionary Muslim thinking, which would introduce a law punishing blasphemy by death is clearly a grave danger for freedom of thought (see *The Times* 18.6.94).

8 For Iran, Ayatollah Khomeini argued in 1971 that the reasons for the twelfth Imam's occultation were beyond human understanding, so Muslims should not wait for him to reveal himself but try to establish Islamic government in his absence (Chehabi 1991: 73).

9 See Gibb 1949: 127–64; Nicholson, in Arnold and Guillaume 1943: 210–38. For anthropological accounts of complex variants of sūfism in different social and political conditions, see Evans-Pritchard 1949; Gellner 1969; Eickelman 1976. Cf. also Davis 1987: 26–8, 44–58; Lewis 1955–6.

10 A Vincentian Father (1952) *The Book of the Miraculous Medal* (5th edn), London: Sands, an officially sanctioned publication. Cf. Firth 1973: 230 *et seq.*

11 A detailed, markedly neutralist consideration of Marian visions and miracles has been given by Victor and Edith Turner, anthropologists and Catholics, 1978 (especially chapter 6).

9 THE TRUTH OF RELIGION?

1 'One of the main uses of the word "true" seems in fact just to enable us to lend assent to assertions with whose precise content we are not for some reason conversant' (Findlay 1963: 216).

References

Allier, Raoul (1925) *La Psychologie de la Conversion chez les Peuples Non-Civilisés*, 2 vols, Paris: Payot.

Arnold, Thomas, W. (1928) *Painting in Islam: A Study of the Place of Pictorial Art in Muslim Culture*, Oxford: Clarendon.

Arnold, Thomas W. and Guillaume, Alfred (eds) (1943) *The Legacy of Islam* (rev. edn), Oxford: Oxford University Press.

Aveneri, Schlomo (1969) *Karl Marx on Colonialism and Modernisation*, Garden City: Doubleday.

Badur, A. K. (1964) 'Réformisme Islamique et politique en Malaisie', *Archives de Sociologie des Religions* **17**: 68–84.

Bailey, F. G. (ed.) (1973) *Debate and Compromise: The Politics of Innovation*, Oxford: Blackwell.

Basilov, V. (1980) 'The study of religions in Soviet ethnography', in Gellner (ed.): 231–42.

Beeson, Trevor (1974) *Discretion and Valour: Religious Conditions in Russia and Eastern Europe*, London: Collins.

Bell, Charles (1931) *The Religion of Tibet*, Oxford: Clarendon.

Bent, N. (1967) *The Death of God Movement*, New York: Paulist Press.

Berger, Peter L. (1969) *The Social Reality of Religion*, London: Faber [orig. pub. as *The Sacred Canopy* (1967) Garden City: Doubleday].

Birnbaum, Norman (1971) 'The crisis in Marxist sociology', in J. David Colfax and Jack L. Roach, *Radical Sociology*, New York: Basic Books: 108–31.

Bouquet, A. C. (1948) *Hinduism*, London: Hutchinson.

Brown, C. C. (1927) 'Kelantan Malay', Papers on Malay Subjects (2nd ser.), Singapore: Government Printer.

Brown, W. (1946) *Personality and Religion*, London: University of London Press.

Bultmann, Rudolf [1958] (1960) *Jesus Christ and Mythology* (trans.), London: SCM Press.

— — (1969) *Faith and Understanding* **I** (trans. Louise Pettibone-Smith), London: SCM Press.

Burckhardt, Jacob (1945) *Civilization of the Renaissance*, Oxford: Phaidon.

Burke, Edmund (1790) *Reflections on the Revolution in France*, London: Dodsley.

Burridge, K. (1969) *New Heaven, New Earth*, Oxford: Blackwell.

Carpenter, Edward (ed.) (1966) *A House of Kings: The History of Westminster Abbey*, London: John Baker.

Chehabi, H. E. (1991) 'Religion and politics in Iran', *Daedalus* **120** (3): 69–91.

Clifford, Hugh (1897) *In Court and Kampong*, London: Grant Richards.

Cochrane, Glynn (1970) *Big Men and Cargo Cults*, Oxford: Clarendon.

Cock, A. A. (1918) 'The cosmological argument for the existence of God', *Proceedings of the Aristotelian Society*, 10 June.

Connelly, Marc (1941) *Green Pastures*, London: Penguin.

Conze, F. (1951) *Buddhism: Its Essence and Development*, Oxford: Bruno Cassirer.

Cuisinier, Jeanne (1936) 'Dances magiques de Kelantan', *Travaux et Mémoires d'Institut d' Ethnologie*, **XXII**, Univ. Paris: Université de Paris.

– – (1957) *Le Théâtre d'Ombres à Kelantan*, Paris: Gallimard.

Cullen, Countee (1929) *The Black Christ and Other Poems*, London and New York: G. P. Putnam's Sons.

Cumont, Franz [1909, 2nd edn trans. 1911] (1956) *Oriental Religions in Roman Paganism*, New York: Dover.

Danby, H. (1933) *The Mishnah*, London: Oxford University Press.

Davis, H. Francis, Thomas, Ivo and Crehan, Joseph (eds) (1971) *A Catholic Dictionary of Theology*, London: Nelson.

Davis, John (1987) *Libyan Politics: Tribe and Revolution*, London: Tauria.

– – (ed.) (1982) 'Religious organization and religious experience', ASA Monograph **21**, London: Academic Press.

Davison, J. (1825) *An Enquiry into the Origins and Intent of Primitive Sacrifice*, London:

Donaldson, Dwight M. (1933) *The Shi'ite Religion*, London: Luzac.

Doughty, C. M. [1888] [1921] (1926) *Travels in Arabia Deserta*, new one-vol. edn [originally 2 vols], London: Cape.

Downs, R. E. (1967) 'A Kelantan village of Malaya', in Julian H. Steward (ed) *Contemporary Change in Traditional Societies*, **I**: 105–86.

Eickelman, Dale F. (1976) *Moroccan Islam. Tradition and Society in a Pilgrimage Center*, Austin: University of Texas.

Endicott, K. M. (1970) *An Analysis of Malay Magic*, Oxford: Clarendon.

Evans-Pritchard, E. E. (1940) *The Nuer*, Oxford: Clarendon.

– – (1949) *The Sanusi of Cyrenaica*, Oxford: Clarendon.

– – (1953) 'The sacrifical role of cattle among the Nuer', *Africa*, **23**: 181–98.

– – (1954) 'The meaning of sacrifice among the Nuer', *Journal of the Royal Anthropological Institute* **84**: 21–33.

– – (1956) *Nuer Religion*, Oxford: Clarendon.

– – (1962) 'The divine Kingship of the Shilluk of the Nilotic Sudan', *Essays in Social Anthropology*, London: Faber: 66–86.

Favre, P. (1875) *Dictionnaire Malais-Français*, 2 vols, Paris: Maison-neuve.

Findlay, J. N. (1963) *Language, Mind and Value*, London: Allen & Unwin.

Firth, Raymond (1943) 'The coastal people of Kelantan and Trengganu', *Geography Journal* **101**: 195–205.

— — (1959) *Social Change in Tikopia*, London: Allen & Unwin.

— — (1964) 'Essays on social organization and values', London School of Economics Monograph, *Social Anthropology* **28**, London: Athlone.

— — (1965) *Primitive Polynesian Economy* [1939] (2nd edn), London: Routledge & Kegan Paul.

— — (1966) *Malay Fishermen: Their Peasant Economy* [1946] (2nd end), London: Routledge & Kegan Paul.

— — (1967a) *Tikopia Ritual and Belief*, London: Allen & Unwin.

— — (1967b) 'The work of the Gods in Tikopia', London School of Economics Monograph, *Social Anthropology* **1, 2**. [1940], London: Athlone.

— — (1969) 'Extraterrioriality and the Tikopia Chiefs', *Man* (Journal of the Royal Anthropological Institute), new series, **4**: 354–78.

— — (1970) *Rank and Religion in Tikopia*, London: Allen & Unwin.

— — (1971) Elements of Social Organization [1951] (3rd edn), London: Tavistock.

— — (1973) *Symbols Public and Private*, London: Allen & Unwin.

— — (1974) 'The sceptical anthropologist? Social anthropology and Marxist views on society', *Proceedings of the British Academy of 1972*, **58**: 177–213.

— — (1979a) 'The sacredness of Tikopia's Chiefs', in William A. Shack and Percy S. Cohen (eds) *Politics in Leadership: A Comparative Perspective*, Oxford: Clarendon: 139–68.

— — (1979b) 'Work and value: reflections on ideas of Karl Marx', in Sandra Wallman (ed.) *Social Anthropology of Work*, ASA Monograph **19**, London: Academic Press: 177–206.

Firth, Rosemary (1966) 'Housekeeping among Malay peasants', London School of Economics Monograph, *Social Anthropology* **7** (2nd edn), London: Athlone.

Fisher, H. A. L. (1933) 'Our new religion', *Thinkers' Library* **31**, London: Watts.

Fortes, M. (1940) 'The political system of the Tallensi of the Northern Territories, Gold Coast', in M. Fortes and E. E. Evans-Pritchard (eds) *African Political Systems*, Oxford: Oxford University Press: 239–71.

— — (1945) *The Dynamics of Clanship among the Tallensi*, London: International African Institute/Oxford University Press.

— — (1949) *The Web of Kinship among the Tallensi*, London: International African Institute/Oxford University Press.

— — (1959) *Oedipus and Job in West African Religion*, Cambridge: Cambridge University Press.

Foss, Michael (1969) *The Founding of the Jesuits 1540*, London: Hamish Hamilton.

Frazer, J. G. (1890) *The Golden Bough: A Study in Comparative Religion*, 2 vols, London: Macmillan.

— — (1909) *Psyche's Task: A Discourse concerning the Influence of Superstition on the Growth of Institutions*, London: Macmillan.

Fung Yu-Lan (1947) *The Spirit of Chinese Philosophy* (trans. E. R. Hughes), London: Kegan Paul, Trench, Trubner.

Fustel de Coulanges, Numa Denis (1873) *The Ancient City: A Study of the Religion, Laws, and Institutions of Greece and Rome* (trans. Willard Small), Garden City: Doubleday.

Geertz, Clifford (1960) *The Religion of Java*, Glencoe, Ill.: Free Press.

— — (1968) *Islam Observed: Religious Development in Morocco and Indonesia*, New Haven: Yale University Press.

Gellner, Ernest (1963) 'Sanctity, purity, secularisation and nationalism in North Africa', *Archiv de Sociologie des Religions* **15**: 71–86.

— — (1969) *Saints of the Atlas*, London: Weidenfeld and Nicolson.

— — (1981) *Muslim Society*, Cambridge: Cambridge University Press.

— — (ed.) (1980) *Soviet and Western Anthropology*, London: Duckworth.

Gibb, H. A. R. (1949) *Muhammedanism: An Historical Survey*, Oxford: Oxford University Press.

— — (1962) 'Studies on the civilization of Islam', ed. Stanford J. Shaw and William R. Polk, Boston: Beacon.

Gimlette, J. D. (1913) 'Some superstitious beliefs occurring in the theory and practice of Malay medicine', *Journal of the Straits Branch Royal Asiatic Society*, number **65**: 25–35.

— (1929) *Malay Poisons and Charm Cures* [1915] (3rd edn), London: J. & A. Churchill.

Gimlette, J. D. and Thomson H. W. (1939) *A Dictionary of Malayan Medicine*, London: Oxford University Press.

Gobineau, Joseph-Arthur (1933) *Les Religions et les Philosophies dans L'Asie Centrale* [1865], Paris: Gallimard.

Goode, W. J. (1951) *Religion among the Primitives*, Glencoe, Ill.: Free Press.

Gray, J. B. (1925) *Sacrifice in the Old Testament: Its Theory and Practice*, Oxford.

Gusdorf, G. (1948) *L'Expérience Humaine de Sacrifice*, Paris:

Guthrie, W. K. C. (1955) *The Greeks and Their Gods*, Boston: Beacon.

Hamid, K. A. (1946) *Ibn Maskawaih: A Study of his Al-Fauz Al-Asghar*, London: Luzac.

Harrison, Jane (1903) *Prolegomena to the Study of Greek Religion*, Cambridge: Cambridge University Press.

— — (1912) *Themis*, Cambridge: Cambridge University Press.

— — (1913) *Ancient Art and Ritual*, London: Williams & Norgate.

Haskins, C. H. (1957) *The Renaissance of the Twelfth Century*, New York: Meridian.

Hastings, J. (ed.) (1908) *Encyclopaedia of Religion and Ethics*, London: T. & T. Clark.

Hawthorn, Harry B. (ed.) (1955) *The Doukhobors of British Columbia*, Vancouver: University of British Columbia.

Herskovits, M. J. (1938) *Dahomey*, 2 vols, New York: J. J. Augustin.

Hirn, Yrjö (1912) *The Sacred Shrine: A Study of the Poetry and Art of the Catholic Church*, London: Macmillan.

Hobbes, Thomas (1904) *Leviathan, or the Matter, Forme and Power of a*

Commonwealth, Ecclesiastical and Civil [1651] A. E. Waller (ed.), Cambridge: Cambridge University Press.

Howells, W. (1949) *The Heathens*, London: Gollancz.

Howison, J. (1801) *A Dictionary of the Malay Tongue*, London: Arabic and Persian Press.

Huart, Cl. (1941) *'Bāb': Handwörterbuch des Islam*, Leiden: Brill.

Hubert, H. and Mauss, M. (1899) 'Essai sur la nature et la fonction du sacrifice', *L'Année Sociologique*, **2**, 1897–98.

Hughes, E. R. (ed.) (1942) *Chinese Philosophy in Classical Times*, London: Dent.

Hurgronje, C. Snouck (1906) *The Achehnese*, 2 vols (trans. O. W. S. O'Sullivan), Leiden: Brill; London: Luzac.

James, E. O. (1933a) *Christian Myth and Ritual*, London: Murray.

— — (1933b) *Origins of Sacrifice*, London: Murray.

— — (1940) *The Social Function of Religion*, London: Hodder & Stoughton.

James, William [1902] (1929) *The Varieties of Religious Experience*, Gifford Lectures, London: Longmans.

Jansen, G. H. (1979) *Militant Islam*, London: Pan.

Jay, Robert R. (1963) *Religion and Politics in Rural Central Java*, New Haven: Yale University.

Kearney, D. (1950) *All About Fatima*, Corl: Mercier Press.

Kenyatta, Jomo (1938) *Facing Mount Kenya*, London: Secker & Warburg.

Kessler, Clive S. (1974) 'Muslim identity and political behaviour in Kelantan', in W. R. Roff (ed.) (1974): 272–313.

— — (1978) *Islam and Politics in a Malay State: Kelantan 1838–1969*, Ithaca: Cornell University Press.

Kingsley, Charles ('Parson Lot') (1848) *Letters to the Chartists, II: Politics for the People*, London: J. W. Parker: 58–59.

Koran, The [1909] (trans. J. M. Rodwell), London: Dent.

Krader, Lawrence (1972) *The Ethnological Notebooks of Karl Marx*, Assen: Van Gorcum.

Krige, E. J. and J. D. (1943) *The Realm of a Rain Queen*, London: Oxford University Press.

Küng, Hans (1995) *Christianity: Its Essence and History*, trans. John Bowden, London: SCM Press.

Kuper, Hilda (1947) *An African Aristocracy*, London: Oxford University Press.

Kurtz, J. H. (1863) *Sacrificial Worship of the Old Testament* (trans. J. Martin), Edinburgh:

Lanternari, V. (1963) *The Religions of the Oppressed: A Study of Modern Messianic Cults* (trans. Lisa Sergio), New York: Knopf.

Lawrence, P. (1964) *Road Belong Cargo*, Manchester: Manchester University Press.

Leuba, J. H. (1912) *A Psychological Study of Religion*, New York.

Lewis, I. M. (1955–6) 'Sufism in Somaliland: a study in tribal Islam', *Bulletin of the School of Oriental and African Studies* **17**: 581–602; **18**: 145–60.

—— (ed.) (1966) *Introduction: Islam in Tropical Africa*, London: International African Institute/Oxford University Press: 4–96.

—— (1979) 'Kim Il-Sung in Somalia: the end of Tribalism?' in William A. Shack and Percy S. Cohen (eds) *Politics in Leadership: A Comparative Perspective*, Oxford: Clarendon: 13–44.

—— (1991) *Ecstatic Religion: An Anthropological Study of Spirit Possession and Shamanism*, London: Penguin.

Lienhardt, Godfrey (1961) *Divinity and Experience: The Religion of the Dinka*, Oxford: Clarendon.

Loisy, Alfred (1948) *The Birth of the Christian Religion (Le Naissance de Christianisme)* (trans. L. P. Jacks), London: Allen & Unwin.

Lowie, R. H. (1936) *Primitive Religion*, London: Routledge.

Machievelli, Niccolò [1903] *The Prince* (trans. Luigi Ricci), London: Grant Richards.

Macintyre, Alasdair (1969) *Marxism and Christianity*, London: Duckworth.

McLellan, David (1973a) *Marx's Grundrisse*, St. Albans: Paladin [1st edn London: Macmillan].

—— (1973b) *Karl Marx: His Life and Thought*, London: Macmillan.

Madelung, Wilfred (1980) 'A treatise of the Sharīf al-Murtadā on the legality of working for the government', *Bulletin of the School of Oriental and African Studies* **41**. 18 31.

Malinowski, B. (1925) 'Magic, science and religion' in J. A. Needham (ed.) *Science, Religion and Reality*, London: Sheldon Press: 19–84.

Mann, Horace K. (1925) *The Lives of the Popes in the Middle Ages*, **9**, London: Kegan Paul, Trench, Trubner.

Maritain, J. (1940a) *Science and Wisdom*, (trans.) London: Bles.

—— (1940b) *Scholasticism and Politics*, (trans.) London: Bles.

Marsden, W. (1812) *A Dictionary of the Malayan Language*, London: Cox & Baylis.

Marx, Karl (1927) 'Zur Kritik der Hegelschen Rechtsphilosophie', in Karl Marx and Friedrich Engels (eds) *Historische-Kritische Gesamtausgabe Werke: Schriften Briefe* **II**(1), Frankfurt A.M.: Marx-Engels Archiv Verlagsgesellschaft: 607–21.

—— (1963) *Karl Marx: Selected Writings in Sociology and Social Philosophy*, ed. T. B. Bottomore and Maximilian Rubel [1956], Harmondsworth: Penguin.

—— (1976) *Capital: A Critique of Political Economy*, **1**, 'Introduction': Ernest Mandel, (trans. Ben Fowkes), Harmondsworth: Penguin.

Marx, Karl and Engels, Frederick [1970] *Selected Works*, in one volume, (2nd printing) London: Lawrence & Wishart.

Mattuck, I. (1954) *Aspects of Progressive Jewish Thought*, London.

Mayr-Harting, Henry (1991) *The Coming of Christianity to Anglo-Saxon England* (3rd edn), London: Batsford.

Mazenod, L. (1943) *Avant-propos, L'Art Roman en Suisse*, Genève: Lucien Mazenod.

Mead, Frank S. (1956) *Handbook of Denominations in the United States* (rev. edn), New York: Abingdon.

Meek, C. K. (1937) *Law and Authority in a Nigerian Tribe*, London: Oxford University Press.

Mendelson, E. Michael (1975) *Sangha and State in Burma: A Study of Monastic Sectarianism and Leadership*, ed. John P. Ferguson, Ithaca: Cornell University Press.

Middleton, John (1960) *Lugbara Religion*, London: Oxford University Press.

Minorsky, Vladimir (1955) 'Iran: opposition, martyrdom and revolt', in Gustave von Grunebaum (ed.) *Unity and Variety in Muslim Civilization*, Chicago, Chicago University Press: 183–206.

Money-Kyrle, R. (1930) *The Meaning of Sacrifice*, London: Hogarth.

Moorman, J. R. H. (Lord Bishop of Ripon) (1967) *A History of the Church in England* (2nd edn), London: Adam & Charles Black.

Muhammed Salleh b. Wan Musa with S. Othman Kelantan (1974) 'Theological Debates: Wan Musa b. Haji Abdul Samad and his Family', in *Kelantan Religion, Society and Politics in a Malay State*, Kuala Lumpur: Oxford University Press: 153–69.

Nadel, S. F. (1940) 'The Kede: a Riverain State in Northern Nigeria', in M. Fortes and E. E. Evans-Pritchard (eds) *African Political Systems*, London: International African Institute: 165–95.

— — (1954) *Nupe Religion*, London: Routledge & Kegan Paul.

Nasr, Seyyed Hossein (1975) *Islam and the Plight of Modern Man*, London: Longman.

Nicholson, R. A. (1914) *The Mystics of Islam*, London: Bell.

— — (1943) 'Mysticism' in Arnold and Guillaume (1943) 210–38.

Nightingale, J. (The Rev) (1821) *The Religions and Religious Ceremonies of All Nations* (new edn), London: Sir Richard Phillips.

Outram, W. (1677) *De Sacrificiis libri duo* (trans. J. Allen (1817) as *Two Dissertations on Sacrifice*), London.

Palmer, Paul, S. J. (1953) *Mary in the Documents of the Church*, London: Burns Oates.

Parkin, D. (ed.) (1985) *The Anthropology of Evil*, Oxford: Blackwell.

Parsons, Talcott (1944) 'The theoretical development of the sociology of religion', *Journal of the History of Ideas*, **5**.

Peacock, James L. (1978a) *Purifying the Faith: The Muhammadijah Movement in Indonesian Islam*, Menlo Park, Calif.: Benjamin/ Cummings.

— — (1978b) *Muslim Puritans: The Psychology of Reformation in Southeast Asian Islam*, Berkeley: University of California.

Qureshi, A. J. (1945) *Islam and the Theory of Interest*, Lahore: Ashraf.

Randolph, B. W. (1923) *Marriage Orders and Unction*, Congress Books **32**, London.

Rattray, R. S. (1923) *Ashanti*, Oxford: Clarendon.

Rentse, Anker (1936) 'The Kelantanese shadow play (Wayang Kulit)', *Journal of the Malayan Branch of the Royal Asiatic Society*, **XIV**: 284–301.

Richards, Audrey I. (1969) 'Keeping the King divine', *Proceedings of the Royal Anthropological Institute for 1968*, 23–35.

Richardson, Alan and Bowden, John (eds) (1983) *A New Dictionary of Christian Theology*, London: SCM Press.

Ritchie, A. D. (1945) *Civilization, Science and Religion*, London: Penguin Books.

Roff, Margaret Clark (1974) *The Politics of Belonging: Political Change in Sabah and Sarawak*, Kuala Lumpur: Oxford University Press.

Roff, William R. (1967) 'The origins of Malay nationalism', *Yale Southeast Asia Studies* 2, New Haven: Yale University Press.

— — (ed.) (1974) *Kelantan: Religion, Society and Politics in a Malay State*, Kuala Lumpur: Oxford University Press.

Sansom, G. (1932) *Japan: A Short Cultural History*, London: Cresset Press.

Schapera, I. (1955) *A Handbook of Tswana Law and Custom* (2nd edn), London: International African Institute/Oxford University Press.

Scholem, Gershom G. (1955) *Major Trends in Jewish Mysticism*, London: Thames & Hudson.

Seligman, C. G. (1911) 'The cult of Nyakang and the Divine Kings of the Shilluk, 4th report vol. **B**, 216–32, Wellcome Tropical Research Laboratories, Gordon Memorial College Khartoum, Dept. Education, Sudan Govt., Bailliere, Tindall & Cox.

Shaw, G. E. (1926) 'Malay industries, Part III: rice planting', *Papers on Malay Subjects* 1st series, reprint, Kuala Lumpur: Government Printer.

Shivapadasundaram, S. (1934) *The Saiva School of Hinduism*, London· Allen & Unwin.

Siegel, James T. (1969) *The Rope of God*, Berkeley: University of California Press.

Skeat, Walter William (1900) *Malay Magic*, London: Macmillan.

Smith, W. Robertson (1907) *Lectures on the Religion of the Semites* [1889] (new edn), London: Adam & Charles Black.

Soothill, W. E. (1929) *The Three Religions of China* (3rd edn), Oxford: Oxford University Press.

— — (1930) *The Lotus of the Wonderful Law*, Oxford: Clarendon.

Sorokin, P. (1941) *Social and Cultural Dynamics*, **IV**, New York: American Book Company.

Southern, R. W. (1970) *Mediaeval Humanism and Other Studies*, Oxford: Oxford University Press.

Stebbing, L. Susan (1937) *Philosophy and the Physicists*, Harmondsworth: Penguin.

Steinilber-Oberlin, E. (1938) *The Buddhist Sects of Japan* (trans. from French, Marc Logé), London: Allen & Unwin.

Stocks, J. L. (1934) 'On the nature and grounds of religious belief' (Riddell Memorial Lecture), Oxford.

Strothmann, R. (1934) *Takiya: Encyclopaedia of Islam* 4, M.Th. Houtsma, *et al.* (eds), Leyden: Brill: 628–30.

Sundkler, Bengt G. M. (1948) *Bantu Prophets in South Africa*, London: Lutterworth Press.

Swettenham, F. A. (1905) *Vocabulary of English and Malay Languages* (5th edn) **I**: Shanghai: Kelly & Walsh.

Swift, Michael (1966) 'Malay peasant society in Jelebu', London School of Economics Monographs, *Social Anthropology* 29, London: Athlone.

Talmon, Yonina (1966) 'Millenarian movements', *European Journal of Sociology* 7: 159–200.

Temple, W. (1924) 'Some implications of theism', in J. H. Muirhead (ed.) *Contemporary British Philosophy*, London: Allen & Unwin: 414–28.

Thornton, W. M. (1930) 'The scientific background of the Christian creeds', (Riddell Memorial Lecture) Newcastle-upon-Tyne: University of Durham.

Toynbee, A. (1946) *A Study of History* (abridged C. D. Somervell), London: Oxford University Press.

Trimingham, J. Spencer (1959) *Islam in West Africa*, Oxford: Clarendon.

Trumbull, H. C. (1885) *The Blood Covenant*, New York: Charles Scribner's Sons.

Turner, Victor (1974) *Drama, Fields and Metaphors: Symbolic Action in Human Society*, Ithaca: Cornell University Press.

Turner, Victor and Turner, Edith (1978) *Image and Pilgrimage in Christian Culture: Anthropological Perspectives*, New York: Columbia University Press.

Tylor, Edward B. (1873) *Primitive Culture*, 2 vols. (2nd edn), London: John Murray.

Van Leeuwen, Arend Theodor (1972) *Critique of Heaven*, New York: Scribner's.

— — (1974) *Critique of Earth*, New York: Scribner's.

Vesey-Fitzgerald, Seymour (1931) *Muhammadan Law: An Abridgement according to Various Schools*, Oxford: Oxford University Press.

von Grunebaum, Gustave E. (1955) 'Islam: essays in the nature and growth of a cultural tradition', *American Anthropological Association* 81.

— — (ed.) (1955) *Unity and Variety in Muslim Civilization*, Chicago: Chicago University Press.

Wach, J. (1947) *Sociology of Religion*, London: Kegan Paul.

Wagner, G. (1940) 'The political organization of the Bantu Kavirondo', in M. Fortes and E. E. Evans-Pritchard (eds) *African Political Systems*, London: International African Institute/Oxford University Press: 197–236.

Webb, C. C. J. (1929) 'Religion and the thought of today' (Riddell Memorial Lecture), Oxford.

Wilkinson, R. J. (1903) *A Malay-English Dictionary*, Singapore: Kelly & Walsh.

— — (1906) *Malay Beliefs*, London: Luzac.

— — (1932) *A Malay-English Dictionary* (Romanized), 2 vols, Mytilene: Savalapoulos & Kinderlis.

Wilson, Bryan R. (1961) *Sects in Society: A Sociological Study of Three Religious Groups in Britain*, London: Heinemann.

Wilson, H. H. (1958) 'Religious sects of the Hindus', in Ernst R. Rost (ed.), Calcutta: Susil Gupta.

Wilson, Monica (1959) *Communal Rituals of the Nyakyusa*, London: International African Institute/Oxford University Press.

Wilson, Peter J. (1967) *A Malay Village and Malaysia: Social Values and Rural Development*, New Haven: HRAF Press.

Winstedt, R. (1951) *The Malay Magician, being Shaman, Saiva and Sufi* (rev. edn), London: Routledge & Kegan Paul.

Winzeler, Robert L. (1974) 'The Social Organization of Islam in Kelantan', in William R. Roff (ed.): 253–71.

Worsley, P. (1957) *The Trumpet Shall Sound*, London: Macgibbon & Kee.

Yap, P. M. (1952) 'The Latah reaction: its pathodynamics and nosological position', Journal of Mental Science, **XCVIII**.

Yerkes, R. K. (1953) *Sacrifice in Greek and Roman Religion and Early Judaism*, London: Adam & Charles Black.

Yinger, J. Milton (1970) *The Scientific Study of Religion*, New York: Macmillan.

Zimmer, H. (1946) 'Myths and symbols in Indian art and civilization', ed. Joseph Campbell, *Bollingen series* **VI**, New York: Pantheon.

Index